Also by Helen Singer Kaplan

Progress in Group and Family Therapy
with Clifford J. Sager, M.D.

The New Sex Therapy

The Illustrated Manual of Sex Therapy

Making Sense of Sex

DISORDERS OF SEXUAL DESIRE

616.6
KAP

and Other New Concepts and Techniques in Sex Therapy

HELEN SINGER KAPLAN, M.D., Ph.D.

Clinical Associate Professor of Psychiatry
and Director of Human Sexuality Program
of the New York Hospital—Cornell Medical Center

SIMON AND SCHUSTER
New York

Copyright © 1979 by Helen Singer Kaplan, M.D., PhD.
A Brunner/Mazel Publication
All rights reserved
including the right of reproduction
in whole or in part in any form

Published by Simon and Schuster
A Division of Gulf & Western Corporation
Simon & Schuster Building
Rockefeller Center
1230 Avenue of the Americas
New York, New York 10020

Distributed in Canada by BOOK CENTER, 1140 Beaulac St., St. Laurent 382, Quebec
Manufactured in the United States of America

1 2 3 4 5 6 7 8 9 10

Library of Congress Cataloging in Publication Data
Kaplan, Helen Singer, date.
    Disorders of sexual desire and other new concepts
and techniques in sex therapy.

    Bibliography: p.
    Includes index.
    1. Sexual disorders.   2. Sexual disorders—Case
studies.   3. Sex therapy.   4. Sex therapy—Case
studies.   I. Title.
[RC556.K319]   616.6   79-23384

To Charles

CONTENTS

APPENDIX 201

LIST OF CASE STUDIES

INTRODUCTION

FIVE YEARS HAVE PASSED since publication of *The New Sex Therapy*. During this period a great deal has been learned about the human sexual response, about the sexual dysfunctions, and about sex therapy.

It has been deeply gratifying to me that the essential elements of the theoretical constructs and clinical material presented as hypotheses five years ago appear to have survived. In fact, not only have the basic tenets been supported and confirmed by the extensive clinical experience which has accumulated in these years, but they have also been extended beyond the treatment of sexual dysfunctions and applied to other kinds of problems.

More specifically, the psychosomatic concept of sexual dysfunctions has remained a useful working model. From this viewpoint, the sexual dysfunctions are seen as the product of the physiologic concomitants of anxiety. Thus, the objective of treatment is to diminish this sexually related anxiety, thereby restoring genital functioning.

Masters and Johnson's hypothesis that the source of sexually disruptive anxiety is often much simpler and more consciously perceived than was postulated by traditional psychoanalysis and psychiatry has also, on the whole, been confirmed. Thus, a substantial number of patients with sexual dysfunctions respond to brief sex treatment methods which effectively resolve such superficial anxieties as performance anxiety and mild obsessive "spectatoring."

The biphasic concept, i.e. the notion that excitement and orgasm disorders are separate syndromes, has been confirmed by clinical observations and is also supported by the response to the specific treatment strategies devised for these dysfunctions. The separation of excitement and orgasm phase dysfunctions has improved the prognosis of the orgasmic disorders of males and females considerably.

Finally, the integration of behavioral with psychodynamic treatment techniques which was pioneered by sex therapy has proved a powerful therapeutic tool which holds the potential for rapid conflict resolution in a variety of clinical situations which are not sexually related.

However, the same clinical experience which has supported many of the basic tenets of sex therapy has also taught us that, while the fundamental theoretical structure of the original concepts was sound, it was also incomplete. And while the basic clinical techniques proved effective on the whole, they required further development and refinements in order to reach a wider spectrum of patients. In response to these limitations, new insights and hypotheses have emerged and clinical techniques have been extended and improved in creative ways. These new developments have not usurped or demolished the "old" new sex therapy, but, on the contrary, have enriched and strengthened it. Indeed, I believe that the incorporation of these current advances represents an important phase in the maturation and development of the infant, but now clearly viable, field of sexual therapy.

THE LAST FIVE YEARS IN SEX THERAPY

Confirmation of the basics, as well as the addition of new insights, has emerged out of the accumulated and shared experiences of many dedicated and talented contributors who are working in this field. The promise of rapid and effective treatment of sexual problems has attracted clinicians from a wide spectrum of orientations and tempted them to experiment with the new sex therapies. The experiences have proved, on the whole, gratifying. This acceptance by professionals, as well as public demand for services, has produced a rapid proliferation of sex therapy clinics and programs in the U.S. and abroad. As a result, a variety of styles of sexual therapy has developed, but all retain the basic format: integration of structured sexual tasks with psychotherapeutic exploration of resistances.

Many thousands of sexually troubled couples have been treated by these new sex therapies. With the growth of clinical experience, the need for greater communication and interchange has developed. Conferences and journals have brought together the psychoanalytically minded, the behaviorists, the family and couples therapists who employ systems models, as well as the physiologically oriented gynecologists and urologists. Happily, instead of the potential Babel which could have resulted from such a diversity and which might have led to an abandonment of the Tower, the sexual response and its disorders have proved a catalyst for integration and amalgamation of a wide spectrum of ideas and experiences, along with the development of new and vital hybrids.

Not surprisingly in the light of the intense activity and interest in this field, important new insights and innovations have emerged from various sources. Sometimes similar discoveries have been made by several contributors independently. Thus, insights into disorders of sexual desire, which represent the most important recent conceptual advance in the field, have come from several independent sources. My own attention was directed towards the desire phase and its disorders as a result of my studies of treatment failures. Dr. Harold Lief, who has contributed and published valuable clinical and theoretical material on this topic, has come to the same conclusion—namely that the previously neglected desire phase of the sexual response is of crucial clinical significance—on the basis of different data. Thus, the ideas about the desire phase presented in this book are not exclusively mine. They represent a significant development which has been shaped by the contributions of many workers in the field of sex therapy.

FAILURES IN SEX THERAPY

Sex therapy has proved to be an exceedingly effective technique which has helped many patients with sexual problems who were believed, before the advent of this therapeutic modality, to be essentially beyond help. However, even this marvelous technique has its failures, and a substantial number of patients with sexual dysfunctions do not respond. I have studied a group of patients whose sexual symptoms were not cured by sex therapy and compared them to successfully treated patients. This study of treatment failures was undertaken in order to improve our methods and outcome and also to sharpen and refine our theoretical constructs about sexuality, sexual disorders, and treatment.

I have been fortunate to have available for study a rich and varied population: 1) a large number of sexually dysfunctional patients treated by our own group with sex therapy and modified sex therapy methods; 2) some former sex therapy patients undergoing long-term therapy; and 3) some treatment failures from other sex therapy programs.

During the last five years, my group* and I have treated some 1,000 patients with sexual complaints. A detailed account of the statistical aspects of this experience including a description of the population, selection criteria, method and outcome and follow-up with each specific syndrome will be published at a later date. The outcome data cited in this book are preliminary and derive from work that is still ongoing. They are presented here only for the purpose of giving the reader a sense of the overall results from which the ideas and hypotheses contained in this book were drawn.

We found that approximately 63 percent of the patients were cured of their sexual symptom, 7 percent were judged to have improved, and 30 percent interrupted treatment or were treatment failures. A comparison of the successful and unsuccessful cases has uncovered several significant prognostic factors. Most of these hold no surprise. They include age, the severity of associated psychopathology, the symbolic meaning of the sexual symptom and the extent to which it serves as a defense against underlying conflict, the quality of the relationship, homosexual problems, the presence of significant anxiety and depression in the symptomatic patient and in the partner as well, and the presence of hidden medical problems. The latter are more important as a cause of treatment failure of males. Of most interest, however, is the discovery that the prognosis of desire phase disorders is substantially poorer than that of the excitement and orgasm phase dysfunctions. Further, even in cases of successful treatment of inhibited sexual desire (ISD), the course of treatment tends to be stormier and more complex.

I have also had the opportunity to study in depth 26 of my former sex therapy patients who were undergoing long-term therapy. These include both patients whose sexual symptom has been cured by sex therapy and some who have been treatment failures. The patients whose sexual symptom was relieved sought help for other problems, while those who were not helped by sex therapy continued to explore their sexual problem in long-term treatment. This experience has

---

* Mildred Witkin, Ph.D., Merle Kroop, M.D., Michael Perelman, Ph.D., Richard Symons, Ph.D., Jerry Lanoil, Ph.D., Erica Sucher, M.S.W., Arleen Novick, M.S.W., Patricia Levi, M.D., Harris Peck, M.D., and Larry Moodie, M.D. comprise the group who contributed to this material.

yielded a perspective of the dynamic infrastructure of the sexual symptom which shapes the clinical course and outcome of each case.

This "vertical" view further confirms the notion that desire problems constitute a separate clinical subgroup and that significant differences exist between desire phase disorders and those of excitement and orgasm. More specifically, patients suffering from blocked desire have, as a group, deeper and more intense sexual anxieties, and/or greater hostility towards their partners and/or more tenacious defenses than those patients whose sexual dysfunctions are associated with erection and orgasm difficulties. But interestingly enough, there are exceptions and I do see a few erectile and orgasm problems that are associated with the deeper kinds of pathology I have come to expect with inhibited sex desire.

Attempts to re-treat with lengthier psychosexual therapy methods 13 couples who failed to be helped by conventional sex therapy in other programs were also most instructive and also supported the hypothesis that ISD is a separate and more difficult syndrome. First, it was striking that all but three failures could be attributed to the fact that the patients were suffering from desire phase problems which had not been recognized by the previous therapists. Most often, these patients had been treated for prematurity or anorgasmia or erectile dysfunction, when the fundamental problem was actually an undetected inhibition of desire. It is not surprising, therefore, that these patients were not cured, since only a small percentage of desire phase dysfunctions responds to standard sex therapy.

This population of treatment failures has been re-treated with the lengthier modified psychosexual therapy techniques which we are employing for desire disorders. We have found that accurate diagnosis of desire inhibition improves outcome but does not ensure success. Some of these patients have improved or been cured, but others remain refractory and do not respond to our treatment techniques.* Cases illustrating both kinds of outcome are described in the following chapters.

Of the many valuable lessons learned from the studies of failures in sex therapy, two conclusions are of overriding importance:

1) *The biphasic model of the human sexual response and its dysfunctions is inadequate to accommodate current data.* The validity of the biphasic model, i.e., the separation of the excitement and the orgasm phases and

---

* The re-treatment data will be published when follow-up studies are completed.

disorders, has been confirmed again and again by clinical experience. However, a third and separate phase, which had previously been neglected, must be included for conceptual completeness and clinical effectiveness. Sexual desire has a separate physiology, a distinctive pattern of pathogenesis, and special therapeutic requirements. Thus, the *triphasic model* which encompasses all three phases—*desire, excitement* and *orgasm*—makes sense out of and organizes the data about the sexual response and its disorders, and also promises to improve the clinical management of the sexual dysfunctions.

2) *A significant number of patients who suffer from sexual dysfunctions are not cured by standard brief therapy methods.* The exact outcome figures will probably vary with the psychiatric characteristics of the patient populations; results may be expected to be poorer with "sicker," i.e., more disturbed, patients and couples, such as those seen in a psychiatric outpatient department. This is because the standard sex therapy methods seem to be effective primarily for those sexual problems which have their roots in mild and easily diminished anxieties and conflicts. Fortunately, a large number of patients fall into this category, especially those suffering from orgasm phase dysfunctions. However, there are sexually dysfunctional individuals whose symptoms are rooted in more profound sexual and marital conflicts and for whom the brief sex therapy techniques are not effective. In our experience, a small proportion of orgasm dysfunctions, some of the more difficult impotence problems, and the majority of desire phase difficulties fall into this category.

Clearly, we need to develop more effective methods to serve this population which is not helped by standard sex therapy. Many workers in the field, ourselves among them, are engaged in this quest.

Our own approach consists of a modified and lengthened form of sex therapy. This method retains the basic ingredient of sex therapy— the integration of prescribed sexual experiences with psychotherapeutic exploration of intrapsychic and interactional defenses and resistances—but the technique has been modified to meet the needs posed by the deeper and more varied underlying difficulties of these patients. Treatment has been lengthened and made more flexible and individualistic. Heavier emphasis is placed on the fostering of insight, on active psychotherapeutic intervention during the office sessions. In comparison to conventional sex therapy, the level of intervention is of necessity "deeper," extending beyond performance anxiety and addressing itself to such problems as unconscious success anxiety and intimacy phobias.

This modified form of psychosexual therapy makes sense from a theoretical point of view and also shows promise of extending the range of treatment effectiveness to a greater number of patients. However, these methods are still in a developmental stage and remain to be systematically evaluated and compared to other treatment methods.

OBJECTIVES AND CONTENTS OF THIS VOLUME

The main objectives of this book are: 1) to describe the desire phase dysfunctions and current treatment approaches and 2) to integrate this new material into the existing, still valid body of knowledge about human sexuality and sex therapy.

In Area I, *The Triphasic Concept of Human Sexuality*, the physiology, clinical features, psychopathology, etiology, treatment and prognosis of the desire, excitement and orgasm phases are reviewed, updated and compared with each other.

Area II describes the *Desire Phase Disorders of Males and Females* and the treatment approach we are in the process of developing. Twelve cases of desire phase dynsfunctions illustrate typical clinical features and psychodynamics, as well as showing different responses to treatment. Both treatment failures and successful cases are reported.

Area III, *Strategies in Psychosexual Therapy*, describes some new insights and hypotheses about the etiology and treatment of the more difficult sexual dysfunctions. Advancements and refinements in the techniques of psychosexual therapy, especially as they apply to the desire phase disorders, are described. These are actually extensions of the integration of behavioral and psychodynamic techniques; they have grown out of attempts to develop effective brief interventions for the more deep-seated sexual dysfunctions, among which desire problems are so heavily represented.

Finally, new tables on the effects of illness and drugs on the sexual responses have been included in the appendix. These are based on tables which appeared in *The New Sex Therapy*. This material makes more sense and is more useful when organized according to the triphasic model. The three phases of the sexual response are governed by neurophysiologic systems which have different loci and different responses to chemicals and stress. Therefore, particular drugs and medical illnesses tend to affect specific phases. Unless the doses are toxic or the illness overwhelming, few drugs or diseases impair the entire sexual response. Some drugs and some medical ailments disturb only libido, others affect only erection, and still others impair only orgasm. With this in mind, the charts on the sexual effects of medical illness and drugs have been organized according to which phase of the sexual response is affected in order to make them more useful to the clinician.

The book presents 22 case histories. These are used to illustrate theoretical issues, as well as to convey the flavor and feeling of the therapeutic process. The underlying dynamics of many of the cases are explained in constructs derived from psychoanalytic theory. For example, the terms oedipal and preoedipal superego are frequently employed. This represents my theoretical bias that some analytic concepts, such as unconscious motivation and conflict, the structural theory, etc. are useful working models to account for and predict otherwise mystifying human behavior, within as well as outside of clinical situations.

However, these concepts are used as working hypotheses which seem useful in some clinical situations. Other psychodynamic models, such as the interpersonal theories derived from Sullivan or the modern offshoots of psychoanalytic theory such as Gestalt and transactional analysis (TA), offer attractive theoretical alternatives which may be equally applicable in some clinical situations.

The key theoretical formulations presented in this book, specifically the psychosomatic concept of the sexual dysfunctions, the hypothesis of remote and immediate causes, and the clinical and theoretical integration of experiential and psychodynamic treatment modalities and behavioral and psychodynamic concepts operate on a different and more fundamental theoretical level of description and are therefore independent of any specific psychodynamic system.

H.S.K.

AREA I

THE TRIPHASIC CONCEPT OF HUMAN SEXUALITY

DESIRE, EXCITEMENT AND ORGASM

Throughout history, until just a few years ago, the human sexual response was seen monistically, as a single event that passed from lust to excitement and was climaxed by the orgasm. All the sexual dysfunctions were also perceived as though they were a single clinical entity. No distinction was made between premature ejaculation or impotence or lack of libido or sexual avoidance. All males who could not perform or enjoy sexual intercourse were termed impotent, while all women with sexual difficulties were labeled frigid.

It followed that treatment was also undifferentiated. Since all sexually dysfunctional patients carried the same diagnosis, they also received the same therapy. At the same time, the etiology of sexual pathology was not clearly understood and so the nature of treatment was empirical. Male patients with all kinds of sexual complaints might receive hormone or nonspecific dietary and rest cures, depending on the style of their doctor. Not surprisingly, treatment for sexual problems was not very successful.

3

The psychosomatic concept of medicine advanced the management of sexual complaints by calling attention to the previously neglected psychogenic determinants. But this approach was marred by two errors. First, the psychoanalytic establishment, consistent with the prevailing monistic concept, regarded all sexually troubled patients—the fetishists, asexuals, those with disturbances of romantic attachments, the sexually phobic, patients with gender disturbances, impotence, anorgasmia, vaginismus, etc.—as variants of the same psychopathological population. The second error involved the belief that the cause of sexual difficulties was specific and profound. It was thought that all sexual problems were produced by specific and serious unconscious conflicts about sex which were acquired during specific developmental phases in early childhood. Thus, all sexually inadequate patients were believed to be in need of psychoanalytically oriented treatment which has the capability of resolving such unconscious conflicts.

The old monistic view of the human sexual response thus impeded advances in the field. Progress in understanding human sexuality required the separation of the component parts from the undifferentiated mass. As soon as this was understood, the multiplicity of determinants that can impair sexuality were recognized, which in turn opened the way for the development of rational treatment procedures.

Gradually, it was recognized that the sexual response is not *an indivisible entity, vulnerable to a single pathogen, subject to only one disorder, and amenable to a single treatment regimen. On the contrary, the human sexual response is composed of three separate but interlocking phases which are each vulnerable to disruption in a specific manner by multiple physical and psychic pathogens, and which produce a variety of disorders that are responsive to specific and rational treatment strategies.*

Before the three phases could be accurately discriminated, it was necessary to obtain a clear description of the physiology of the sexual response of men and women. In contrast to our advanced understanding of all other biological functions, this was not available for sex until very recently. This scientific asexuality cannot be attributed to the fact that sexual physiology is too complex for our investigative tools. On the contrary, compared to other biological responses, such as, for example, the highly complex physiology of the brain, sex is far simpler and much easier to study and understand. But emotional prejudices precluded the scientific study of sex. It was Masters and Johnson who first had the courage and the good sense to regard the human sexual response as a

*natural biologic function and who observed male and female sexual
behavior accurately under the same kinds of laboratory conditions which
serve the study of other biological systems such as digestive and
respiratory physiology. Their work yielded the first clear and accurate
description of the human sexual response. Masters and Johnson divided
the sexual response into the four well-known stages:* excitement,
plateau, orgasm *and* resolution. *While this system does not
correspond to the underlying physiologic phases, it has descriptive
validity and has facilitated the development of further insights.**

*The first breakaway from the monistic view of sexual disorders was
made by urologist James Seaman. In a paper published in 1956 he
separated "ejaculatory impotence" from the undifferentiated wastebasket
of the male dysfunctions. While he did not explicitly differentiate the
orgasm and excitement phases and their disorders in the male, he did
devise a specific and highly effective treatment method for premature
ejaculation, which, although Seaman did not explicitly state this, was
designed to modify the immediate and specific causes of this disorder.
Thus, Seaman ushered in the biphasic era of human sexuality.*

*The analogous separation of the two genital phases of the female did
not occur until much later, in the 1970s. It was pointed out in* The
New Sex Therapy *that it makes good theoretical sense and improves
clinical effectiveness to separate the excitement phase from the orgasm
phase disorders in females, just as it does in males. In the female, also,
the syndromes differ clinically and are the product of different causes;
therefore, treatment is more rational and effective when it is specific for
orgasm or excitement phase problems. This conceptual separation led
the way to the development of the self-stimulation treatment techniques
which modify the immediate and specific antecedents of the female
orgasm dysfunction. These methods have improved the outcome of the
treatment of the female orgasm inhibitions immensely, to a degree which
is comparable to the improvement in the outcome of premature
ejaculation which resulted from Seaman's technique.*

*Thus, the biphasic concept represented a significant theoretical
advance in the field which led to important clinical developments. But
the understanding of the sexual response and its dysfunctions was still*

---

* Masters and Johnson's stages have the following relationship to the three physiologic phases described herein. The orgasm stage corresponds to the orgasm phase. Masters and Johnson's excitement and plateau stages refer to different degrees of the vasodilatory excitement phase. Resolution merely refers to the absence of sexual arousal. Desire is not included in the Masters and Johnson scheme, which describes only the genital phases of the sexual response.

incomplete and the clinical data were still not sufficiently accounted for until the recent recognition of a third, a central phase, the phase of sexual desire.

The three phases are physiologically related but discrete. They are interconnected but governed by separate neurophysiological systems. Metaphorically, orgasm, excitement, and desire may be thought of as having a "common generator," but each has its own "circuitry." And the existence of a separate "wiring" system or neural circuits creates the possibility for separate and discrete inhibition of the three phases. Certain kinds of trauma, if sufficiently intense, disturb the entire system, but often only one component is disrupted. One set of causes is likely to "blow the fuses" of the orgasm circuits, another type of conflict may "disconnect the erection wires," while a different group of variables is likely to cause interference in the "libido circuits" of the brain.

The different sexual dysfunctions make sense when they are viewed as consisting of impairments of one of the three phases. When the orgasm phase is disrupted, the clinical syndromes of premature and retarded ejaculation of males and their analogue, orgastic inhibition of females, result. Excitement phase inhibition produces impotence in males and "general sexual dysfunction" of females, which is a rather poor term for the syndrome wherein a woman does not become excited and does not lubricate adequately during sexual activity. Desire phase inhibition occurs in both males and females and is evidenced by low libido in both genders.

When sexual conflict is severe, all three phases of sexual response may become impaired and the person becomes totally asexual. But discrete inhibition of one of the phases, with sparing of the others, is more prevalent in clinical practice. Thus, one commonly finds patients who desire sex, have problems with erection, but can ejaculate with a flaccid penis; or men who are very interested in sex, have no erectile difficulties, but cannot control their orgasms; or women who have no desire for sex, but who can lubricate and even have an orgasm on stimulation. To repair these various malfunctions efficiently one does not simply "kick the television set"; one intervenes at discrete points with specific therapeutic tools.

An understanding of the sexual dysfunctions and the rationale behind the treatment rests first on an understanding of the biological **infrastructure** *of the sexual response. The physiology of the two genital phases of the sexual response has been described in* **The New Sex**

Therapy *in 1974. This description is in the main still accurate and up-to-date except that a few more details about the physiology of erection have been clarified since that time. That volume also contained hypotheses about etiology and suggestions about the treatment of the various syndromes. The extensive clinical experience which has been accumulated in the past five years has on the whole confirmed these early notions, but it has also yielded more refined hypotheses regarding the causes and treatment of the excitement and orgasm phase disorders.*

In the following sections, current concepts of the physiology, etiology and therapy of the orgasm and excitement phases are reviewed briefly and, in addition, current concepts and hypotheses about the physiology, etiology and treatment of desire phase disorders are discussed. Although some of this material is already available and in that sense repetitious, it is included here in order to bring the information on the two genital phases up-to-date, to provide a comprehensive overview of the three phases, and to integrate the early material with the new thinking about the desire phase.

1

THE PHYSIOLOGY

OF THE

SEXUAL RESPONSE

SEXUAL DESIRE is an appetite or drive which is produced by the activation of a specific neural system in the brain, while the excitement and orgasm phases involve the genital organs. In both males and females the excitement phase is produced by the reflex vasodilatation of genital blood vessels. By contrast, orgasm essentially consists of reflex contractions of certain genital muscles. These two genital reflexes are served by separate reflex centers in the lower spinal cord.

THE DESIRE PHASE

The neurophysiologic and neuroanatomic bases for sexual desire have not yet been delineated with the same degree of accuracy as other drives, such as hunger, thirst and the need to sleep. Current concepts regarding the biology of the sexual appetite are based on relatively few experimental studies, inferred from clinical evidence, and drawn by analogy from our general knowledge of brain functioning and of the neurophysiology of the other biological drives.

The experimental evidence from pharmacologic studies, from ablation experiments, from neurophysiologic investigations and from behavioral observations indicates that the sex drive is basically similar to the other drives in that it: 1) depends on the activity of a specific anatomical structure in the brain; 2) contains centers that enhance the drive in balance with centers that inhibit it; 3) is also served by two specific neurotransmitters—an inhibitory and an excitatory one; and 4) has extensive connections with other parts of the brain which allow the sex drive to be influenced by and integrated into the individual's total life experience.

Sexual desire or libido is experienced as specific sensations which move the individual to seek out, or become receptive to, sexual experiences. These sensations are produced by the physical activation of a specific neural system in the brain. When this system is active, a person is "horny," he may feel genital sensations, or he may feel vaguely sexy, interested in sex, open to sex, or even just restless. These sensations cease after sexual gratification, i.e., orgasm. When this system is inactive or under the influence of inhibitory forces, a person has no interest in erotic matters; he "loses his appetite" for sex and becomes "asexual."

This relationship between neural activity and experience is also characteristic of the other drives. For example, the sensation of hunger is similarly produced by the physical activation of anatomically specific "hunger" circuits and centers in the brain. Appetite suppressive medication such as dexedrine physically inhibits the activity of the appetite centers and so causes the person to "lose his appetite."

Just how the neural activity of the sex circuits is translated into the experience of sexual desire is not yet understood precisely. Is it the electric activity of the network's neurons which moves us? Are we literally "turned on" like a light? Or does activity of the neurons in these networks release chemical intermediaries? Is our love life regulated by "shots" of endogenous aphrodisiacs secreted when the sex centers are activated? Do the "juices really flow" when we see or smell or feel an attractive and seductive sexual partner?

Anatomy

While these mysteries remain, the anatomy of the sexual system is fairly well understood. The sex center of the brain consists of a network of neural centers and circuits. Both inhibitory and activating centers have been identified. These are known to be located within the limbic system, with important nuclei in the hypothalamus and in the preoptic region. The limbic system is located in the "limbus" or rim of the brain. It is an archaic system which governs and organizes the behavior that ensures not only individual survival but also the reproduction of the species. Towards those ends it contains the neural apparatus that generates and regulates emotion and motivation. The limbic system exists even in primitive vertebrates, and has remained essentially unchanged even in man. However, it has been integrated into our complex brains so that it often seems to have disappeared. Yet is is very much alive and influential and comprises the biologial substrate of our complex emotional and sexual experience.

The sexual system has extensive neural connections with other parts of the brain. All of these pathways have not as yet been located precisely, but much of the structure, function and connections of the sexual system can be inferred from behavior, i.e., from introspection and from clinical observations of the vicissitudes of the libido. For example, it is highly probable that the sexual centers have significant connections, neural and/or chemical, with the pleasure and the pain centers of the brain. When we have sex, the pleasure centers are stimulated and this accounts for the pleasurable quality of erotic behavior. But when we are in pain, we don't feel like sex because the pain centers inhibit the sexual system.

All drives are regulated by a dual steering mechanism: the avoidance of pain and the seeking of pleasure. Indeed, all of human behavior is organized around the seeking of pleasure and the avoidance of pain, i.e., the seeking of stimulation of the pleasure center and the avoidance of pain center stimulation.

Neural centers have been identified in the brains of mammals which mediate the experiences of pleasure. When these centers are stimulated electrically, animals will clearly prefer the sensation produced by this stimulation over food, water, sex, and maternal behavior. Recent studies have indicated that chemical receptor sites are located on the neurons of the pleasure centers which respond to a chemical that is produced by brain cells. This is called endorphin because it resembles morphine in its chemical characteristics, as well as in its physiologic effects of causing euphoria and alleviating pain. It may be speculated that eating and sex and being in love, i.e., behaviors which are experienced as pleasurable, produce this sensation by stimulation of the pleasure center, electrically or by causing the release of endorphins, or by both mechanisms.

The sex drive seems relatively more responsive to pleasure than to pain. Thus, sexual frustration, while certainly not pleasant, does not produce the intense pain and agony which are elicited by starvation or bodily injury. Drives which serve the goal of self-preservation seem to be capable of producing much greater pain and to be more urgently controlled by pain avoidance than the reproduction drives, which are motivated more by pleasure-seeking.

Because of this pleasurable quality of sexuality, it may be inferred that the sexual circuits have intimate connections with the pleasure centers of the brain, and/or release a chemical for which receptor sites exist in the pleasure circuits. But sexual desire must also be anatomically and/or chemically connected with the pain centers, for if a sexual object or situation produces pain—i.e., is experienced as dangerous or destructive—it will cease to evoke desire. In other words, pain has the capability of inhibiting sexual desire.

Aversive or pain centers which are in close approximation to the pleasure centers have also been identified in the brain of mammals. If these are stimulated electrically, the animal expresses acute distress and may never again engage in whatever behavior he was doing at the time of the shock. A chemical mediator for pain which is analogous to endorphin probably exists, but it has not yet been identified. The pain centers are activated by the perception of physical injury or by the anticipation of such danger. And when they are active, they have priority over and can inhibit functions which are extraneous to the individual's survival, since our brains are organized so that pain has priority over pleasure, which makes sense from an evolutionary perspective. Individual survival must come before reproduction, and when we perceive that we are injured or in danger, the pain center becomes activated and governs our functions so that all our energies are focused on finding solutions (fighting, running, outmaneuvering, finding alternative strategies), instead of becoming distracted by and vulnerable because of our sexual urges. The ability of these aversive centers to inhibit the sexual centers, which has clear adaptive value, is also the biological basis for the neurotic inhibition of libido.

Behavioral observations also suggest that the sex circuits are extensively interconnected with those parts of the brain that analyze complex experience and also with the memory storage and retrieval systems. There is evidence that sexual desire is highly sensitive to experimental factors which determine and shape, in large measure, the objects and activities which will and will not evoke our desires.

It may also be speculated that neural connections exist between the central sex centers and the spinal reflex centers that govern genital functioning. Input from the higher centers can enhance or diminish the genital reflexes. Thus, when libido is high, when a person feels sexy and sensuous, erection and lubrication are full and rapid, and orgasm is easily achieved. In fact, erection and even orgasm may at times be achieved purely on the basis of external stimuli and fantasy without any physical stimulation of the genitals. But the opposite is also true. When desire is absent and the sexual experience is flat and joyless, the threshold for the genital reflexes is much higher. When one is not turned on it can take "forever" and the physical stimulus must be intense before the genitals will function.

Physiological Mechanisms

Information regarding the physiologic mechanisms, the electric and chemical events which govern the sexual system, is just beginning to be accumulated, and the information is still too fragmentary to build a coherent conceptual structure.

Ablation experiments, pharmacologic studies, and investigations that employ electrical stimulation of the brain indicate clearly that activating mechanisms are in balance with inhibitory mechanisms. Clinical observation can give us a good idea of what will enhance the sexual appetite, i.e., what will stimulate the activating mechanisms and/or release the inhibitory mechanism from inhibition.

In the natural state, libido and the sex circuits are governed by biological rhythms as well as by the availability of an attractive partner. Animals whose reproductive behavior is regulated by an estrus cycle are more subject to biological rhythms than man is. For example, female animals whose sexual receptivity is governed by the estrus cycle display a total absence of sexual desire and avoid sex except during periods of "heat," which are controlled by hormones. In infrahuman females, both sexual attractiveness and sexual receptivity depend on *estrogen*. The central action of estrogen on the brain makes them receptive, while the peripheral action makes them attractive. Specifically, estrogen causes the vaginal cells of some species of animals to manufacture *pheromones* which release sexual desire in the male. In human females, estrogen does *not* enhance sexual desire and its role in female attractiveness remains controversial. But humans, too, fluctuate to some extent in their sexual desire on a biological basis. The biological sex rhythms of humans are probabaly mediated by sex hormones via their influence on the sex centers of the mammalian brain.

The role of *testosterone* in human sexuality seems clearer. It is the "libido hormone" for both genders. In the absence of testosterone, there is little sexual desire in both males and females in all species studied so far, including humans. Presumably this effect is due to the crucial role testosterone plays in the functioning of the sex centers of both genders, although the mechanism of this action is not clearly understood as yet.

Recent evidence indicates that a small peptide molecule, a hormone secreted in the brain called luteinizing hormone-releasing factor (LH-RF), may enhance sexual desire even in the absence of testosterone or when testosterone is ineffective. This finding has raised interesting questions, such as: Does LH-RF act directly on the sex centers of the brain? Can it be used clinically to increase libido? As yet, LH-RF is a mystery, but it has important clinical implications and merits further investigation.

It has been speculated that the sex hormones, testosterone and perhaps LH-RF, influence sexual behavior by some interaction with the neurotransmitters which are the mediators of neural impulses within the sexual circuits. Evidence suggests that serotonin or 5-HT acts as an inhibitor, and dopamine as a stimulant, to the sexual centers of the brain.

Bonding, the connection to an attractive and receptive male, stimulates the sexual centers in all animals which reproduce by sexual union, including humans. Female rabbits ovulate and become sexually receptive in the presence of an attractive male. And when we are in love, libido is high. Every contact is sensuous, thoughts turn to Eros, and the sexual reflexes work rapidly and well. The presence of the beloved is an aphrodisiac; the smell, sight, sound, and touch of the lover—especially when he/she is excited—are powerful stimuli to sexual desire. In physiologic terms, this may exert a direct physical effect on the neurophysiologic system in the brain which regulates sexual desire.

But again, there is no sexual stimulant so powerful, even love, that it cannot be inhibited by fear and pain.

Although it has been established that significant anatomic and neurophysiologic differences exist in certain parts of female and male mammalian brains, this is not true for the sex centers. There is no evidence that the sexual desire centers of males and females differ anatomically or even physiologically. In fact, neurophysiologic studies have shown that the two genders have similar neurologic bases for sex. For example, both genders require testosterone for activation, and the anatomic loci for penile erection and clitoral congestion, as well as of the orgasm centers and pathways, are the same for both genders.

However, there seem to be major gender differences in the stimuli that evoke desire. Desire in male animals is normally aroused by the smell, sight and other sensory cues provided by a receptive female, by a female in "heat," while desire in receptive females is evoked by the presence of a sexually active, courting male. However, in complex humans, objects of desire are highly conditionable and influenced by experience and it is extremely difficult, if not impossible, to discriminate between biologic and experiential bases of sexual desire.

In our culture, a slightly different spectrum of factors seems to be associated with inhibition of the sexual desire of males and of females. For example, while both men and women may be "turned off" if they are angry at their partner, this is more often true of women. The majority of women seem to lose their desire for a partner towards whom they feel hostile. This is also true of some men, but less frequently, and more males than females can experience intense desire for a partner with whom they are angry.

Again, the biologic basis for the inhibition of desire lies in its neural organization. The complex connections of the sex center to other parts of the brain and the dependence on a fine balance of hormones and neurotransmitters make desire subject to the influence of a wide range of biologic and experimental variables. Further, the neurologic mechanism is constructed in a manner such that it can be "turned off" when the brain has "decided" that it is not to the individual's advantage to pursue sexual pleasure.

Disorders of the Desire Phase

Hypoactive sexual desire and inhibition of sexual desire (ISD) are common syndromes of males and females. The hypoactive individual is asexual; he behaves as though his sexual circuits have been "shut down." He loses interest in sexual matters, will not pursue sexual gratification, and if a sexual situation presents itself, is not moved to avail himself of the opportunity. It may be speculated that hypoactivity of sexual desire can result from the lack of activity of the sexual centers or from their active inhibition.

Inhibition is often selective in that the genital functioning of men and women with sexual anorexia may be maintained. These individuals may be able to experience erection or lubrication-swelling and orgasm, but in a mechanical manner, without much pleasure.

THE EXCITEMENT PHASE

In both men and women the physiologic signs of sexual excitement are produced by the reflex vasodilatation of the genital blood vessels. During sexual arousal two centers in the spinal cord, one at S_2, S_3, and S_4 and one at T_{11}, T_{12}, L_1, and L_2, become activated and cause the arterioles which invest the genitals to dilate. This vasodilatation causes these organs to become swollen and distended and changes their shape to adapt them to their reproductive function. The reflex dilatation occurs in both genders. However, because of anatomic differences in the male and female genitals, this swelling takes different forms and so produces changes which are different but complementary. The penis becomes hard and enlarged to penetrate the vagina and the vagina balloons and becomes wet to accommodate the penis.

Male Excitement—Erection

In the male, the cavernous spaces of the corpora cavernosa of the penis fill with blood and distend the penis against its tough, rigid outer sheath. This changes the flaccid, soft penis into a hard and erect organ capable of penetrating the vagina. The penis is maintained hard and erect by a high pressure hydraulic system which uses blood as its fluid.

Erection is attained and maintained by a complex physiologic system which produces an increased flow of blood to the penis while at the same time decreasing the flow of blood out of the penis. This increases the amount of blood and traps it inside the penis at a relatively high pressure.

The increased amount of blood is shunted into the cavernous

sinuses which distend, thus enlarging the penis. The enlargement is contained by the tough fascia which encases the penile cylinder. The pressure of the increased blood against this sheath hardens the penis and makes it erect. The increased penile flow during excitement is known to be caused by a dilatation of the penile arteries. This is brought about by parasympathetic impulses from the erection centers which cause the muscles in the arterial walls to relax. The mechanism responsible for decreasing penile outflow is not yet entirely clear. Some hypotheses hold that it is caused by reflex constriction of the penile veins. An alternate hypothesis suggests that special penile valves control the outflow, while still another postulates that the outflow and also the shunting of blood to the cavernous sinuses are controlled by "polsters" or small smooth muscle structures located only on the penile blood vessel walls.

The erectile response is primarily a parasympathetic one, although surgical and pharmacological evidence suggests that some sympathetic component is also required for potency, possibly by controlling outflow of erectile blood. However, it is well-known clinically that an intense sympathetic response, such as that produced by fear and anxiety, can instantly drain the penis of extra blood and so cause a psychogenic loss of erection.

Female Excitement

In the female, the excitement phase is also accompanied by reflex vasodilatation of the genital organs. Of course, the anatomy of the female genitals is different. For one, the vulva is much less complex and specialized than the penis. There are no caverns, "polsters," or vascular shunts and the organs are elastic and not rigidly contained like the penis. The genital vasodilatation does not produce erection and there is no evidence of a specifically controlled outflow of blood. Instead, during excitement there is a generalized swelling of the labia and of the tissues surrounding the vaginal barrel.

The "orgasmic platform" which was described by Masters and Johnson as occurring in the plateau stage (the most intensely developed part of the excitement phase) is probably a cushion of swollen and distended tissue which is produced by diffuse genital vasodilatation. Other manifestations of female excitement include the genital "blushing," i.e., heightened coloring of the labia, and the vaginal wetness or lubrication which is the cardinal sign of female excitement. Vaginal lubrication consists of transudate from the blood which distends the genital area during excitement.

It is believed that, like male erection, the physiologic concomitants of female excitement, lubrication and swelling, which are produced by the local vasodilatory reflexes, are governed primarily by the parasympathetic nervous system, which controls the vasodilatation of blood vessels.

Erection in the male is governed by two spinal reflex centers, involving thoracic and lumbar segments, and one at the sacral level. Clinical evidence from spinal cord accident victims suggests that the upper center responds to psychic stimuli, while the lower one is stimulated by tactile input from the genitals. The lower reflex center can function without any higher input or outflow. This accounts for the well-known clinical fact that patients whose spinal cord has been transected above the erection centers can have erections by tactile stimulation of the genitals, on a reflex basis, even when sensation is lost below the level of injury.

Under normal circumstances the excitement reflex centers receive input from the brain and provide outflow to the brain. These connections provide the biological basis by which excitement can be enhanced or inhibited, the pleasurable sensations augmented or blocked by experiential factors.

The neural apparatus that governs the female excitement phase has not yet been delineated precisely. It may be speculated, in view of the analogous embryologic development of the reproductive and nervous systems of the two genders, that the spinal reflex centers as well as the higher neural connections are analogous in males and females.

Disorders of Excitement Phase

Disorders of the male excitement phase are called impotence. This consists of difficulties in attaining or maintaining an erection. This may occur with or without associated disturbances of libido or ejaculation.

Female excitement disorders are marked by difficulty with lubrication and swelling during love-making.

The complex physiology of male erection and the need to create a temporary high blood pressure system make this phase of the male sexual response the most vulnerable to biological factors, as well as to anxiety. It follows that impotence or erectile dysfunction is a highly prevalent sexual disorder. By contrast, dysfunctions of the female excitement phase, i.e., the isolated inhibition of lubrication and swelling, is a relatively uncommon clinical syndrome, except as the result of such local physiologic factors as estrogen deficiency with senile vaginitis. Excitement phase dysfunction of females can exist as a discrete syndrome, but the painful and uncomfortable experience of coitus with a dry and nondistended vagina can cause a secondary inhibition of desire and/or avoidance of sex.

THE ORGASM PHASE

The orgasm phase of the sexual response is, like excitement, a genital reflex that is governed by spinal neural centers. Sensory impulses which trigger orgasm enter the spinal cord in the pudendal nerve at the sacral level, and the efferent outflow is from T_{11} to L_2. The spinal reflex centers for orgasm are in close anatomic proximity to those which govern bladder and anal control. For this reason, in injuries to the lower cord, orgasm, urinary and defecatory control may all be impaired. Orgasm does not, as does excitement, involve a vascular reflex but consists in both males and females of reflex contractions of certain genital muscles.

The male orgasm is made up of two independent but coordinated reflexes which make up its two subphases: emission and ejaculation.

Emission consists of the reflex contraction of the smooth muscles which are contained in the walls of the internal male reproductive organs: the tubuli epididymides, the vas deferens, the seminal vesicles and the prostate gland. This contraction deposits a bolus of seminal fluid into the posterior urethra. The internal vesical sphincter snaps shut, placing the seminal bolus into an enclosed space. This emission response is not pleasurable; it is reported to be perceived as a slight physiologic signal which has been called the "sensation of ejaculatory inevitability" by Masters and Johnson.

In the healthy male, emission is followed a split second later by rhythmic, .8 per second contractions of the striated muscles which are located at the base of the penis, the ishio and bulbo cavernosi muscles. The effect of these contractions is to propel the seminal fluid out of the penis in a series of squirts. These contractions are accompanied by the typical pleasurable orgastic sensations.

Female orgasm is strictly analogous to the second phase of male orgasm. Lacking the Wolffian derived internal male reproductive organs, there is, of course, no emission phase in the female. Adequate stimulation will, however, evoke a rhythmic contraction occurring at the rate of 8 per second, just as during the ejaculatory part of the male orgasm, of the same muscles, the ishio and bulbo cavernosi. In the female these are located around the vaginal introitus. These contractions are accompanied by the pleasurable sensations of orgasm.

In the male tactile stimulation of the glans and shaft of the penis results in the orgasm reflex, while in the female evidence suggests that stimulation of the embryologically and neurologically analogous area, the clitoris, produces orgasm.

Emission in the male is governed by the sympathetic nervous system. During emission, stimulation of the alpha adrenergic receptors of the smooth muscles of the male reproductive orgasms are stimulated, causing them to contract.

The neural connections which control the second part of the male, as well as the female, orgasm, which consists of contractions of striated muscles, are probably controlled by a different reflex center which has not as yet been identified.

The reflex center for orgasm in males is located in the sacral spinal cord, near the centers that govern defecation and urination reflexes. It is believed that the female orgasm center is similarly located. Spinal cord victims can have the physical component of orgasm and so father children. This can occur as a result of local stimulation of the genitals, as long as this center is intact, even if they experience no sensation. But under ordinary circumstances, the orgasm center receives input from the brain, and also contributes its output to the higher centers.

These connections between the spinal orgasm centers and the higher brain provide the physiologic apparatus for learned inhibition of orgasm. Orgasm, unlike erection, which is not subject to voluntary control, can be, and under normal circumstances is, under the individual's voluntary control. This means that there are probably neural circuits that connect the orgasm center to voluntary motor and conscious perception areas of the brain. It may also be speculated that orgasm has close connections with the pleasure center of the brain. It is this connection which under normal circumstances makes the experience of orgasm so pleasurable.

Disorders of the Orgasm Phase

Clinical syndromes produced by disorders of the orgasm phase include: inadequate ejaculatory control or premature ejaculation, retarded ejaculation, and its female analogue, orgastic dysfunction of females. Orgasm inhibitions of both males and females fall along a spectrum of severity from total anorgasmia to mild situational difficulties in reaching a climax. An interesting subvariety of retarded ejaculation is a syndrome I have called *partial retardation* (PRE) (cf. *The New Sex Therapy*)—PRE patients have a normal emission response, but the second phase ejaculation is selectively inhibited. Clinically these men experience a "seepage" of semen but no orgastic squirting and no ejaculatory pleasure. Return to the flaccid state is commonly delayed in these patients.

OTHER SEXUAL PROBLEMS AMENABLE TO SEX THERAPY

The great majority of the sexual dysfunctions that are seen in clinical practice can be classified as disturbances of the desire, excitement, or orgasm phases of the sexual response. All of these are psychophysiologic disorders caused by sexually related anxiety and all are, to some degree at least, amenable to sexual therapy. However, two other syndromes should be included here because they, too, are associated with sexual anxiety and they, too, are often amenable to sexual therapy.

The first consists of a group of psychophysiologic sexual disorders which are the product of involuntary painful spasms of muscles of the genital and reproductive organs. Vaginismus in females and certain types of ejaculatory pain in males fall into this category.

Sexual phobias, with their attendant avoidances, are also common sexual complaints. They are not psychophysiologic, nor are these disorders related to a specific phase. Sexual phobias are included here primarily because these syndromes are frequently amenable to sex therapy.

Muscle Spasms of Sexual Organs

Vaginismus is caused by the conditioned reflex spasmic contraction of the muscles guarding the vaginal introitus. This syndrome is not related to a specific sexual phase, but occurs whenever vaginal entry is attempted. This is a common cause of unconsummated marriage and is highly responsive to sex therapy. In milder form, this genital spasm causes dyspareunia. Entry is possible in such cases, but intercourse is painful.

An analogous cause of dyspareunia of the male is *psychogenic ejaculatory and post-ejaculatory pain*. In this syndrome, the man experiences a sharp pain at the moment of ejaculation or, more typically, a short time after he ejaculates. This pain may last for minutes or hours or even days. It is frequently so intense as to be disabling. Examination sometimes reveals that the cremasteric muscles are in spasm, pulling the testicles tightly against the perineum. It may be speculated that the pain is produced by the spastic contraction of the cremasteric and/or the smooth muscles of the internal male reproductive organs.

Sexual Phobias

Many persons experience sexual difficulties because they have developed phobic avoidances of erotic feelings and/or certain sexual activities. Commonly avoided sexual behaviors or situations include penetration, oral sex, anal sex, masturbation, kissing, caressing, looking at genitals, semen, vaginal secretions, pubic hair, getting undressed, etc. Such patients experience acute anxiety and panic attacks in the phobic situation. They commonly also develop anticipatory anxiety and strong avoidance of any activity that might lead to the frightening sexual situation. A patient may suffer only from sexual phobia. Or the phobia may be associated with sexual dysfunctions. For example, phobic avoidance of sex often complicates the clinical picture of vaginismus and of ISD.

Phobias of all kinds, including sexual phobias, are responsive to a variety of rapid treatment methods. Behavior therapy, integrated methods which combine behavioral and psychodynamic tactics, and drug therapy have been found to be effective for treating phobias and phobic avoidance states. But if a sexual phobia is not recognized, standard sex therapy is ineffective and may even aggravate a patient's problem because the erotic exercises tend to evoke too much anxiety.

However, sexually phobic patients can often be helped by psychosexual therapy, provided that the treatment is flexible enough to accommodate to their specific and individual needs and the tasks are designed to evoke the optimal level of anxiety to desensitize the patient.

CHAPTER

2

THE ETIOLOGY OF THE

SEXUAL DYSFUNCTIONS

On one level, the sexual dysfunctions, as well as the sexual phobias, are caused by a single factor: anxiety. Sexually related anxiety may be considered the "final" common pathway through which multiple psychopathogens may produce sexual dysfunctions. This sexually disruptive anxiety is always evoked by and related to sex, but it is not specific in content or intensity. It can have many origins and intensities and can play various roles in the psychodynamic structure of the person and in the relationship. It can result from deep unconscious conflict derived in early childhood or it can be the product of simple performance fears. It can be the result of fears of sexual success or fears of sexual failure. Deep fears of rejection and vulnerability that derive from past events can cause sexual problems, as can simple power struggles that have their basis in current reality. The patient may be entirely conscious about what causes his sexual dysfunction or his anxiety can operate on a deeply unconscious level and leave him mystified. *But the physiological concomitants of anxiety are always the same no matter what its source or depth or intensity, no matter what the relationship to conscious experience, and no matter what the level of insight.*

If anxiety is evoked when a person tries to have sex, it will produce the identical psychophysiologic disturbances of function. In that sense there is no specificity; a man can lose his erection simply because he is worried that he will not perform that evening, an anxiety of which he is painfully aware, or because the sexual act with his wife evokes anxiety that derives from oedipal incest taboos acquired during early childhood, of which he is totally unconscious, or because he hears a burglar downstairs. On a physiological level the event is identical in all the cases and the penis does not know the difference. In all these cases, the brain has "decided" that it is too "dangerous" to have sex. The physiologic components of the negative affect which is evoked when he tries to make love will inhibit the spinal centers which control the inflow and outflow of blood, and the blood will drain out of his penis instantly, producing impotence, no matter what the original stimulus was.

If anxiety is the common denominator of all the sexual dysfunctions, what determines symptom choice? Why does one man with sexually related anxiety lose his desire while another becomes impotent and still another fails to achieve control over his ejaculation? And why, if anxiety is indeed the universal cause of sexual dysfunction, do the different syndromes respond to different treatment regimes?

The question of specificity in psychosomatic disorders is complex and is by no means fully understood. However, in the area of the sexual dysfunctions some parts of the puzzle are becoming clearer.

It has been proposed that one determinant of symptom choice is the individual's psychophysiologic response pattern, which is highly specific. According to this view, a person's physical response to emotion is as specific and individual as his fingerprint. From early childhood on, one person will respond to any form of stress with an increased flow of gastric acid, another's muscles will tense up, while a third's genital blood vessels will be particularly responsive. This characteristic response pattern predisposes one person to develop specific psychosomatic disorders, another to inhibit his orgasmic response, and the libido of another to be more vulnerable. To a certain extent this is true and accounts in some measure for symptom choice.

In addition to "individual response specificity," clinical experience with the sexually dysfunctional population suggests that three psychological variables contribute to the choice of symptom: 1) The *time* at which anxiety and the defenses against this anxiety arise within the sexual experience will to some extent determine what kind of symptom the patient will develop. 2) The quality or intensity, but not the content, of the remote or underlying anxiety is another determinant. 3) The different dysfunctions are associated with specific immediate antecedents or specific defenses against sexually related anxiety. The nature of these specific antecedents will determine the type of symptom developed because the symptom results from the interaction between these defenses and the sexual response.

TIMING OF ANXIETY

Sexual symptoms are produced by the interaction of anxiety with the physiologic expression of sex and different symptoms are produced when anxiety arises at different times or points in the sequence of the sexual response.

Desire phase problems occur when the anxiety is aroused very early in the sequence of desire-excitement-orgasm. In these patients the first stirrings of sexual pleasure will evoke anxiety with its attendant repression. In fact, sexual desire may be defended against even before that, at the mere contemplation or anticipation of a sexual opportunity.

Excitement phase problems are caused by anxiety which is evoked later, at varying points in the course of love-making, when the person is already physically aroused. Some patients feel anxiety as soon as they have an erection, and so lose it then; others are tranquil until the point of penetration, but lose the erection at that time, while still others are plagued by anxiety while they are in the vagina and so become flaccid before they ejaculate.

Orgasm phase problems occur when anxiety and defenses against this are evoked late, at the highest point of arousal just prior to orgasm and so these patients' sexual response is normal until the climax, which is impaired.

Clinical observations suggest that the more severe and intense the sexual anxiety is, the earlier in the sexual sequence it tends to arise. Thus patients whose anxiety is most severe tend to develop desire phase problems, while those with the mildest anxieties will "tolerate" sexual pleasure for a while before they get anxious and typically develop orgasm difficulties. Again, this correlation is not absolute and clinical exceptions exist.

QUALITY OF THE REMOTE CAUSES

In the past it had been the prevailing hypothesis that sexual dysfunctions invariably grow out of deep and serious underlying conflicts. According to psychoanalytic theory, the nature of these conflicts, the conditions under which they were acquired, and the patient's age at acquisition are highly specific. In brief, it was believed that male dysfunctions are caused by the unconscious fear of castration or injury if the man were to be fully sexual. This conflict was believed to derive from an inadequate resolution of the oedipal crisis at the age of four or five. The identification with the father was thought insufficient to allay fears of competition and retaliation from him for the universal wish to have sex with mother. Adult life sexual situations evoke these old fantasies and fears. Wife is mother and retaliation is unconsciously anticipated. This results in sexual anxiety and dysfunction.

Female dysfunctions were also attributed to anxieties produced by unresolved oedipal and preoedipal conflicts which predisposed the female to unconsciously view sex as a competitive act for which she would be punished by mother. In addition, it was felt that some women were envious and angry at males because of their superior anatomic endowments and cultural opportunities and were therefore impaired in their capacity to love and to enjoy sex with a man. "Penis envy" also was believed to result in female sexual dysfunction.

Other psychoanalytic theorists have different views, but they are equally specific and all see sexual dysfunctions as arising during childhood. Thus, for example, Sullivan's theories held that the responses of persons important to the child, his "significant others," shape adult sexuality. In other words, a parent's negative attitudes about sex, even if they are expressed only on a nonverbal level, influence the child to the extent that he may become so conflicted that he is not able to function sexually in adult life.

Family and marital therapists called attention to the hidden emotional forces in a couple's relationship which may spawn sexually disruptive anxiety. Deep angers deriving from power struggles and other interactional problems that have their genesis in parental transferences towards the spouse, as well as anxieties which have their roots in simple communication failures, may disrupt a couple's sexual relationship.

Masters and Johnson and some of the behavior therapists have shown us that superficial or milder anxieties can also produce dysfunctions. Simple learned anxieties, performance anxieties, "spectatoring," and mild, culturally engendered guilts have been implicated in the etiology of the sexual dysfunctions by these investigators.

In fact, clinical experience with patients who complain of sexual disorders does not support the specificity hypothesis. A wide spectrum of underlying causes, varying in content and ranging from the mildest to the deepest and most tenacious, can be associated with sexual symptoms. All the causes cited by these clinicians may be associated with sexual problems. If a critical level of anxiety is aroused in the sexual situation, dysfunction will result irrespective of the underlying source and the conditions of acquisition or of the reality of the danger.

When this population is studied from the perspective of the triphasic concept, it appears, however, that while the *content* of the sexual conflict is highly variable, the *quality* of the underlying anxiety is not evenly distributed among the three groups of dysfunctions. It appears that patients with desire phase dysfunctions, as a group, are afflicted with more serious intrapsychic and/or marital problems, while the patients with orgasm problems are more often, but not invariably, found to have relatively milder and less tenacious underlying problems. Excitement phase disorders fall in the middle of the spectrum. Sometimes impotence is associated with moderate kinds of underlying anxiety. Another proportion of this population belongs with the mild kinds of remote causes which usually produce orgasm phase disorders, while another significant segment of impotent males have the deeper kinds of problems which are more characteristic of desire phase inhibition.

The observations suggest that, while the immediate causes of the various dysfunctions tend to be fairly specific, the content of the deeper causes that give rise to these immediate ones is not. However, there does appear to be some specificity with respect to severity or intensity. The etiology or causes of the sexual dysfunctions may be thought of as lying on a continuum from mild and transient and easily extinguished to deep, tenacious, and intense and resistant to treatment.

I have a good deal of discomfort with this formulation because of the lack of definition of "intensity" or "depth" or "mildness" of conflict or anxiety. These qualities cannot be measured, and physiological concomitants of anxiety or conflict do not correlate with the psychic "depth"; there are no rating scales to measure these qualities.

And yet this is the only formulation that makes sense. Trained clinicians show a high degree of agreement in their judgments of the quality of the underlying anxiety of particular causes: "That is a deep problem"; "His anxiety is pervasive and intense"; or, "This is a simple learning problem"; "He just has some performance anxiety." The "quality" construct is used here only as a working hypothesis, as a useful explanatory model, to be discarded when more accurate parameters which will lend themselves better to scientific validation are developed.

To minimize confusion, I will try to define or describe what I mean by mild and intense and deep and superficial with respect to underlying causes. On what I call the mild side are uncomplicated performance anxieties, overconcern for the partner, the anxieties produced by unrealistic sexual expectations of oneself and one's partner, transient fears of rejection, mild residues of childhood guilt and shame about masturbation and sexual pleasure, etc. These are either "pure" (i.e., they are feared in reality) or the product of mild underlying causes: mild power struggles, lack of assertiveness, mildly negative childhood messages, even mild remnants of oedipal and sibling rivalry problems. These milder anxieties tend to be recognized consciously by the patient and are highly amenable to the brief psychosexual treatment procedures with their emphasis on reducing anxiety and promoting confidence and open, reassuring communications between the partners.

Success and pleasure anxieties, fears of intimacy and commitment, and deeper fears of rejection may also underlie the sexual dysfunctions. These may be termed the "mid-level" group of remote causes. In contrast to performance fears, these are not usually consciously recognized by patients. These types of conflicts do not usually yield to standard sex therapy techniques, which are primarily designed to deal with fears of sexual *failure* rather than with success fears. However, sex therapy can be modified to accommodate such dynamics. These "mid-level" success conflicts are not usually strongly defended against and resistances against admitting these into conscious awareness are usually not intense. The brief psychosexual treatment techniques which are designed to confront these issues rapidly and actively are often quite effective with these patients. However, conflicts about sex and success and pleasure may be derivative of earlier and deeper problems. If these are still actively operative, brief treatment techniques are not likely to be successful.

Finally, truly profound and tenacious sexually related anxieties may produce sexual symptoms. Included in this etiologic group are the more serious relationship problems, the hostile and neurotic associations, and those sexual conflicts which have their roots in childhood injury and the destructive adaptations to these injuries. These often, but not always, involve oedipal and preoedipal problems. Problems may also derive from unresolved sibling rivalries and intense performance anxieties, as well as strong family messages which have made sex or love or pleasure dangerous and guilt-provoking. These intense causes almost always operate on an unconscious level and are deeply threatening to the patient. Characteristically, during therapy the patient will resist attempts at rapid confrontation with an interpretation of such material, so that brief treatment is not likely to be successful in cases where the quality of the sexual anxiety and conflict are of this intensity.

In sum, the hypothesis has been advanced that the three groups of dysfunctions are not equally represented along a continuum of severity of causes. Patients who have desire for sex and who can experience excitement—whose problem is limited to the orgasm phase—tend to cluster around the milder remote causes and are highly amenable to treatment. By contrast, patients whose dysfunction affects the desire phase tend to be heavily represented in the severe category of causality.

There are exceptions to both generalizations. Some patients whose sexual response is inhibited on the level of the desire phase have only minor or mild underlying anxieties. These are among the few in this group who can be cured by the rapid sex therapy techniques. On the other hand, some impotent and anorgastic patients are deeply disturbed and highly resistant to treatment. Excitement phase problems have a wide spread along this hypothetical continuum. They fall along the entire spectrum but tend to cluster around the center.

THE HYPOTHESIS OF SPECIFIC IMMEDIATE CAUSES

Anxiety is handled or defended against in a variety of ways. The classic defense mechanisms described by psychoanalytic theories first called our attention to the different strategies people employ in coping with anxiety. The sexual anxiety associated with the sexual dysfunctions similarly evokes defense mechanisms which are typical for that individual, for that situation and for that level of anxiety. Thus, one person *suppresses* his erotic sensations because they make him anxious, while another will *obsessively* attempt to *control* them. These individuals will develop different symptoms: The suppressor will fail to learn ejaculatory control while the obsessor will be unable to release his orgasm. *The interaction of the specific defenses against sexually related anxiety with the sexual response produces the specific syndrome.* A detailed examination of the specific experiences of sexually dysfunctional patients reveals that the psychic events—the specific sensations which are experienced during sex and immediately preceding the occurrence of the symptom—are quite distinctive for the various dysfunctions. It appears that the different sexual dysfunctions are associated with specific, immediate antecedents which evoke sexually disruptive anxiety or disruptive defenses against this.

The degree of *correlation* between specific antecedent and specific symptom varies with the syndrome. For example, complaints associated with genital muscle spasm, i.e., vaginismus and certain dyspareunias, as well as the orgasm phase disorders, are most closely associated with a specific antecedent, i.e., the physiologic concomitants or defenses against anxiety, while desire and excitement dysfunctions are more variable in that respect. In other words, prematurity is almost always associated with distraction at high levels of sexual excitement, while impotence is often, but not invariably, produced by performance anxiety.

Vaginismus

Vaginismus is always associated with a conditioned spasm of the perivaginal musculature. This spasm is a reaction to fear evoked by vaginal penetration, which is always the immediate cause or antecedent that produces vaginismus. The original cause of the penetration fear and the spasm, that is, the remote cause, is highly variable. In my experience, the vaginal spasm originally may be caused by physical pain on intercourse, by rape, by guilt about real or fantasied incestuous experiences, by conflict about pleasure, by fear of or anger at the partner, etc. Insight is not a determinant in the formation of the symptom. These remote origins are remembered by some patients, but for others they are inaccessible and irretrievable to memory. The intensity of the underlying anxiety varies substantially, and the symptom is not related to a specific phase.

Dyspareunia Associated with Genital Muscle Spasm

Psychogenic ejaculatory pain and post-ejaculatory pain and the female dyspareunia caused by mild vaginismus are always caused by an involuntary, intense, painful spasm of certain genital muscles.

A varity of deeper or more inaccessible causes may be associated with this syndrome. In-depth studies of female patients have revealed a variety of sources: guilt about intercourse and erotic pleasure, fear of penetration, and anger at the partner. In males the underlying causes range from mild masturbatory guilt to profound and severe sexual conflict. Sometimes no underlying cause can be detected.

Premature Ejaculation

In most cases, premature ejaculation is associated with the man's failure to perceive the erotic sensation of the late excitement stage which occurs prior to orgasm. Premature ejaculators will often report that they experience an atypically steep curve of excitement. Instead of the gradual rise of excitement, which many normal men experience, they go from low levels of excitement directly and steeply to the intense sensations of excitement which are premonitory to orgasm. Early mild excitement is well tolerated by these men, but high levels of excitement seem to evoke anxiety and its defense which in this case is repression, suppression or distraction from the clear perception of the erotic sensations. This defense mechanism or immediate anteced-ent produces the symptom of inadequate ejaculatoy control, for the perceptual defense against the sensations of erotic pleasure interferes with the normal process of learning ejaculatory control. It may be speculated that in order to acquire control over this or for that matter any other reflex, one must be able to experience and register the sensations that occur premonitory to the discharge of that reflex. Without the perception of orgasm together with high excitement, the process of sensory-sensory integration upon which learning is based is lost. The same is true of learning control of urination. The child must be able to feel and register the sensations of a full bladder if he is to learn control.

While the immediate cause of premature ejaculation is specific, the original or remote causes responsible for the anxiety evoked by intense sexual excitement and for the erection of perceptual defenses against this are highly variable in content. In my clinical experience, a wide variety of remote causes may be associated with inadequate ejaculatory control. Most of these patients get anxious when sexual pleasure is prolonged and intense, but the reason for this varies. Some, as Masters and Johnson pointed out, have trained themselves to climax quickly because of the pressured conditions of their early sexual experiences. Some have performance anxiety, fearing they will come too quickly or lose their erection, while some are angry at the partner or ill at ease with her. Many have anxiety related to all pleasure— they tend to eat as quickly as they climax and do not relish their food any more than their sensuous feelings. Others seem to suffer from the remnants of unresolved oedipal and preoedipal and sibling rivalry problems, and infantile transferences which cause them to feel anxious when pleasure is too great and lasts too long. But in the majority of these patients—no matter what the source or content of the anxiety— the quality of this sexual anxiety is mild or moderate and easily extinguished.

Inhibition of Orgasm

In males as well as in females inhibition of orgasm appears often, but not universally, to be the product either of inadequate penile or clitoral stimulation or of obsessive self-observation during high levels of sexual arousal, i.e., "orgasm watching."

It is not possible to have an orgasm without stimulation that is sufficiently intense so that it reaches the reflex threshold. A detailed examination of the experience of anorgastic patients frequently reveals that the stimulation they receive during sexual contact is not adequate for this purpose. This is more often true of women. Ignorance of sexual physiology, unconscious avoidance of sexual pleasure and problems with assertion may underlie this behavior.

The more common immediate cause of orgasm dysfunction is the obsessive focus on the erotic sensations that are premonitory to orgasm during stimulation that would be adequate if there were no inhibition. These patients, like the premature ejaculation group, also seem to experience anxiety at high levels of excitement. In contrast to the premature ejaculators, who defend against such "late" sexual anxiety by "not perceiving," these orgasm-blocked patients do the opposite. They obsessively focus on the sensations in an attempt to control anxiety. This interferes with the normal functioning of the sexual reflexes because it causes inhibition.

This mechanism is not specific to the orgasm reflex; all reflexes which are subject to voluntary control can be inhibited when conscious attention is focused on their process. This experience creates the opportunity to associate the sensations premonitory to orgasm wth the orgastic sensations. Such sensory-sensory integration may be the mechanism for learning normal control of all reflexes. It is the principle upon which the treatment of inadequate ejaculatory control is based, and it is also the rationale behind treatments of enuresis, or inadequate bladder control.

However, this mechanism for learning normal control can go too far, until the smooth operation of the reflex is impaired by an inappropriately intense focus of attention. This is true of the patellar reflex, which cannot be elicited by the neurologist's hammer when the patient is staring at her knee. Distraction by having the patient grasp her hands will frequently release the knee "jerk." It is also true of functions composed of complex coordinated reflexes, such as dancing or swallowing. "Self-consciousness" makes us awkward and the orgasm reflex is no exception. Inhibition is likely to occur in both men and women when the focus of attention is obsessive, i.e., in the service of anxiety reduction rather than in the service of pleasure.

Evidence for this hypothesis derives from questioning patients about their specific experiences while making love. Such patients, if they are insightful, tend to report: "I start thinking, now will I come, will it happen this time?" or "Is this what is supposed to happen? Am I feeling the right thing?"

The point of sexual excitement at which the anxiety which mobilizes the defense against orgasm is evoked is highly specific for each patient, but this defense, "spectatoring," is operative in most patients with orgasm dsyfunctions.

The remote causes, that is, the reasons which cause the patient to become anxious and obsessive during high levels of sexual excitement, are highly variable in content. In-depth studies of anorgastic women reveal that fears of losing control of aggressive as well as of sexual impulses often lie beneath the inhibition. These are evoked at high levels of excitement. Fears of urinating, unrealistic fantasies about the dangers or the pleasures of orgasm, performance anxieties related to fears of failure to have an orgasm or to have it quickly enough, unconscious competitive feelings towards other women, fears of rejection, fears of death, and fears of pleasure and sexual success are also found in this population.

Retarded Ejaculation

Males with retarded ejaculation suffer from a slightly different spectrum of underlying causes. Although some are also afraid of sexual failure and others of sexual success, more often there is evidence of anger towards women and lack of trust in the relationship.

Of course, all the causes mentioned above may be derivative of deeper and more unconscious conflicts, but the quality of the underlying anxiety of anorgastic women and of men with mild situational retarded ejaculation tends in the great majority of patients to be mild and highly responsive to brief treatment. Those relatively few patients whose orgasm inhibition is a defense against deeper fears make up the bulk of treatment failures.

Excitement Phase Dysfunctions

Impotence is associated with a specific immediate cause or antecedent—anxiety which arises during the sexual act. Impotence is *not* a consequence of a defense against anxiety; rather it is a physiologic concomitant of anxiety and a sign that defense mechanisms are *not* effective.

Many impotent men experience performance anxiety or the fear of sexual failure, but such performance anxiety, while it is clinically highly prevalent, is not the only immediate cause of impotence. I believe that many factors can create anxiety while a man is making love and this can drain the penis of the extra blood needed for erection, even if it is not associated with performance fears. Clinical experience with impotent men reveals that many do experience the thought, "I wonder if it will work tonight," just before they lose their erection. But other impotent men conjure up different anxiety-laden thoughts during love-making and some experience anxiety which has no specific conscious content.

The performance anxiety which is so often associated with impotence is sometimes "pure," i.e., it has no other roots except the anticipation and fear of sexual failure. Such problems are highly amenable to non-demanding treatment techniques which reassure the patient and restore his confidence. However, such anxiety is often only the conscious manifestation of deeper conflicts. The mere thought, "Maybe I won't have an erection tonight," need not necessarily be associated with anxiety of sufficient intensity to drain the penis of blood. In the secure person who has a good relationship, such a thought will not produce impotence, but when there is deeper unrecognized anxiety about sex, then the consciously perceived penile performance anxiety can tap intense sources of conflict which may be beyond the man's conscious awareness. For example, if a man is immature in his relationships with women and is therefore unduly fearful of rejection, he will be uncomfortable unless he performs perfectly, unless he "gets an A for mother's approval." When he equates sex with a performance to be judged by his partner, sex becomes marred by anxiety, which is related on a deeper level to primitive fears of abandonment. Or, if a man harbors unconscious fears of sexual success, if he has not resolved his early developmental struggles, and intercourse means symbolically a forbidden and hazard-ous oedipal competition, then he may "prevent himself" from func-tioning by conjuring up self-destructive doubts about his performance. Characteristically, patients are not consciously aware of their active role in evoking the anxiety-provoking thoughts which result in impotence. On a conscious level the patient panics about his ability to perform, while unconsciously he needs to avoid a successful performance. When the manifest fear of failure is a cover for an unconscious fear of success, simple behavioral techniques designed to dispel performance anxiety cannot be expected to work.

Thus, again, it appears that the immediate cause of erectile failure, performance anxiety, can be the basic problem or it can be associated with a wide range of deeper causes. These vary in both content and intensity. Some impotent men suffer only from true performance fears and lack of confidence which is easily dispelled, while others are plagued by deep-seated, intense and tenacious conflicts about sexual pleasure and sexual success.

Inhibited Sexual Desire

The immediate causes of inhibited sexual desire (ISD) are the most elusive, and have not yet been clarified precisely. The following represents a working hypothesis about the antecedents to the inhibi-tion of sexual desire which has emerged from the study of the immediate and specific sexually related experiences of this patient population.

Desire inhibition patients, like those who suffer from the genital dysfunction, experience sexually related anxiety and also significant hostilities towards their partners. In this population the anxiety is evoked earlier in the sexual sequence, when sex is merely anticipated or becomes a possibility, or as soon as the initial sensations of erotic desire or interest are experienced. These early stirrings are threatening and the patient characteristically defends against the anxiety evoked by *suppressing* his desire rapidly and involuntarily, often before it can develop fully and emerge into conscious awareness. Some of the patients I have studied do this by tapping the normal psychophysiologic mechanism for suppressing desire. They conjure up or focus on negative thoughts or on the partner's most unattractive features or on the disadvantages of the situation. It may be speculated that the associated negative affect effectively inhibits the sexual and pleasure centers. Other patients merely distract themselves with asexual thoughts or activities and so form a perceptual barrier to sexual stimuli.

The mechanism of focusing on negatives to suppress desire is the mirror image, or the opposite, of conjuring up sexual fantasies in the service of liberating sexual desire.

Still other patients erect additional defenses against sexual feeling by developing a pattern of phobic avoidance of situations that may arouse them. This pathological sequence is analogous to the one which may operate in anorexia nervosa. Anorexic patients also suppress the sensations of hunger by conjuring up noxious thoughts about being fat and may also develop a phobic avoidance of food.

ISD patients characteristically have no insight into the mechanism of active suppression, but in fact may complain and seek help for their low libido. However, a detailed study of the experiences of these patients indicates that libido is not low because desire does not arise, but rather such patients have learned to "turn it off," usually at the point when the first erotic sensations are felt or anticipated.

Some of these patients are so threatened by sex, so unwilling to engage in erotic interchange with their partners, that they manage to avoid any situation which might evoke sexual feelings. In case the patient has, "despite himself," allowed himself to experience some sexual activity, he or she will usually report that she/he feels "nothing," because the "turn off" occurs so rapidly and automatically that it is not even consciously perceived. The experiences of some ISD patients in sexual therapy lend support for the hypothesis of the operation of a "turn off" mechanism rather than an absence of desire. A study of the experiences of such patients in response to the pleasuring exercises which are prescribed in the course of sex therapy reveals that highly sensitive and introspective patients will sometimes report that the partner's gentle loving caresses begin to "feel good," i.e., evoke pleasure, but almost instantly these pleasurable sensations are replaced by negative feelings and thoughts. Just when he begins to enjoy sensuous or erotic feelings, the patient may suddenly feel uncomfortable, tense, angry, anxious, or repelled by the partner. Focus on unattractive or unacceptable features about the partner is an extremely common mechanism.

Other ISD patients feel no such negative sensation. They report only an absence of feeling, a kind of anesthesia. If ISD patients do have sex, they may be able to function genitally. Characteristically, they feel little during the excitement phase, but they do feel some pleasure just before or fleetingly during orgasm. Some of these patients have negative *post* coital feelings, experiencing depression or anxiety or the impulse to detach or even "cleanse" themselves from the partner.

In-depth studies of such patients suggest that they suppress their desire because on some level they *do not want* to feel sexual. For many underlying real and irrational reasons sexual desire has become dangerous or objectionable. The reasons for a sexual "turn off" may be quite realistic. The inhibition of sexual impulses and feelings when one is in a dangerous or inappropriate situation constitutes a normal adaptive mechanism. For example, it is normal and appropriate not to feel or express sexual desire when the partner is unavailable or sadistic, when he is a family member or a business associate, or when he is physically unattractive. Nor is it abnormal to feel no desire when there is real danger, or when sexual activity is always disappointing and there is no hope for improvement, or when there is bitter anger or disillusionment within the relationship. The inhibition of desire becomes pathological only when it occurs in an inappropriate situation—when the patient does not feel desire for an attractive and appropriate partner; when desire is dampened by unprovoked anger, by mistrust of a spouse who is in reality giving and loving.

Irrational deeper causes of ISD include intrapsychic as well as relationship problems. In my experience, ISD can be associated with fears of success, pleasure and love; intense performance fears; fears of rejection; neurotic power struggles based on infantile transference towards the partner; anger, mistrust and envy of the partner; fears of intimacy; deep sexual conflicts that have their roots in the patient's early development; and anger caused by poor communication between the couple.

At times desire is inhibited because of mild and easily modifiable underlying causes, but usually deeper and more intense angers and anxieties often play an etiologic role in this syndrome.

3

SPECIFIC TREATMENT

STRATEGIES FOR

SEXUAL DYSFUNCTIONS

MASTERS AND JOHNSON originally proposed a structured treatment format which was general, i.e., the same treatment regime was recommended for couples suffering from all forms of sexual "inadequacy." However, as clinical experience has deepened and extended our understanding of the sexual dysfunctions, it has become apparent that while the dysfunctions all have a great deal in common, in that they are all produced by sexually related anxiety, there also are significant differences in the psychopathological structure of orgasm, excitement and desire phase disorders. In the preceding chapter, the pathogenesis of the various syndromes was discussed in terms of differences in both the immediate and the deeper causes. The recognition of such differences has led to the development of specific and more effective treatment strategies.

The first objective of psychosexual therapy is to modify the immediate antecedents or causes of the sexual symptom. These are different and specific for the various syndromes. During the process of symptom modification, underlying resistances tend to emerge and these are dealt with to the extent that this is necessary in the office sessions. These resistances are the product of the deeper causes which underlie the immediate antecedents of the prematurity, impotence, etc. In contrast to the specific character of the immediate causes, these deeper problems are *not* specific. The psychological issues that emerge during treatment tend to be similar for all kinds of problems and are not related to a specific phase or syndrome. Therefore, the *psychodynamic techniques* and strategies employed in sex therapy tend to be similar for all the dysfunctions.

On the other hand, the experiential techniques, the structured sexual tasks or *sigs* which are assigned to the couple, are employed to modify the immediate and specific causes of the various dysfunctions, and are of necessity different for the various syndromes. Thus, differences in the psychosexual treatment of the sexual dysfunctions pertain to the behavioral aspect of sex therapy only.

The following is a review and update of the specific behavioral strategies that are currently employed for the treatment of the different syndromes. The suggested exercises are conducted within a flexible time frame. When the patint is comfortable with one step, he proceeds to the next, at his own pace, which is dictated by his and his partner's anxiety level.

INADEQUATE EJACULATORY CONTROL
(PREMATURE EJACULATION)

The aim of the treatment of premature ejaculation is to facilitate learning voluntary control over ejaculation by fostering the patient's awareness of, and increasing his tolerance for, the pleasurable genital sensations that accompany the intense sexual excitement which precedes orgasm. Any method which encourages the man's concentration on pre-orgastic erotic sensations, including the "squeeze" and the "stop-start" methods, can be used to implement this goal. The following variation of the stop-start method is employed by our group:

The patient is advised to concentrate on his erotic sensations only and not to attempt to "hold back."

1) The partner stimulates the patient's penis manually, until he feels that he is near climax. He then asks her to *stop*. A few seconds later, when he feels the acute sensations diminish, he

asks her to *start* again. He climaxes on the fourth period of stimulation.

2) The stop-start stimulation of the penis manually by the partner is repeated, this time using a lubricant. We use petroleum jelly. This procedure simulates the sensations produced by the vaginal environment.

3) Stop-start stimulation is conducted intravaginally, in the female superior position. The woman straddles her partner with his erect penis inside her vagina. His hands are on her hips to guide her motions. She moves up and down until he feels he is near climax and motions her to stop. Then he signals her to start again. He climaxes on the third period of stimulation. At first he does not thrust during this exercise. After he attains control he proceeds to thrusting.

4) Stop-start intravaginally is conducted in the side-to-side position.

5) Stop-start intravaginally in the male superior position.

6) Stop-slow intravaginally. After the patient has learned control by stopping at a high plateau of excitement, if necessary he can improve his control by slowing rather than coming to a complete stop at high excitement levels. This "stop-slow" sig may be employed when the man is having difficulty integrating his new ejaculatory control into his behavior.

ORGASM INHIBITION IN MALES AND FEMALES

The objective of the treatment of orgasm inhibition is to modify the patient's tendency to obsessively observe his/her pre-orgastic sensations and to foster abandonment to erotic feelings, which is a necessary condition of orgastic release. These aims can be implemented by structuring the situation so that the patient receives effective penile or clitoral stimulation under the most tranquil conditions that can be arranged. At the same time, he/she is distracted from the obsessive self-observations. The usual means of distraction is fantasy, but external distractions such as reading or observing pictures or films may also be employed to circumvent the difficulties some patients experience with fantasy.

The following method is employed by our group unless the evaluation reveals reasons to modify the treatment plan.

*Total Anorgasmia—Males and Females**

If the patient is totally anorgastic, the initial aim of treatment is to have the patient experience an orgasm while she is alone, as follows.

1) Self-stimulation of the penis or clitoris—this is first done manually. If manual stimulation is not sufficient to overcome the resistance to orgasm, the intensity of the stimulus is increased. Towards this end males employ a lubricant and females a vibrator.
2) Concomitant distraction by imagery. This may entail concentration on the person's favorite erotic fantasy, on reading erotic literature or on viewing erotic pictures, or on a non-erotic neutral image. The mental imagery occurs while the patient is stimulating him/herself.

Anorgasmia with a Partner—Males and Females

After the patient is comfortable with his/her own sexual feelings and orgasm, or if she/he can only reach orgasm when he/she is alone, the next step entails learning to have an orgasm in the presence of the partner. Since shared sex is usually far more anxiety-provoking than sex when one is alone, orgasm alone usually precedes shared orgasm unless there is profound resistance to masturbation.

The steps to shared orgasm are:

1) Self-stimulation to orgasm in presence of partner. This should occur with a gradual increase in intimacy. First the partner turns his back while the patient stimulates herself. Then he can hold her while she stimulates herself. One partner can stimulate herself to orgasm after the other has climaxed, but the patient should not attempt to reach orgasm during intercourse at this stage of treatment.
2) Manual genital stimulation by the partner to orgasm, while the patient uses his/her customary fantasy for distraction. (This is preceded by sensate focus I and II as needed. See p. 146)

---

* Anorgasmia is far more prevalent in females.

Coital Anorgasmia

Treatment for this complaint essentially consists of progressive in vivo desensitization to orgastic release during vaginal containment. The treatment procedures for males and females are slightly different at this point.

Retarded Ejaculation

1) Orgasm is reached by manual self-stimulation of genitals in the presence of the partner. This is done progressively nearer to the partner's vagina, until orgasm can comfortably be achieved near the mouth of the vagina.
2) Orgasm is achieved by manual stimulation by the partner.
3) The partner stimulates the man's penis manually to a point close to orgasm. Then the penis is inserted into the vagina at the moment of orgasm.
4) The procedure is repeated but the penis is inserted into the vagina progressively earlier until the need for manual stimulation diminishes.
5) Concomitant manual and vaginal stimulation of the penis. The female stimulates the base of her partner's penis manually as he thrusts in and out of the vagina. This maneuver supplies additional stimulation. It is sometimes used to supplement the progressive desensitization, described in steps 1 through 4.

Partial Ejaculatory Retardation

The immediate antecedents of this syndrome are similar if not identical to the immediate causes of general retardation of the entire male ejaculatory reflex, and treatment follows the same tactics: relaxation and stimulation concomitant with distraction by fantasy.

Female Coital Anorgasmia

The aim of the treatment of female coital anorgasmia is to diminish any anxieties, if these exist, that are provoked by penetration because this will lower the woman's orgastic threshold. In addition, the patient is trained to maximize the relatively low level of clitoral stimulation provided by penetration, and to accustom herself to have orgasms in this manner. Most woman can learn to have orgasm on coitus with concomitant clitoral stimulation with these techniques. But only a relatively few are successful in achieving coital orgasm without "clitoral assistance."

The method we employ for the treatment of coital anorgasmia uses the following sequence:

1) Self-stimulation with pelvic thrusting. Under usual circumstances women reach orgasm during coitus by actively thrusting the pelvis against the partner's pubic bone and not, as during masturbatory, manual or oral stimulation, by passive reception of stimulation. Therefore, coitally anorgastic women are first taught to stimulate themselves to orgasm by thrusting their pelvis down against their stationary hand. This pattern of orgastic release improves the probability of learning climax during coitus.

2) The bridge maneuver. This consists of concomitant clitoral stimulation and vaginal intromission. While the penis is inserted, the woman or her partner stimulates her clitoris until she reaches orgasm. This is most comfortable in the side-to-side or rear entry positions. Intromission is delayed until the woman is highly aroused by foreplay.

3) Progressively earlier cessation of clitoral stimulation while the penis is inserted in order to climax without "clitoral assistance."

Many apparently normal women do not learn to climax during intercourse without clitoral assistance, at least by these methods. Such couples are counseled to adapt their love-making to the woman's pattern of climax, without considering this "settling for second best."

EXCITEMENT PHASE DISORDERS OF THE MALE (IMPOTENCE OR ERECTILE DYSFUNCTION)

The performance anxiety which is so frequently associated with impotence can be diminished in many cases by structuring the sexual interactions so that they are nondemanding and reassuring. The patient is encouraged to substitute the nonpressuring goal of pleasure for the stress-producing goal of performance, and the sexual situation is arranged so that it is highly stimulating but has a low level of demand for performance or pressure. The basic Masters and Johnson method accomplishes these goals in a substantial number of patients:

1) Sensate focus I—This consists of taking turns caressing or "pleasuring" each other's bodies without genital stimulation.
2) Sensate focus II—This consists of taking turns body pleasuring and also includes gentle, nondemanding genital stimulation which may proceed to erection but not to orgasm.
3) Brief intromission without orgasm in the female superior position. The woman inserts her partner's penis into her vagina, thrusts a few times, and gets off before there is any anxiety or erection loss. The man reaches orgasm by manual stimulation, which is provided by himself or by his partner, depending on which is more comfortable for him.
4) Intromission to orgasm in the female superior position.
5) Intromission to orgasm in the male superior position.

This method is highly effective in those cases where the etiology is a simple fear of failure. However, many impotent men are basically afraid of sexual success and require a more flexible treatment approach which is designed to accommodate their specific needs. The following tasks may be used to circumvent or "bypass" sexual anxiety which is not primarily related to performance fears. They are designed to reduce the pressure on the man still further, and also to provide him with the tools to deal with his anxiety should this arise.

1) The use of fantasy concomitant with genital stimulation, especially during anxious moments.
2) Having the wife learn to accept clitoral stimulation as an alternative to coitus, thus relieving the pressure on the man.
3) Teaching the couple the use of self-stimulation at times of tension.

Partial Impotence

It may be speculated that males who cannot ejaculate with a full erection on a psychogenic basis have reinforced the incomplete erections by ejaculating in that state. This reinforcement sequence may be regarded as the immediate cause of the syndrome of partial impotence. Treatment is based on the rationale of extinguishing that response, and reinforcing full erection instead.

The man or his partner stimulates his penis. He is advised not to allow himself to climax unless he is fully erect. If he feels that he is near orgasm he stops until he is fully erect. Finally, when he has a full erection, he climaxes. This is a frustrating but effective treatment procedure.

EXCITEMENT PHASE DISORDERS OF FEMALES (GENERAL SEXUAL DYSFUNCTION OF FEMALES)

The aim of treatment of this rather uncommon disorder is to reduce the anxiety which is evoked during the excitement phase, and which inhibits its expression. The original Masters and Johnson method is effective, although there are advantages to employing some flexibility to accommodate to the patients' individual dynamic needs.

1) Sensate focus I—Taking turns at pleasuring or caressing each other's bodies without genital stimulation.
2) Sensate focus II—Taking turns at pleasuring each other's bodies with gentle, nondemanding genital stimulation which does not proceed to orgasm.
3) Slow, teasing genital stimulation by partner. The vulva, clitoris and vaginal entrance and the nipples are caressed. This is interrupted if the woman feels near orgasm, and then continued a little later, when arousal has diminished somewhat.
4) Coitus is withheld until the woman is well lubricated. To avoid frustration and to reduce pressure on the woman, the partner is advised to have extracoital orgasms during this phase of treatment.
5) Slow, teasing nondemanding intromission in the female superior position under her control, for the purpose of focusing on her vaginal sensations.

When the patient's anxiety does not diminish sufficiently with these desensitizing exercises, we suggest bypass via distracting erotic imagery during stimulation, to give her a "tool" for managing her anxiety.

DESIRE PHASE DISORDERS OF
MALES AND FEMALES

The sexual excercises employed in the treatment of ISD are designed to confront the patint with his/her active though unconscious and involuntary avoidance of sexual feelings and activities and/ or the tendency to focus on negative images and thoughts and to suppress sexual feelings which may emerge despite the patient's defenses against this.

In addition, as has already been mentioned, desire phase disorders seem, with some exceptions, to be associated with more severe and tenacious underlying psychopathology than is typically associated with the genital dysfunctions. Consequently, psychosexual treatment of these disorders often necessitates much more extensive psychotherapeutic intervention than does the treatment of orgasm and excitement phase disorders.

The structured sexual experiences are designed to reduce sexual anxiety and to promote sexual pleasure. At the same time, they play the role of a "probe" to rapidly ferret out and foster the emergence of deeper anxieties and resistances and make these available for psychotherapeutic exploration in the sessions. The blocks against sexual desire must be clearly identified and resolved or bypassed before sexual desire can return.

In these disorders the sequence of treatment is much more variable than with prematurity or secondary impotence. The therapist decides on exercises according to the specific dynamic needs of the couple. However, in order to illuminate these dynamics, it is often useful to begin treatment with the "classical" Masters and Johnson therapeutic sequence, which is employed in the excitement phase disorders:

1) Sensate focus I—Taking turns pleasuring or caressing each other's bodies without stimulating the genitals.
2) Sensate focus II—Taking turns pleasuring each other's bodies and gently stimulating primary erotic areas and genitals, but not to orgasm.
3) Self-stimulation—If the woman is inhibited in her desire and also anorgastic she first learns to have an orgasm by herself. If both partners are orgastic they masturbate together in each other's presence.
4) Exploring fantasies—In blocked patients the exploration of

fantasies is often useful, both to increase desire and to reveal psychological blocks.

5) Sharing erotic fantasies with partner.
6) Sharing erotic material with partner.
7) Slow and nondemanding intromission.
8) Focus on the emotional interaction of the couple before love-making. The couple is instructed not to attempt any sexual activity unless both feel calm and receptive.

VAGINISMUS

The treatment of vaginismus is designed to extinguish the conditioned spasm of the muscles surrounding the vagina by means of systematic in vivo desensitization. Any technique which uses gradual dilatation of the spastic introitus is effective. Our method employs the following sequence:

1) Inspection of vaginal opening by the patient using a mirror.
2) Daily insertion of one of her fingers into her vaginal opening until comfortable. A lubricant may be used in all the dilatation exercises. Also, graduated dilators may be substituted for fingers.
3) Daily insertion of two fingers into vaginal opening until comfortable.
4) Daily insertion of three fingers into vaginal opening until comfortable.
5) Insertion of one or two fingers into vaginal opening by partner.
6) Insertion of penis without thrusting under patient's control. This is usually most comfortable in the female superior position.
7) Insertion with thrusting.

When vaginismus is mild enough to permit penetration, but severe enough to make intercourse painful, gradual dilatation of the vagina is also highly effective. The use of a lubricant is helpful.

EJACULATORY PAIN DUE TO MUSCLE SPASM

The muscle spasm which occurs immediately after ejaculation, and which is the immediate cause of this syndrome, is treated by systematic in vivo desensitization. Towards this objective, a variety of psychological anxiety-reducing methods, such as reassurance and explanation, may be employed, as well as procedures which relax muscles by physical means.

The patient is educated about the origin of his pain. He is reassured as to his medical and sexual health. Then he is advised to masturbate while in a tub of warm water which tends to relax muscle tension. Some fantasies are more likely to be associated with pain, and these are explored in the therapy sessions. Chlordiazepoxide and thioridazine are capable of relaxing the genital muscles and are helpful as an aid in extinguishing this conditioned response.

SEXUAL PHOBIAS

The immediate cause of sexual phobias and their attendant avoidance behavior is acute anxiety and panic which is evoked by sexual feelings and/or activities. Sexual phobias respond to the same treatment procedures as other kinds of phobias. Specifically, when the sexual phobia is part of a phobic-anxiety syndrome, treatment with tricyclic or MAO inhibitor drugs is appropriate.* Evidence indicates that many sexually phobic patients can be helped by these drugs, which protect them against the panic attacks they experience in the phobic situation. The residual anticipatory anxieties can then be diminished with systematic in vivo desensitization by means of gradual sexual exercises and sometimes with systematic sexual assertiveness. In those cases where no medication is required, a combination of very gradual in vivo desensitization and psychotherapeutic support and confrontation with resistances is often effective. It is not possible to construct a sequence of tasks which is appropriate for all phobic patients, because the anxiety patterns are highly individual.

UNCONSUMMATED MARRIAGE

The successful management of uncomsummated marriage rests on the accurate diagnosis of the specific immediate causes responsible for the problem. A couple may be unable to have intercourse for a

---

* For specific information on drug dosages, actions and side effects, the reader should consult the texts on psychopharmacology listed in the Bibliography.

variety of reasons. These include a sexual phobia on the part of either partner, ignorance, dyspareunia or sexual dysfunction. Treatment will, of course, vary with the specific cause.

THE THERAPEUTIC BALANCE

It should be emphasized that the behavioral strategies outlined for the various syndromes describe only the experiential aspect of sexual therapy. The exercises are designed primarily to modify the specific immediate antecedents of the symptom. This by itself cures many patients. But sexual symptoms often have deeper roots, which are not specific to each syndrome. Sexual anxieties of all kinds and anger at the partner may underlie any of the syndromes. These deeper problems may be resistant to behavioral methods alone, i.e., to the removal of the symptom, but clinical experience has demonstrated that they are often responsive to brief, active psychotherapeutic interventions. In our hands this takes the form of rapid confrontation of resistances, interpretation of some unconscious conflict, together with active, warm support of the patient and the relationship, and encouragement of enjoyable sexual pleasure. Therapy may be individually or couple oriented according to the specific clinical requirement. These psychotherapeutic methods, together with the experiential modalities, are employed for all the disorders as they are needed to deal with resistances that emerge in the course of treatment.

The format of psychosexual therapy is flexible, particularly with respect to the relative roles played by behavioral and psychotherapeutic modalities. The balance varies considerably with each case. One of the important determinants of the relative emphasis of experiential and psychotherapeutic tactics is the intensity of the anxiety which underlies the symptom and/or the severity of associated relationship difficulties. The more intense and deeply rooted the anxiety, the more difficult and tenacious the resistances, the heavier the reliance on therapeutic techniques. These will be used either to bypass or to confront and resolve these resistances to the modification of the immediate antecedents of the symptom.

Clinical experience suggests that, compared with the other dysfunctions, orgasm phase disorders tend to be associated with mild conflicts and resistances. Thus, behavioral techniques play a relatively more important role in their treatment. In these disorders, the structured experiences are often intrinsically therapeutic and constitute the active therapeutic ingredient. In cases of simple orgasm inhibition, psychotherapeutic support is often merely ancillary to the experiential aspect of the treatment, and is used primarily to remove simple resistances to the vital behavioral exercises.

The opposite is true of the desire phase disorders, which are often the product of deeply rooted, tenacious conflicts. In the desire phase syndrome, the psychotherapeutic interaction between the therapist and the patient and/or couple is usually the primary therapeutic ingredient. The structured sexual interactions are often not powerful enough to be intrinsically therapeutic. They are used primarily to help the patient gain insight rapidly by confronting him with his resistances to sexual pleasure, and also to evoke previously unrecognized conflicts so that these become available for active exploration, circumvention or resolution.

PROGNOSIS OF SEXUAL DYSFUNCTIONS ASSOCIATED WITH ORGASM, EXCITEMENT AND DESIRE PHASE INHIBITION

The following estimates of treatment outcome are not based on systematic research. They are the product of a survey of the literature, of our own preliminary outcome data, and of personal communications with colleagues. They are not to be interpreted as claims of effectiveness, but rather as estimates based on a consensus of clinical observations. It is my sense that time will prove these observations to be essentially realistic, especially as to the differences in outcome when the data are broken down according to specific phases. These differences lend support to the triphasic concept and to the hypothesis that the quality of the conflict associated with the different syndromes varies.

When the treatment outcome of the various dysfunctions is examined from the perspective of the triphasic concept, striking differences in prognosis emerge. Orgasm phase dysfunctions have by far the best prognosis. In our program approximately 90 percent of anorgastic females and males with inadequate ejaculatory control are relieved of their symptom after three to 20 sessions, with an average of 12 sessions. The outcome of treatment of retarded ejaculation varies with the severity. It is my impression from personal communications with colleagues that these results are similar to those attained by other programs and clinicians with respect to treatment of orgasm phase dysfunctions.

Estimates of the effects of sex therapy on impotence range from a 50 to an 80 percent cure rate. Length of treatment in our experience varies from 10 to 20 sessions, with an average of 16 sessions. There is a wide variation in the prognosis of impotence. Simple secondary impotence which is caused by performance anxiety has an excellent prognosis, perhaps in the 80 to 90 percent range. Simple secondary impotence behaves clinically like the orgasm phase disorders and carries a prognosis of over 80 percent success. But the difficult cases— those whose impotence is primary and those with more severe underlying conflicts—seem dynamically like ISD, with a prognosis in the 10 to 20 percent range. It is my impression that the outcome with impotence varies more with the characteristics of the patient population than does the outcome of the orgasm phase disorders.

The population seeking help for sexual problems seems to be changing. The simple cases are disappearing, and today patients, at least in the large urban centers, are more sophisticated and also seem to include more seriously disturbed persons. Consequently, the outcome for impotence seems to have become poorer. It is my impression that a 60 percent overall cure rate for impotence is currently fairly standard in various programs.

There are as yet no outcome statistics for the treatment of desire phase dysfunctions. I believe, however, that these disorders carry by far the worst prognosis. While it is unusual for an orgasm phase dysfunction *not* to be cured by traditional sex therapy, one feels a sense of surprise when a desire problem *does* clear up rapidly in treatment. My estimate is that only 10 to 15 percent of patients suffering from ISD are cured within the average 14 sessions which are traditional in sex therapy. Clearly there is a need to develop more effective treatment methods for this population. It is for this reason that the modified and longer psychosexual treatment techniques which are described in the next chapters were developed.

AREA II

DESIRE PHASE DISORDERS OF MALES AND FEMALES

Inhibited sexual desire is a distinct clinical entity. It is related to the other sexual dysfunctions in that it involves sexual anxieties, but it also differs in many important respects. Specifically, as a group, patients suffering from blocked desire have deeper and more intense sexual anxieties, greater hostility towards their partners, and more tenacious defenses than those patients whose sexual dysfunctions are associated with erection and orgasm difficulties.

The concept of ISD gains clarity when it is compared with anorexia nervosa, with which it has some interesting similarities and analogies, both with respect to the nature of the psychopathological structure and the clinical course and treatment response of the two disorders. In both syndromes, a biological drive which is the expression of specific neurophysiologic activity of the brain is inhibited by unconscious psychological factors. Also, both disorders have a poor prognosis for spontaneous recovery. Anorexia was highly unresponsive to traditional insight methods of treatment but much progress has been made recently by the application of active, integrated therapeutic methods. These more effective approaches may be conceptualized as intervening on a behavioral level which modifies the immediate antecedent of appetite suppression. This is supplemented by also working on deeper psychological levels dividing the patient's family and intrapsychic dynamics. With some exceptions ISD patients also tend to be resistant and have a relatively poor prognosis with all treatment methods currently employed. Even sex therapy, which improved the outlook for the genital sexual dysfunctions dramatically, has been disappointing with respect to the desire disorders. While a small proportion of ISD patients do respond to the traditional, rapid, time-limited sex therapy methods, too many patients fail to improve. One factor in the high failure rate may be related to the fact that the immediate causes of the suppression of sexual appetite have not yet been clearly delineated. In addition, these techniques probably do not deal extensively enough with deeper conflicts which so often play a crucial role in desire problems.

The attempt to improve the treatment of ISD is based on observations regarding the immediate and specific antecedents of the suppression of sexual feelings, and on the hypothesis that outcome of ISD may improve if both these immediate causes and their deeper psychic roots are dealt with in treatment. This has led to the development of an approach which combines features of the traditional insight and the new sex therapies. The mthod consists of a modified form of sex therapy, which might be called **psychosexual therapy.** *This is lengthier, more flexible and more dynamically oriented than classical sex therapy. The combined and integrated use of structured sexual experiences with psychotherapeutic exploration is retained, but greater emphasis is placed on insight therapy.*

The objective of this approach is to exploit the great advantage of sex therapy—that of intervening directly and effectively on the level of the immediate causes of the sexual symptom, which is often neglected in psychotherapeutic modalities, while relying more heavily on psychotherapeutic exploration of unconscious resistances to accommodate the more complex dynamics and more tenacious and deeper remote causes typically found in this patient population. This modified form of sex therapy is currently being explored for the treatment of all of the more difficult sexual dysfunctions, including ISD.

The following three chapters detail the diagnoses, etiology and treatment approaches of desire phase dysfunctions. Case studies are included throughout, with additional Clinical Illustrations in Chapter 7.

4

DEFINITION, DESCRIPTION

AND DIAGNOSIS

EPIDEMIOLOGY

HYPOACTIVE SEXUAL DESIRE is probably the most prevalent of all the sexual dysfunctions. Harold Lief has reported that 40 percent of patients applying to the Marriage Counsel of Philadelphia for help with sexual problems were suffering primarily from what he terms inhibited sexual desire, or ISD. This is consistent with our own experience. Since we have begun to take cognizance of disturbances in libido we have also found that desire problems are extremely common in our population.

DEFINITION AND DESCRIPTION

The nomenclature committee of the American Psychiatric Association has organized its classification of the sexual dysfunctions according to the triphasic concept of the sexual response and has recognized ISD as a clinical entity. In *DSM III* (the third edition of the *Diagnostic and Statistical Manual* of the APA), Desire Phase Inhibition is defined as follows:

302.71 Psychosexual Dysfunction with Inhibited Sexual Desire

A. Persistent and pervasive inhibition of sexual desire. The basis for the judgment of inhibition is made by the clinician taking into account age, sex, occupation, the individual's subjective statement as to intensity and frequency of sexual desire, a knowledge of norms of sexual behavior, and the context of the individual's life. In actual practice, this diagnosis will rarely be used* unless the lack of desire is a source of distress either to the individual or to his or her partner. Frequently this category will be used in conjunction with one or more of the other dysfunction categories.

B. The disturbance is not caused exclusively by organic factors and is not symptomatic of another clinical psychiatric syndrome.

For conceptual clarity, the term ISD is reserved here for those situations of abnormally low libido in which an etiologic diagnosis has been made, i.e., when it is established that sexual desire is inhibited by psychic factors. The term *hypoactive sexual desire* (HSD) is preferable when the etiology of low libido has not yet been determined.

The term *sexual avoidance* employed by Masters and Johnson to describe persons who have a low frequency or absence of sexual activity can be confusing. Inhibition of desire is but one of several possible causes of asexual behavior and a patient may develop a pattern of avoidance of sexuality whether he feels sexual desire or not. It is true, however, that some patients who have ISD also develop phobic avoidance of sex, and this is of clinical importance.

DIAGNOSIS

Reliable and valid norms of human sexual behavior are not yet available and in the final analysis the diagnosis of ISD is made by comparing the patient's experience with a sense of what the normal range of sexual desire is. This is based on deduction rather than on the kinds of direct scientific observation and measurement which are available for the genital responses. Thus, our concepts of the normal parameters of the sexual drive of men and women are inferred from various statistical surveys of the frequency of intercourse and orgasm, as well as from diverse clinical observations and from personal experience.

This is not exactly scientific terra firma. However, it is not feasible to wait until more accurate data have been accumulated to attend to

---

* In our experience lack of sexual desire is in fact a highly prevalent complaint, and we frequently use this diagnosis.

the urgent needs of this patient population. There is enough of a sense of what the normal range of sexual interest is for practical purposes, and while there is confusion in borderline situations, professional consensus is adequate to define the *extreme* and clearly pathological *deviations from the norm*. In other words, if a young man of 20 has never been attracted to a girl, seldom has a sexual thought or fantasy, and does not masturbate, he would probably be regarded by most clinicians as having a pathologically low libido. Similarly, most experts would agree that if a married woman of 39 never feels sexual desire, is attracted neither to her husband nor to anyone else, and never fantasizes or masturbates, she has an abnormally low sexual appetite. Or, if a person is preoccupied with sex and masturbates 10 times every day to orgasm, it is safe to venture that there would be little professional dispute that the patient's response is excessive.

But is a frequency of once every two weeks normal for a busy executive in his forties or is this pattern a product of inhibition? Is sex once a month by a couple in their fifties pathological or normal? Data in addition to frequency of sexual activity are required to make a sensible judgment in such cases.

A history of significant *changes in libido* suggests that the patient's desire has become pathologically impaired and is not simply low normal. Few clinicians would disagree about the diagnosis of diminished libido if a patient reports that he had pleasurable sexual intercourse with his wife twice a week for many years but lately has sex only once every two months or so, and then is primarily moved not by passion, but by concern that his wife is feeling rejected.

Of course, the clearest evidence of libido inhibition is a *situational pattern of inhibition of desire*. There is little doubt that the man who has no interest in his loving beautiful wife who wants a sharing intimate relationship, but can only feel desire for young women strangers with whom he never converses when he has sex, should be considered to have an inhibition of desire. Situational inhibitions of desire rule out a medical etiology, depression, and a constitutionally low but uninhibited libido.

The Normal Sexual Experience

The diagnosis of hypoactive sexual desire (HSD) rests in part on a comparison of the patient's sexual history with the norm. Therefore, a sense of what constitutes normal sexual development is important. Again, this can be described only in the most general terms at this incomplete state of our knowledge. But some generalizations can be made. It seems that in the healthy individual, *some form of sexual appetite is present throughout life no matter what his cultural origins are.* As with any human trait, e.g., height, intelligence, etc., the intensity of the sex drive varies widely, and in some cases, it may be difficult to determine what is pathologic and what is a normal variation. In other words, some normal persons apparently have such a low sex drive that their experience overlaps that of persons suffering from pathologic HSD.

Sexual appetite changes in intensity with age and takes a gender-specific course of development. Infants seem to already have some capacity for erotic feelings. These are evoked when their genitals are stimulated. When a tiny clitoris or penis is touched in the course of bathing and dressing, the infant expresses pleasure by smiling and cooing. Children, if they are not stopped, will masturbate and later play sexual games which may entail looking at and touching each other's genitals. We tend to forget or repress much of these early sexual fantasies and experiences but some memory is normally retained. And when during a psychosexual evaluation the patient remembers *no* prepubescent erotic feelings or sex play or fantasies, one can assume a certain amount of early sexual inhibition or repression.

There is a substantial increase in sexual desire at puberty. This is probably correlated both with the maturation of the cerebral circuits which govern sexual expression and with the increase in testosterone which is produced by the gonads at this time and which activates these circuits.

After puberty sexual development takes a different course in the two genders. In the male sexual desire seems to peak around 17 years and then slowly declines. The normal adolescent male is intensely interested in sex, is easily aroused, and in the absence of a partner will masturbate, while conjuring up erotic fantasies, with frequencies varying from several times a day to several times a week. If there is no sexual outlet, he will experience frustration. This phenomenon is so predictable that if the sexual history of a male reveals no adolescent increase in sexual desire as reflected in masturbation and/or fantasy and/or actual intercourse, one may suspect a problem in psychosexual development.

The intensity of the male sex drive diminishes gradually after adolescence. At middle age he still desires sex, but often can go without sexual outlets for longer and longer periods of time without experiencing frustration. Throughout his life, however, his sexual desire can be aroused under exciting circumstances.

Females also experience an increase in libido at puberty. However, this appears less intense than that of adolescent males. Girls seem more easily discouraged from sexual expression than boys. Thus, the absence of adolescent masturbation in a female psychosexual history does not carry the same clinical significance of severe sexual repression as it does in the male. In our current culture, the female sex drive does not decline after adolescence, but slowly increases and peaks somewhere around the age of 40. Then female sexual desire also slowly declines. In general, female sexual desire is more variable than that of males. While women have a greater orgastic potential, their sexuality is also more easily suppressed.

It was believed by Sigmund Freud that the biologic sexual urges of males are more compelling than those of females. Clinical evidence supports this notion, at least to the extent that the sex drive of young males is stronger than that of aging men and also of women, particularly of young women. This inference is based on the observation that the sexual desire of females seems more easily inhibited than that of males, especially during youth when sex drive in males is so intense. In other words, ISD can be produced in women of all ages and in aging men by relatively minor factors, and it seems to take more substantial and intense negative factors, i.e., harsher punishment, more serious injunctions, etc., to inhibit the sexual desire of a young male. Speculations about the relative contributions of biological and cultural determinants to these gender differences in sexual desire are legion and inconclusive at this time.

Throughout his life the normal person experiences spontaneous sexual desire, and also has the capacity to be aroused by an attractive partner. When the sex drive is high, the person will experience spontaneous desire and will be aroused by a wide range of stimuli. As desire diminishes, the range of stimuli that will evoke the sexual appetite narrows, and more intense psychic and physical stimulation is required to produce a response.

Factors apart from age also affect the sexual appetite. Physical health and mood are important determinants in reproductive behavior. Both genders experience an increase in sexual appetite when in love and both genders experience a decrease in sexual desire when they are under stress. Love is the best aphrodisiac discovered so far.

But even when a man and a woman are happily in love, sexual desire normally fluctuates, so that interest in making love shows some variation. However, it never remains absent for long for normal couples. On the other hand, during periods of stress, even loving, healthy couples may experience a diminished desire to make love, which should return to a normal level when the crisis is mastered.

Clinical Description

The person with low sexual desire will not feel "horny" or interested in sex. He will not be moved to seek out sexual activity, nor will he fantasize about sex. He might comment, "I don't even look at pretty girls on the street anymore." Also, in contrast to normal experience, sexual desire evoked by stimulation of the genitals will be absent or greatly reduced. The reflexes may, in fact, work if stimulation is permitted; i.e., the person may have an erection or lubricate and/or have an orgasm. But this experience is not really satisfying in the presence of a low desire state. Pleasure is fleeting, perhaps just before orgasm, and is limited to and localized in the genitals. Patients describe such experiences as similar to eating a meal when one is not really hungry. In situations which would normally arouse their sexual desire, inhibited patients will report an absence of feeling or even negative sensations of irritation, tension, anger, anxiety and/or disgust. "When he kisses me, I just want to curl up and go to sleep."

Some persons whose desire is low will not engage in sex. In fact, some avoid sexual situations with various degrees of intensity. These patients may develop a phobic avoidance of sex. Others will engage in sex for reasons apart from desire—usually to avoid hurting a partner's feelings or to reassure themselves that they "can still do it." Sometimes such experiences of sex without desire can be good. There may be a feeling of warmth or coziness. The person may feel generous about giving the partner a "gift." But sometimes if sex is attempted in such a low desire state, the gential reflexes may not function well, and a secondary performance anxiety may develop, complicating the clinical picture.

Clinical Variants of ISD

Disorders of sexual desire can be described as primary or secondary and can exist globally or situationally. *Primary HSD* is a rare condition which is marked by a lifelong history of asexuality. The patient is devoid of sexual interest to the extent that he does not even masturbate. Primary HSD is characteristic of constitutionally low sex drive and certain disease states, as well as of severe psychopathologic states such as schizophrenia and chronic depression. Persons whose libido is severely repressed on the basis of neurotic conflict may also present an asexual picture.

Secondary HSD, in which there is a loss of sex drive after a history of normal sexual development, is much more common than primary inhibition. Secondary loss of libido may be produced by a variety of physical factors and is also seen after psychological crises such as marriage, the birth of children, a traumatic rejection or object loss, anger at or disillusionment with a partner, or nonsexually related stress such as a job loss or an accident.

When there is a *global loss of sex drive*, the person ceases to desire or be interested in sex at all. He experiences no erotic wishes, fantasies or thoughts and, if male, may even cease to have morning erections. Global or total loss of libido is typically associated with depressive states, severe stress and physical causes.

The most common clinical variant is *situational HSD*. This is the typical picture found in psychogenic inhibited sexual desire. Characteristically, the person feels desire only in situations that are psychically "safe." It is usually the most appropriate and most desirable partner who represents the "psychic danger" that results in the inhibition of desire. Thus a man may feel desire for and be sexually active with prostitutes or strangers or a woman who treats him sadistically or women of a lower social class. But his sex drive becomes inhibited with his intelligent and attractive girlfriend with whom he would like to be intimately and tenderly connected.

One such 36-year-old man presents a typical story. He lies next to his extremely beautiful and loving wife in bed every night and feels no desire. In fact, if he should occasionally find himself erect, he experiences discomfort and hastily moves away from her to avoid any physical contact. But he visits prostitutes two or three times a week and has a normal sexual response in these situations.

Also typical of the situational ISD group is the woman who feels very erotic during the many years of her precoital experiences. She felt desire and erotic pleasure during "petting," but she loses sexual interest after she has engaged in coitus, or after marriage, or after childbirth, i.e., in situations which on a symbolic and unconscious level represent danger.

Inhibition of Sexual Desire and the Paraphilias

Situational inhibition of sexual desire may be thought of as lying at the borderline of the sexual deviations or variations or "paraphilias." The focus of interest in these conditions has traditionally been on the "deviant" object or "perverse" activity which evokes desire. But there seem to be two components in these conditions, as well as in homosexuality: 1) inhibition or absense of heterosexual desire; and 2) desire for an object or situation which does not interest the majority of persons.

According to the gay point of view, heterosexual desire is absent or diminished but not inhibited in the homosexual. But an alternative hypothesis holds that the common denominator of paraphilias and of some forms of homosexuality is an *inhibition of desire for* heterosexual coitus. In that sense sexual variations or paraphilias may be considered as special instances of situational ISD. Persons whose erotic desire is primarily or exclusively evoked by fetishistic objects, by sadomasochistic activities, by an animal, by cross-dressing, by exhibiting or looking, and also by a partner of the same gender, etc.—by any of the variations or paraphilias—is usually able to experience no or little desire in situations which most persons would find erotic, i.e., an intimate sexual relationship with an attractive partner of the opposite gender. The heterosexual situation is not psychologically "safe" and desire is inhibited as a means of avoiding the danger. The fetish serves the psychic function of "bypassing" this desire inhibition. Symbolically, the sexual situation is rendered safe by the use of a fetish, which thus allows the person to experience sexual pleasure which would otherwise be denied him. There is usually no insight into these dynamics.

The dynamics of situational ISD are identical. In the cases mentioned above, desire is inhibited only for the "dangerous" sexual situation, for "father" or "mother" or "intimacy" or "commitment" or "competition." In other situations, i.e., with "strangers" in "undesirable" sexual situations with persons of lower intelligence or lesser power, anxiety with its attendant inhibition is not mobilized. The differences between lust for less than ideal or special sexual partners which are "safe" and the variations are not dynamic, but largely cultural. In both cases, desire for appropriate intimate heterosexual sex is inhibited but the person is able to enjoy erotic pleasure by avoiding this situation and choosing a "safe" one. In our culture, uncommitted sex or sex with a prostitute is not defined as perverse, while sex with an animal, or with a child or with a member of the same gender is labeled as a paraphilia, variation or perversion.

Fantasies about variant sexual objects or situations serve to circumvent the anxieties mobilized by similar sexual conflicts. They also circumvent the dangers posed by the heterosexual situation and so allow the person to experience sexual pleasure without resolving his basic sexual conflicts. Probably a fantasy "bypass" is effective in circumventing conflicts which are the same in content but of a lesser intensity than those that are operative in the paraphilias where the fantasy is acted out.

It may be speculated that there is a range or spectrum of the intensity of the conflicts which underlie inhibition of sexual desire. If a person is extremely fearful about sexual expression, his desire may become totally repressed and he becomes asexual, i.e., loses his libido totally. On the mild end of the spectrum, in the range of normalcy, are the mild inhibitions; libido is inhibited only in specific situations, and sexual pleasure can still be experienced in "safe" situations. Such persons may be confined to having sex with strangers and prostitutes, and their mild blocks can be circumvented by means of fantasy. Between these extremes lie the paraphilias. Here sexuality is blocked to the extent that while heterosexual sex is precluded, erotic pleasure can be experienced if the conflict is bypassed symbolically by the fetish or by other variations or perversions.

According to this view, perversions, fantasies, paraphilias, and special interests in sex are constructive, in that they permit the individual to experience erotic pleasure and satisfaction which would otherwise be blocked. Such devices operate as if they protect the sexual circuits from the inhibitory forces which might otherwise be mobilized by sexual activity. Naturally, *if* it is possible, resolution of underlying sexual conflict is a better and ultimately a more effective solution than bypassing them by these means. Clinical experience suggests, however, that intense inhibition of sexual desire, especially when it is acquired early, is tenacious and often resistant to treatment, and bypass by means of fantasy or symbolic activity may be the only available alternative that permits a conflicted person to experience sexual pleasure.

ISD and Homosexuality

An interesting clinical variant of primary and situational ISD is seen in young men, who are usually bachelors, often virgins, or who have had very few sexual experiences. They do masturbate with varying frequency and have homosexual or bisexual fantasies that alternate between homosexual and heterosexual. But if they attempt to experience homosexual sex, they tend to become anxious and/or experience little pleasure.

These men tend to be uncomfortable in sexual or potentially sexual situations with women. Basically they are deeply fearful, sometimes to the point of phobic avoidance of female genitals and/or of erotic arousal in a heterosexual situation. However, they express the wish not to be homosexual and seem genuinely to want to be able to enjoy heterosexual relations.

Although these patients have some of the features of "classic" homosexuality (if this exists), in that their desire for heterosexual sex is low or inhibited, the intensity of their desire for sexual contact with other males seems less than that of "genuine" homosexuals, or of homosexuals who have no wish to change their orientation.

In my admittedly limited experience, such patients, provided they are highly motivated, have an excellent prognosis for rapidly acquiring a heterosexual behavior pattern in response to psychosexual therapy. In these cases treatment combines therapeuticaly structured sexual experiences, with a skilled and reassuring partner, and active exploration in the therapy sessions of underlying sexual conflicts as they emerge in response to these experiences. In my experience, the unconscious fear of competition with males is frequently an important dynamic feature is such cases.

The patients we have treated rapidly tend to lose or learn to manage their fear of heterosexual behavior to a point where they are able to and can enjoy heterosexual functioning. However, most continue to employ homosexual fantasies. One may infer from this that the basic pattern of homosexual desire has not been altered in response to brief treatment, even though the men have learned to function with women. However it is not invariably true that only the genital phases change. I have on occasion seen the fantasies and presumably the underlying desire become heterosexual after treatment. Obviously more extensive experience is required before any definitive conclusions can be drawn in this fascinating area.

Differential Diagnosis

The cardinal sign of ISD is a low frequency of sexual activity. However, this alone only denotes hypoactivity, which must, for clinical purposes, first be differentiated from sexual avoidance. In this condition, the frequency of sexual activity can also be low, but because of fear of sex and *not* because desire is diminished. Once it has been established that libido is indeed low, then an etiologic diagnosis must be made. Physiologic and primary psychiatric etiologies must be differentiated from psychogenic ISD and, finally, pathological lack of desire must be differentiated from those normal states where desire is appropriately inhibited or not generated.

Differentiation from Orgasm and Excitement Phase Disorders

One of the most important consequences of the separation of desire phase dysfunctions from excitement and orgasm dysfunctions is that it enables the clinician to sort out this patient population from those suffering from disturbances of the genital phases. Patients who complain of orgasm and excitement phase dysfunctions but who retain normal desire generally have an excellent prognosis when they are treated by sex therapy, but patients who have little or no sexual desire do not respond as well to these methods and require different treatment strategies.

The existence of ISD is not always apparent during the evaluation because patients do not tend to complain of this directly. They are more likely to cite erection and orgasm problems as the chief complaint. It is often much easier and less threatening for the symptomatic patient, as well as for the spouse, to define their problem as a genital dysfunction than to admit that "I feel no desire" or, even more threatening, that "I feel no desire for you."

Whenever the clinical picture includes a low frequency of sexual activity, the clinician should be alert to the possible hidden presence of HSD and question the patient specifically about desire.

Sexual Avoidance

Low frequency or absence of sexual contact may also be a sign of sexual avoidance on the part of one or both of the partners. When sex arouses intense anxiety, a pattern of phobic avoidance can develop, regardless of whether desire is present or not. This is an important diagnostic point, because if sexual avoidance complicates the clinical picture of any of the dysfuctions, e.g., vaginismus as well as ISD, this avoidance presents a clear obstacle to therapy and must be treated and resolved first.

Normal Asexuality

Asexuality is certainly not always abnormal. It has already been mentioned that some persons' sexual appetite falls on the low side of the normal distribution on the basis of constitutional determinants. Such persons are not bothered by the infrequency of their need for sex unless external circumstances exert pressure. Such pressure includes a partner with a relatively higher sexual drive as well as the high sexual expectations currently in vogue in our society. If there is clinical evidence of a relatively low sex drive which is normal for that individual, then the person or couple may need counseling to help them both accept this reality and integrate it into their lives constructively. A person can learn to accept and value himself apart from the strength of his sex drive. A couple can learn to accommodate with sensitivity and love to an imbalance in sexual appetite, as loving couples do with imbalances in other spheres of life.

There are also many circumstances where a person's sexual desire is inhibited on a nonpathological basis. We are biologically constructed so that the emergency emotions which govern survival have priority over those which lead to reproduction. And so fear will *normally* inhibit the sex drive. Therefore, when a sexual situation is dangerous or disadvantageous, the sexual appetite will normally be diminished. For example, it is perfectly normal for a man to lose his sexual desire when he fears that his lover's angry, vindictive, powerful husband is about to enter the bedroom. Or if a woman finds that involvement with a man, whom at first she found attractive, will be destructive emotionally or with respect to her career, it is not abnormal for her interest in him to diminish. It is adaptive and appropriate for her to "turn off" sexually in the face of real danger.

In fact, pathological conditions are produced when an appropriate inhibition of sexual desire does *not* occur. Some persons are sexually obsessed with disinterested, rejecting or even cruel partners, towards which they *should* normally experience a loss of desire. The cruelty, the pain, the frustration of such situations should shut down the desire machinery, but in obsessive love this does not happen. The inability to suppress or "give up" an inappropriate and destructive desire thus also constitutes a pathological state.

Of course, sexual desire is frequently inhibited on the basis of irrational and false dangers; sexual situations which are in reality safe may be perceived consciously or unconsciously as dangerous on the basis of remnants of past experience. These must be differentiated from those situations where a sexual encounter or relationship really *is* destructive to the person. In such situations, the irrational sources of fear, the fantasies of injury consequent to sexual pleasure or intimacy or commitment to a relationship, must be brought into conscious awareness, so that they can be understood and seen realistically before the person can feel sexual desire again.

Finally, despite current propaganda to the contrary, it is not appropriate to find all potential sexual partners or situations attractive. Frequently the evaluation of a couple who complain of loss of sexual desire reveals that there is no real basis for attraction. The partners do not like each other—or her/his hygiene is so poor as to be repulsive—or there is a significant discrepancy in intellectual capacity, etc. The irrationality of these situations lies in the fact that persons think that they *should* be attracted, *should* feel desire when it makes no sense.

One such couple consisted of an extremely obese (350 lbs.-5'3"), unkempt man and his shy, petite wife. His complaint was that she did not desire him sexually. He was correct, but common sense precludes a diagnosis of pathologically inhibited desire in this case.

One need not go so far as limiting normal asexuality to a repulsive or unclean or mentally ill partner. Many persons do not really enjoy sex unless they have an intimate and sensitive relationship with the partner, or unless the partner meets some special emotional needs and/or satisfies a physical or psychological ideal. Such persons may choose to inhibit their sexual feelings until they can find a desirable partner. Celibacy while waiting for the right mate can be a constructive, mature, dignified choice, which should hardly be classified as pathological.

The healthy celibacy in which desire is suppressed until a really satisfying partner becomes available should be differentiated from a neurotic rejection of partners who are in reality suitable. Some patients manage to find something wrong with *every* potential romantic partner. This is a reflection of the unconscious fear and avoidance of sexuality, love, intimacy, or commitment. As with most syndromes, there is a range of the intensity with which persons avoid good relationships and sex. In some persons this rejection operates on first encounter. The person they meet is immediately perceived as too fat, old, lower class, stupid, etc. Such statements as, "He wore a polyester suit," "She had blue eye makeup on," "Did you see the ridiculous chain around his neck?" become rationalizations for the individual's sexual inhibition.

Other ISD patients have little problem in the initial courtship phase of attachment. They have no conflict about making themselves attractive and they make good contact. However, at a certain point of intimacy or commitment, anxiety is mobilized and desire is suppressed. With little insight into this dynamic, they find fault with each partner and detach themselves or sabotage the relationship by becoming withholding or provocative.

Many, but not all, normal persons who are in love do not feel desire for anyone but their partner. Occasionally, a person who feels desire exclusively for his lover will seek "help" in order to also be able to feel desire for someone else with whom he is not in love—say for the spouse. This is not feasible. Exclusive desire for the person with whom one is romantically bonded, together with inhibiton for all others, is a normal phenomenon that should be celebrated rather than treated.

REACTION TO LOW SEXUAL DESIRE

Some persons are nonchalant about the loss of their sexual appetite. Especially if there is no partner pressure, they may go for years without sexual activity and never think about it. Others are deeply concerned about the loss of their sexual drive and feel damaged, diminished and aged by this.

The partners of such patients also show a spectrum of reactions. Some seem to take little notice—in fact, if the sexual relationship was not particularly enjoyable, some partners are even relieved when the relationship becomes asexual. On the other hand, many partners are extremely threatened by their mate's lack of desire. They take this as a personal rejection. Since it evokes deep insecurities and old rejections, they may become depressed and obsessed with the problem.

When a person becomes obsessed with the partner's sexual desire and response, a destructive cycle of behavior can result. Obsessive pressure from the partner can by itself result in inhibition of sexual desire, and can certainly aggravate this condition when it already exists in a mild state. In fact, treatment becomes far more complicated when the partner of the patient who is suffering from an inhibition of desire exerts too much pressure. The partner's anxiety and pressure become an obstacle to treatment which the therapist must resolve before treatment of the primary inhibition problem becomes possible.

The following two cases involve desire problems. They are similar in many respects except that the characteristics of the inhibited women's partners are significantly different.

CASE 1   ADAM AND EVA
        Inhibited Sexual Desire with Phobic Avoidance
        Obsessive Partner
        Successful Outcome

Chief Complaint

The patient, Eva, was a 36-year-old woman married for six years to her 39-year-old husband, Adam. He was a successful architect and she was a former teacher now at home. The couple had one child, a three-year-old boy who was adopted.

The chief complaint was a loss of sexual desire on the wife's part. This was associated with severe sexual avoidance. The woman was so uncomfortable with any physical contact that the couple had no sex at all for three years. She even suffered from hours of anticipatory anxiety when she thought that she might be confronted with a sexual situation.

History

The couple enjoyed a good sexual relationship during the first year of their marriage. This gradually declined as the woman felt less and less desire, and finally she developed a true phobic avoidance of sex.

Two years after their marriage, Eva experienced severe gynecologic problems involving ovarian cysts and pelvic adhesions. This made coitus painful and necessitated four surgical procedures. These were successful and she now feels well physically. During the two years of her illness Eva totally lost her libido but continued to have intercourse with her husband. After a year of joyless and often painful intercourse, she developed a phobic avoidance of any sexual contact.

Adam, the husband, became increasingly tense, anxious and angry at what he perceived as a personal sexual rejection. While Eva was physically ill he was irritable but controlled his anger. When she recovered her health and still did not want sex, he became pressuring, demanding, depressed and preoccupied with this problem to such a degree that he was not functioning well on his job. He developed a preoccupation with the thought, which had no basis in reality, that Eva could and would respond to other men.

Etiology

It was speculated that the immediate causes of the problem were 1) a phobic avoidance of sex which was precipitated by the series of painful illnesses and surgical procedures, and 2) the obsessive pressuring of the husband. But Eva's was not just a simple conditioned avoidance reaction. The situation had evoked past injuries and their attendant defenses. Specifically, Eva harbored strong unconscious conflicts about success and pleasure, unconsciously fearing retribution for pleasure. The patient's family background had been intensely anti-pleasure and induced in her strong unconscious guilt about "winning" in sibling rivalry situations.

She was very much in love with her handsome, successful husband, as he was with her. Also, through her marriage her financial situation was far better than that of any other member of her family, and symbolically her good life constituted "winning," which evoked old conflicts and defenses. Her surgical problems and repeated illnesses were unconsciously seen as punishment for forbidden pleasure and success. Her sexual inhibition represented a fear of further injury should she again allow herself sexual pleasure. In addition to these intrapsychic problems, there were interactional ones. The spouses were engaged in a power struggle and were frequently angry at each other, as she tried to develop an independent identity within the relationship with this dominant, assertive, vital man.

Treatment

The husband's obsessive reaction proved an obstacle to therapy. The treatment plan was to first deal with her avoidance of physical contact by gradual desensitization. Accordingly, sexual therapy began with sensate focus I, i.e., body caressing without touching the genitals. Not surprisingly, his caresses evoked tension and not pleasure in his wife. He could not accept her response and experienced and expressed intense distress. His reaction upset her, made her guilty and inhibited her even further, so that she was reluctant to allow herself to be touched at all, even for a few moments. There was an attempt to bypass the obstacle posed by his anxiety and anger by shifting treatment to self-stimulation in an attempt to work through her unconscious conflict about pleasure. However, his pressuring continued in the form of obsessive questioning about her "progress." In his mind she would not "have to play with herself" if he were "more of a man." His anxious and hostile queries evoked her anger and guilt and prevented her from experiencing her own feelings.

As it became clear that the obstacle posed by her husband's (understandable but unfortunate) anxiety could not be circumvented, treatment was focused on his pressuring. In sessions alone with him, he was confronted with the negative effects of his behavior on the therapeutic process. He came to see that his wife was so occupied with dealing with the upsetting interaction between them that she could not work out her own problem. But insight into the effects of his anxiety was not sufficient to relieve the situation. Some of the deeper roots of his insecurities, as well as of his anger and competitiveness, had to be explored and resolved sufficiently, so he could experience his wife's sexual avoidance without feeling personally threatened. He then became calmer, but the change in his pressuring behavior did not in itself produce a cure in Eva. Nevertheless, the individual work with Adam was necessary for the progress of therapy, since only with the removal of his pressuring could Eva experience and work on her own sexual anxieties and inhibitions. In fact, his acceptance of her as she was—with all her sexual fears—enhanced her trust in him immensely.

Eva's phobic avoidance of sex was worked through in gradual steps with in vivo desensitization. She reached the point where she could tolerate physical contact without feeling tense and anxious, but this in itself did not increase her sexual desire. With support and encouragement during the therapy sessions, Adam did not pressure further at this point.

Some time later in therapy sessions alone with Eva, she came to recognize that now that he no longer behaved in a way that was inhibiting, she was using obsessive and negative thoughts to "protect herself" from sexual feelings. This insight, together with the exploration and some degree of resolution of deeper pleasure and success inhibitions, was significant in that her sexual desire began to return. At first she felt sexual only when her husband was not at home, but gradually she began to feel erotic again in his presence. At this point the couple was again seen in conjoint sessions.

One year later Eva was able to resume sexual intercourse with Adam. At termination of treatment the phobic element was gone. Although sexual desire and erotic pleasure had returned, they still had sexual contact less frequently than during their first year of marriage.

CASE 2   SAM AND SUSIE
        Inhibited Sexual Desire with Phobic Avoidance
        Calm Partner
        Successful Outcome

The patient was a 28-year-old housewife who had been married for four years to a high school principal who was 30 years of age. The couple had twin boys age three years. The couple had been referred by a traditional sex therapy clinic where they had been seen for nine months for weekly sessions. During this time the problem had worsened and the patient had become increasingly hopeless and discouraged. Prior to this experience, Susie had been in psychoanalytically oriented psychotherapy for two years. This had helped the depressions she was then experiencing but the sexual complaint had not improved.

Chief Complaint

The chief complaint was "lack of desire," which turned out to consist of true inhibition of sexual desire complicated by a severe phobic avoidance of any erotic contact.

History

Susie had never experienced sexual desire, even during her adolescence, except during the third trimester of her pregnancy. She was capable of reaching orgasm on clitoral stimulation both by herself and by her husband. However, she did this infrequently. During their four years of marriage the couple had had intercourse only three times (one of these times resulted in the pregnancy). They had had no physical contact at all for two years because any attempt on his part to kiss or hold her resulted in "hysterics," i.e., provoked an anxiety attack.

Sam and Susie had a good relationship and, although they were not very intimate in terms of sharing their feelings, were in love with each other. They were both excellent parents.

Etiology

The immediate cause of the lack of sex was the patient's phobic avoidance of physical contact. There were also deeper problems in the form of a severe unconscious conflict about any kind of pleasure. This patient experienced sharp headaches when she allowed herself to have fun and pleasure. It was speculated that the genesis of her fear of sexual pleasure involved unresolved oedipal conflicts which had been activated by a father transference towards her husband. She had a hysterical character structure.

Treatment

In contrast with Adam, the husband in the last case, Sam did not feel rejected by his wife's sexual avoidance and this did not mobilize feelings of anxiety or anger or competition with other men. He accepted the reality of her sexual anxiety as being her problem and he never pressured her. If he felt sexually frustrated he masturbated without anger and without taking the opportunity of evoking her guilt by portraying himself as her victim.

His bland attitude raised the question of whether he was harvesting some psychic gain from Susie's sexual inhibition. It was speculated that he might pose resistances as she began to improve, but this did not materialize.

The initial focus of sex therapy was on the first obstacle, her phobic avoidance of physical contact. This was implemented by very gradual in vivo sensitization. Her resistances to improvement often took the form of trying to do too much, i.e., if the *sig* were to lie next to Sam in bed and hold his hand, she might try to have him caress her breast, which would, of course, throw her into an intense and counterproductive anxiety state. She was confronted with this and given the responsibility of keeping her anxiety level at an optimum "comfort zone." She realized that if she did nothing and so experienced no anxiety, no progress could be made. If she took too big a step, she would get too anxious for useful progress. She would have to take responsibility for structuring her tasks so that she experienced an optimum level of anxiety.

This she did—and she also made a conscious effort not to sabotage her pleasure. The progressively erotic and intimate tasks and the evolving feelings of pleasure evoked a veritable galaxy of previously unconscious psychic material, as will typically occur with hysterics. Expressions of unconscious material evoked by the treatment were dramatic. Thus, dreams featured "dead relatives buried in the basement that needed to be removed." Her deceased father, who figured in her psychopathology, appeared in her dreams eight times. In the first two dreams he was a central and threatening figure. Thereafter his role in the dreams diminished. Four months after treatment had begun, when significant oedipal material had been revealed and discussed, and when the influence on her life that was created by her relationship with her father diminished, he appeared only "for a fleeting visit" in her last father dream.

I saw the patient alone and also together with her husband for 16 sessions. By that time her phobic avoidance was greatly diminished, but she did not yet experience any notable sexual desire. For reasons of scheduling the couple was transferred to another therapy team. They then focused on conflicts centering around sexual and pleasure guilt and the sexual exercises were continued. She began to take an active role in learning to be "good to herself." Twelve sessions later the couple was having satisfying intercourse once to twice a week.

Susie still does not initiate sexual activities, but she does feel some desire. She does not avoid sex and is able to feel erotic pleasure and excitement and orgasm once she "gets into it." In addition, her relationship with her husband is more open, and her unconscious pleasure anxiety, which had caused her to sabotage her joy in life, has also abated to a point where she feels pride and not anxieties or headaches when she enjoys herself.

HYPERACTIVE SEXUAL DESIRE

In my experience, excessive sexual desire is so rare as to constitute a clinical curiosity when it is a primary symptom. An abnormally intense sexual appetite in females has been termed "nymphomania" and the corresponding condition in the male is "Don Juanism."

Primary hyperactive sexual desire must be differentiated from those high levels of sexual activity that are components of manic and hypomanic states. I have seen two patients who were genuinely distressed by excessive sexual desire. They constantly felt sexually hungry and tense even shortly after orgasm. Both were hypomanic, and both responded to lithium therapy with a more comfortable level of sexual desire as well as with a general calming.

Compulsive and obsessive sexual states must also be differentiated from true excessive sexual desire. Sexual obsessions are highly prevalent. Many patients are constantly preoccupied with their sexuality and may masturbate to orgasm ten times a day or more. However, careful evaluation reveals that these patients really do not experience an excessive or constant desire for sex. Rather they are highly anxious and tense and seek to relieve their discomfort with sexual activity. In all compulsive states, anxiety rises when the compulsive act is prevented. And, indeed, these patients experience a flood of anxiety when they are not engaging in physical stimulation or in seduction. Sexual activity used in the service of tension relief is a compulsion and not truly overactive sexual desire.

One such patient presented with a complaint of impotence. The examination revealed that he masturbated to orgasm six to ten times during the day, interrupting his work as a telephone repairman in order to do this. He then attempted intercourse every night with his wife. Not surprisingly, his erections were less than complete at those times. This increased his anxiety still further and was the reason he sought consultation. When he tried to stop masturbating, the anxiety mobilized by this attempt to refrain was massive and intolerable.

Another patient who was obsessed with fears about his sexual performance tried to employ a compulsive pattern of sexual expression in order to reassure himself. Naturally, this had the opposite effect— since he failed to function perfectly with the many partners (sometimes three different women in one night) which were part of his compulsive pattern, he sought therapy for his "impotence."

This patient managed to persuade a urologist to perform penile implant surgery which did, indeed, give him the perfectly reliable erection he had sought so obsessively. And surgery did him no harm. Afterwards he did, in fact, cease his sexual overactivity, but as obsessives usually will, he found another and related obsession—he became obsessed instead with a fear that he would always be rejected by women whom he valued, no matter what he did. The obsessive's expressed concern is not the true reason he is anxious. In fact, the obsessive concern may be a smoke screen, a distraction from the real and unconscious vulnerability.

Sex therapy is inappropriate for obsessive patients, regardless of whether or not the content of their obsessive preoccupation is sexual. Such patients require specific kinds of treatment, usually long-term. The description of this topic is beyond the scope of our discussion here. More information may be found in the Bibliography.

5

THE ETIOLOGY

OF DESIRE PHASE

DISORDERS

A PSYCHOSOMATIC CONCEPT

SEXUAL DESIRE is an appetite. It is governed by multiple biological and experiential determinants; consequently, a wide variety of physical and psychological factors can disturb its functioning.

An understanding of the physiology of sexual desire is basic to the understanding of its disorders. Sexual desire is a drive that serves the biologic function of species survival. It instills a strong erotic hunger that prods us to engage in species specific behavior that leads to reproduction. It moves us to find a mate, to court, to seduce, to excite, to impregnate, to be impregnated.

The neural organization that governs libido is similar to that which produces hunger, thirst and the urge to sleep. Like these other drives, it is served by its own specific network of centers and circuits. The behavioral correlate of neural activity in these centers is the experience of sexual desire. In the absence of such activity there is no libido.

Like the other drives, sexual desire is organized so that it is kept in balance by inhibitory and activating mechanisms. When the inhibitory centers dominate, sexual desire is diminished; an increase of sexual desire is experienced when the circuits are under the influence of the activating centers. The centers have extensive anatomical connections to other parts of the brain, and by virtue of these connections, sexual desire can be enhanced and inhibited by a number of internal and external forces.

The sex centers and sexual appetite are responsive to hormones, specifically testosterone and LH-RF. Without an adequate hormonal environment they cannot operate and libido vanishes. Also, external stimuli—the aroma, sight, sound and touch that indicate that an attractive partner is at hand—influence the state of desire profoundly.

The connections of the sex centers to the parts of the brain that process and store experience make sexual desire highly sensitive to the past. The suppression of sexual desire can be acquired. We *learn* to inhibit desire in situations that carry negative contingencies, and *learn* to allow desire to emerge in "safe" contexts. In fact, desire is the product of a biologically rooted substrate that is shaped in direction and intensity by events of the past.

Also important from a clinical vantage is the fact that the sex centers are profoundly influenced by emotion. The negative emotions that serve individual survival and motivate us to avoid and defend against danger—fear and anger—have priority over the urge to reproduce. This hierarchy has clear survival value. It makes good sense for the activity of a man's sex circuits to become inhibited so that he does not stop to seduce his mate while he is under attack from a saber-toothed tiger. But this adaptive mechanism can go awry if the "dangers" are not accurately perceived. If an individual reacts to fantasy dangers, if he reacts with alarm to fears that have no basis in reality, his sex drive will become inhibited just as surely as if there was a real tiger in his bed. That is the psychophysiologic basis of the inhibition of sexual desire.

PHYSIOLOGIC CAUSES OF HSD

A normal sex drive requires the anatomic and physiologic integrity of the brain and specifically of the sex centers. It is not surprising, therefore, that libido is often diminished in response to physiologic factors. These must, of course, be ruled out before sexual therapy is attempted. Certain physiologic causes are responsive to specific treatments, and even when they are not, sex therapy for a patient whose drive is hypoactive on a physiological basis is not rational and of course carries a poor prognosis. The most common physiologic factors associated with HSD are depression and severe stress states, certain drugs and illnesses, and low testosterone level.

Depression

Depression is perhaps the most common physiologic cause of HSD. Depression is marked by a diathesis of vegetative symptoms which includes sleep, eating and libido disturbances. It may be speculated that during a depressed state the activity of the centers and circuits that serve such vital functions as eating and sex is diminished. The loss of sexual appetite may be an early symptom of depressive states and may appear even before the patient's mood becomes perceptibly sad. Characteristically, during depression erection and orgasm are not impaired at all or not to the same extent as is libido. Again, sexual therapy is not an appropriate treatment modality when loss of libido is secondary to depression. The underlying depression should be treated first by appropriate means which may include medication and/or psychotherapy. Often, but not always, sexual desire returns spontaneously when the depression lifts.

Stress

Severe stress, such as is experienced on the battlefield, or during a traumatic divorce, or after a job loss or forced retirement, is often associated with a loss of sexual interest. Clinical observations suggest that crisis and stress are also associated with a physiologic depression of the sexual apparatus. For this reason, it is important to assess the patient's current life situation during the initial evaluation. Usually it is wise not to commence sexual therapy during crisis periods, even though patients may displace their anxieties and become obsessed with their sexual functioning. For example, a patient consulted me with an urgent complaint of impotence and lack of desire. At the time of the interview he was in the midst of a bitter marital crisis, his son had been arrested for drug abuse, his business partner had embezzled his life's savings and he was being pursued by the I.R.S. for tax evasion. But he was preoccupied with the fact that he was not very interested in making love to his young mistress. This was hardly the ideal time for sexual therapy! The management of depression as well as of crisis and stress is a complex topic which extends beyond this discussion.

Drugs

The sex centers depend for their proper functioning on a delicate balance of the neurotransmitters serotonin and dopamine, on a specific matrix of sex and pituitary hormones, and probably on yet undiscovered chemical ingredients as well. Anything that upsets these balances, that tinkers with the recipe, may result in a malfunctioning of the centers and so depress libido.

While the specific mechanisms of action are not clear in all cases, clinical evidence suggests that some drugs may produce a diminution of sexual desire; these include narcotics, high doses of sedatives and alcohol, certain centrally acting antihypertensive agents such as those, for example, which contain reserpine and methyl dopa, and drugs which antagonize the action of testosterone. The psychosexual evaluation should, for this reason, always include a survey of substances taken by the patient. If the patient is ingesting any medication that affects sexual desire, an attempt should be made to find alternate drugs if this is consistent with good medical care.

Unfortunately, some physicians are not as sensitive to the sexual side effects of medications as they are to side effects that disturb other functions and fail to search with vigor for drugs or drug combinations that reduce blood pressure while minimizing sexual distress.

When a patient is abusing alcohol, sedatives or narcotics, he should not be accepted for therapy until he has controlled his habit. This view is based on the poor prognosis of these patients and not on a moral judgment.

The effects of drugs on sexual functioning are summarized in Table I of the Appendix.

Hormones

Because the activity of the sex centers depends on testosterone, insufficient levels of this hormone or its physiologic unavailability may produce a diminution of sexual interest in both males and females. This can result from any condition or drug or psychic state which impairs the production of androgens by the testes, ovaries and adrenals. Common factors in testosterone deficiency include the aging process, prolonged stress, surgical removal or disease of the testosterone-producing glands, and hormones and medication, such as provera and estrogen which antagonize the action of testosterone. A low testosterone level should always be ruled out when the evaluation points to a possible organic etiology for HSD. Psychological treatment in such cases is contraindicated because it has no rational basis. Even more important, when HSD is secondary to a testosterone deficiency, replacement therapy will often restore sexual functioning without further psychological intervention. Recent evidence suggests that increased levels of the hormone prolactin may play some role in libido problems.

Medical Illness

Any medical illness or surgical procedure which disturbs the anatomy or physiology of the brain's sex centers such as, for example, renal dialysis, can be associated with low libido states. Such conditions are rather rare, but they do play a role in some cases and should not be neglected. Also, some medical, urological and gynecological disorders cause sexual activity to lose its pleasurable aspect or to become uncomfortable and even painful. Under such circumstances a secondary loss of interest and/or sexual avoidance may occur. Effects of Illness on the Sexual Response are summarized in Table II in the Appendix.

PSYCHOLOGICAL CAUSES OF ISD

When a patient's sexual drive is constitutionally low, or he is deficient in testosterone, or he is depressed, i.e., when the sex centers are hypoactive on a physiologic basis, sexual appetite is low because it is not generated. But in ISD libido is diminished because it is actively, albeit unconsciously and involuntarily, suppressed on the basis of psychological conflict. In clinical practice psychogenic disturbances of libido are more prevalent than those that are secondary to physiologic factors.

Some patients are so strongly defended against their sexual desire that they will actively *avoid* any situations which may evoke it. Such patients will not read erotic literature or look at erotic pictures. They will not discuss sexual topics and may even experience discomfort when a conversation or joke has sexual overtones. They may avoid socializing with a potential sexual partner and will go out of their way to avoid physical contact. Other patients have learned to control their sexual appetite so well they don't need to avoid stimuli which would ordinarily evoke it. They are able to suppress erotic appetite in the face of the most tantalizing stimulation.

The "Turn Off" Mechanism

Examination of the specific and immediate experiences of such patients suggests that the *involuntary and unconscious but active suppression of sexual desire is the immediate cause or antecedent of ISD.*

Most of the patients I have studied tend to suppress their desire by evoking negative thoughts or by allowing spontaneously emerging negative thoughts to intrude when they have a sexual opportunity. They have learned to put themselves into negative emotional states, by selectively focusing their attention on a perception or thought or by retrieving some memory or allowing an association to emerge that carries a negative emotional valence. In this manner they make themselves angry, fearful or distracted, and so tap into the natural physiologic inhibitory mechanisms which suppress sexual desire when this is appropriate and in the person's best interest. In other words, sexual desire is normally inhibited when the individual is in danger or in an emergency. In physiologic terms the sex circuits are blocked by the activity of the fear and "anger" circuits. And some ISD patients I have studied have learned to activate these emergency circuits, evoking or permitting upsetting thoughts, and in this manner suppressing their sexual desire.

A varity of evoked images, associations or perceptions are "selected" for their ability to serve as a "turn off" mechanism—there is no specificity in the content of these negatives. A patient will focus his/her attention selectively on one of the partner's unattractive physical features—his pot belly, her unkempt hair, her fat thighs, the odor of his breath, or his genitals etc.—in the service of shutting down the sex centers. Or the memory of the partner's unacceptable behavior or past injustices may be employed. The evening that lovemaking is in the air, he will focus on her overspending or her neglect to purchase some needed household item, and she will allow herself to be irritated by evidences of his immaturity or anxiety or suddenly recall that he did not buy her an anniversary present. Other persons use negative thoughts about themselves to "protect" them from feeling sexy: "I am too fat"; "My breasts are too small or too large to be attractive"; "I am too old"; "I will come too soon"; "It will take me too long to come"; "I will not be able to have an erection." Other persons choose sexual times to retrieve memories of non-erotic situations to control their erotic mood. Work, children and money are commonly used "turn offs."

In clinical practice, certain typical patterns of experience will signal that the mechanism of self-evoked or selected negatives may be operative. The wife complains that she feels sexy all day. When she talks on the phone with her husband, she feels warm and receptive— but when he walks in the door she is immediately turned off. She suddenly feels critical and irritable. Often, she has produced this anti-sexual mood herself by selectively focusing on some of her husband's negative features as soon as he comes into her physical presence.

Another patient gives a history of intense desire in new or casual relationships, but of loss of libido in more long-lasting or committed situations. A close scrutiny of his experiences reveals that with a new woman he is not critical. He relates only to her genuine positive features and ignores the negatives. In this manner he allows himself to feel the full force of his erotic desires. Then, after he succeeds in engaging her, the opposite happens. Rather than focusing on her lovely dark hair, her slim legs, and her expressive eyes, he now reacts to her poorly groomed nails, her less than stylish clothes, and some pimples on her back. Not surprisingly, his ardor fades.

It may be speculated that in patients who suffer from global ISD, all erotic feelings cause anxiety and evoke the attendant defenses against this. All sexual situations evoke negative thoughts and associations. When the desire inhibition is *situational*, only specific situations evoke sexual conflict and cause the patient to tap into the "turn off" mechanism.

Such negative thoughts serve the opposite purpose as sexual fantasies, which are used to enhance the sexual desire and serve to diminish the anxieties that turn off desire. Erotic imagery buffers the sex circuits and protects them from the negative input which may shut them down. The negative focus described above does the exact opposite. It "opens the switch" which will suppress the sex centers.

The person who is conflict-free about sex mentally does the opposite of the inhibited one, in the sense that he does *not allow* negative feelings or thoughts or distractions to intrude upon his sexual pleasure. He arranges the weekend to be free of business intrusions; he avoids arguments with his partner—in fact, he acts so as to bring out the best in her. In order to put her in a receptive mood, he focuses only on her positive attributes—makes her feel special—all in the service of his pleasure. When he is in a sexual situation, he does not criticize his partner's taste in bedroom furniture, or see figure flaws, or comment on less than brilliant conversation. His behavior instinctively maximizes his erotic experience.

Some persons have a very narrow range of requirements for sexual pleasure. Only partners with very specific characteristics "turn them on." This is adaptive if they are with such a desired partner, but if they never seem to find the right one, the clinician should be alert to the possibility that they are inhibiting themselves in the service of a hidden sexual conflict.

Others can respond to a wide variety of partners; they are much more accepting, finding and relating to the partner's positive attributes so that they are able to enjoy the relationship.

Unconscious Defenses

Individuals are usually not aware of the active role they play in their inhibitions. This process seems to operate unconsciously, automatically and involuntarily. In fact, patients tend to see themselves as victims. They usually have no insight into the fact that they are actively evoking negative images or permitting them to intrude. They do not usually recognize that they have a choice, that they do not have to do this, that they have control over the focus of their attention.

Characteristically, patients will externalize: "I have no sexual interest in her because she is fat (she is inconsiderate, it's the wrong chemistry, I need a more macho guy, I want a man who has better erections etc.)." They are not aware that they actively and selectively, albeit unconsciously, focus on negatives. They tend to report that they "don't feel anything" or they feel uncomfortable, i.e., tense, bored or angry, in response to sexual stimulation, and they feel relief when they manage to avoid sex. However, the detailed study of experiences evoked in such patients by the sexual exercises suggests that there often *are* sexual sensations, albeit fleeting, which the patient immediately anesthesizes himself against or diminishes by evoking counter-erotic feelings such as fear, tension, anger or disgust.

This formulation implies that we have much more control over what we desire and what we do not than we are aware of. We have the capability to control our sexual pleasure, as well as our other feeling states, to a far greater extent than we have been taught to believe. For instance, we are aware, once we are in touch, that we can control and select, to a certain extent at least, what aspect of an experience or person we relate to and this substantially determines the quality of experience. Within certain limits, we can be in charge of our desires. We have more of a choice than we generally believe.

A person will dampen his desire by evoking or focusing on negatives because, on some level of consciousness, the person *does not want to have sex*. He does not want sex at all, or he does not want it with this partner or not in this situation. In other words, his unconsciously expressed wish for sex is not as strong as his unconscious reluctance is.

Patients are generally not aware that they really do not want to have sex. In fact, they may claim the opposite and sincerely ask the doctor to help them feel sexual toward their wife or husband or lover. They also have no insight as to why they don't want to have sex or into what triggers their inhibition. The sources of the sexual conflict are usually unconscious.

Remote Causes of ISD

It has been hypothesized that the immediate cause of ISD is specific and consists of the suppression of sexual desire by evoking, failing to put aside or focusing on negative thoughts. It is difficult at this early stage to determine how universally this mechanism operates, but my preliminary impression is that it is present in a significant proportion of this patient population.

While the immediate antecedent of the symptom may be specific, the remote causes—the conflicts which trigger this response, i.e., which cause the patint to be conflicted about wanting sex—seem to be multiple.

On a deeper level, any and all of the countless reasons which make sex dangerous or undesirable to that individual may be operative. There seems to be no specific content, no special unconscious conflict or fantasy or developmental disturbance that produces this symptom. A variety of intrapsychic as well as interactional factors may contribute to the development of desire inhibition, although ultimately it is always fear or anger, most often but not always beyond the patient's awareness, which makes desire undesirable. These underlying causes can be organized qualitatively, i.e., according to the depth or intensity of the underlying conflict.

Mild Sources of Anxiety

It has already been mentioned that, in general, the sources of anxiety associated with ISD seem to tend to cluster near the more intense or "deep" end of the causal continuum. However, occasionally desire will be inhibited by simple performance anxiety, or the anticipation of lack of pleasure in the act, or mild residual guilt about sex and pleasure. Rather than facing a distressing failure, the person unconsciously "elects" not to feel anything at all. Simple overconcern for pleasing the partner, along with failure to communicate one's own needs, can also cause a person to eschew sexual feelings. Rather than face the "hassle" of unpleasant sex, the person learns to squelch his desire. Also, repeated nonpleasurable, ungratifying sexual experiences, especially if the partner is having pleasure, may, after a while, lead to a loss of interest in sex. More often, in such cases, the patient is a woman. Love-making is too rapid, her partner not sensitive enough to her needs, too orgasm oriented. She anticipates frustration and sees no way to improve the situation. Often she feels it is "her fault" and will not assert herself or seek a way to improve things. Unconsciously, she "refuses" to feel desire rather than be disappointed once again; she does this by conjuring up negative memories every time love-making is attempted. Obsessive pursuit of sexuality by the partner has already been mentioned as common and milder precipitant of ISD. Here the partner's anxious and pressuring behavior evokes such negative sensations in the patient that sexual desire is suppressed. Also in this category of mild causes are the surface guilts, inhibitions and cautions that are the residues of culturally determined anti-sexual injunctions of childhood. If memories of these are evoked in the love-making situation, desire can be repressed thereby.

These "mild" factors can cause some persons to inhibit their sexual feelings. These cases are atypical with respect to their simple etiology, as well as in their excellent response to the rapid, reassuring, pleasure-encouraging sex therapy methods. In such cases, a successful outcome can occur without the patient's insight.

"Mid-Level" Sources of Anxiety—The Unconscious
Fear of Success and Intimacy

More typically, ISD is associated with deeper and more complex psychic problems. The high frequency with which the unconscious fear of success and/or pleasure plays a dynamic role in this disorder is impressive. Especially in those puzzling cases where desire is lacking even though the relationship is excellent and loving and the partner is ideal, the unconscious fear of romantic success is frequently the crucial underlying cause of a sexual "turn off." Sexual pleasure with an especially valued and loved partner is "too much" for such patients. It is not psychologically "safe" and for that reason he unconsciously does not "want" to feel desire. He will then evoke negative images and so inhibit his desire. When success anxiety is mild, it may be desensitized with behavioral methods, circumvented by redefining "success" and focusing on physical pleasure, or with simple confrontation of the existence of the active turn off mechanism. But more frequently these unconscious fears cannot be bypassed; they must be resolved at least to some extent before the patient can enjoy sexual feelings again. The etiology of success and pleasure anxiety and its management in brief therapy are discussed more fully in Chapter 10.

The unconscious fear of intimacy also often plays an etiological role in ISD. Sometimes it seems that people in our culture are more afraid of intimacy than they are of sex. Patients with intimacy problems are not afraid of erotic pleasure per se. They unconsciously fear a close and intimate attachment. Such persons may have good sex in the early stages of a relationship, before it is intimate, but experience a loss of sexual interest after they reach a certain level of closeness with and commitment to the partner.

"Mid-level causes," i.e., pleasure and intimacy conflicts, are highly prevalent in patients with desire problems. This patient group may fail to respond to brief behaviorally oriented methods and may need psychosexual therapy which has been modified and lengthened to increase its capability to foster insight into and resolution of these types of problems. Milder problems in the couple's relationship, as well as milder intrapsychic conflicts, may also fall into this "mid-level" group, who may fail with brief methods but respond to the longer, more psychodynamically oriented methods.

Deep Sources of Anxiety

Unfortunately, the unconscious roots of a desire inhibition are frequently found in profound and complex intrapsychic conflicts and in severe relationship problems. Various schools of thought have hypotheses regarding these. Psychoanalysis has studied such problems at length and analytic formulations regarding the etiology of inhibited libido are similar to those used to explain impotence. This is not surprising because, until recently, desire and erection disorders were both categorized as the single pathologic entity: impotence. Thus, psychoanalytic theory postulates that unconscious fears of injury and/or castration are mobilized when a person who has not resolved his oedipal conflicts encounters a sexual situation in adult life. Such patients tend to form primitive and pathological parental transferences with their sexual partners, which inhibit their sexual expression to various degrees. The husband becomes the "daddy" with whom sex is forbidden. The wife becomes "mother" who rightfully belongs to father. ISD in such cases is a maladaptive defense against incest. Clinical experience indicates that a portion— but certainly not all—of the patients whose desire becomes inhibited could be described in such terms. They "don't want to" feel sexual desire because this is not safe. Sex will expose them to dangers of injury from fantasy competitors.

Recently some psychoanalysts have extended and refined developmental concepts of psychopathology. While the oedipal period retains its importance as an explanatory concept in the etiology of sexual problems, attention has also been focused on even earlier developmental stages as potentially pathogenic. Studies of borderline and narcissistic patients suggest that when early emotional development is abnormal, the capacity to fall and stay in love in adult life becomes impaired. More specifically, it has been postulated that even before the oedipal period the child forms "psychic introjects" in response to his early *interactions* with his parents. As he matures, he integrates these introjects into his psychic organization. Desire and love problems at length and analytic formulations regarding the etiology of fails to internalize and integrate appropriate introjects.

Alternate and somewhat less complex hypotheses have been developed by schools of thought that derive from learning theory and from interpersonal orientations. These center around the exquisite sensitivity of the child to the responses of persons who are emotionally significant to him. According to these theories, the child may learn to inhibit his sexuality, to sabotage his romantic success, and to be guilty about pleasure, if the emotional nonverbal and verbal responses of his family are destructive and not encouraging in these respects.

On a more basic level, the urge to have sexual pleasure and to enjoy romantic love is strong and biologically determined. But other forces—the forces that serve self-preservation—are even stronger. The libido can be twisted, side-tracked, compromised and even blocked entirely by the onslaught of negatives, especially while the libido functions are still vulnerable during childhood and adolescence.

Sometimes such deeply rooted, unconscious conflicts about love and sexuality can be "bypassed" by working on the level of the immediate antecedent of the symptom in brief therapy, but often they are too compelling and must be resolved, at least in part, before the person feels "safe" enough to allow himself to experience desire fully and enduringly with an appropriate partner.

Anger

Fear or anxiety is the major etiologic factor in all the sexual dysfunctions, but anger at the partner is also a highly prevalent cause for the loss of sexual interest. Anger is a final common pathway by which sexuality can become blocked for multiple underlying reasons. Also, anger, like anxiety, can be viewed as varying in intensity and in depth. Anger at one's partner can be the result of mild or easily remediable causes, mid-level causes, or it can have its origin in the most profound intrapsychic and relationship factors. Consequently, anger evoked by silly squabbles, petty annoyances and simple irritations can "turn off" sexual feelings, but this is temporary unless these trivial issues are the "tip of the iceberg" for more serious difficulties.

Power struggles and anger at contractual disappointments may be considered to be "mid-level" problems that can impair sexual feeling. Also in this group are the fights that are provoked by persons who harbor unconscious fears of intimacy and romantic success.

The most serious sources of anger between a man and a woman derive from infantile transferences. He is enraged because his wife-mother will not "feed" him, does not give him enough, and, worst of all, prefers others, brothers and fathers. And she is furious because daddy-husband neglects her for business or is controlling and bossy or threatens her with abandonment.

Regardless of the origin of anger, it is not possible for most persons to feel sexual desire for "the enemy." Anger and love act as mutual inhibitants. If you love someone, anger disappears rapidly. When you are enamoured you are ready to quickly forgive and forget and welcome the sweet resumption of closeness. On the other hand, if you are angry at someone, if you want to hurt him, then it is difficult to give into sexual desire and to be close. You don't "want" to feel desire for this person. You "hold on" to the psychic distance your anger creates. You retrieve the memories of past injustices. An angry partner resists giving and receiving pleasure. Partners engaged in power struggles don't want to be close and intimate. A distrustful partner does not want to make himself vulnerable, while sexual abandonment, which entails lowering of defenses and regression in the service of pleasure, may generate profound feelings of vulnerability. And so it is safer to block the feelings of desire.

In my experience, it is not possible for normal persons to experience sexual desire for a partner with whom they are angry. I believe that anger and sex act as mutual inhibitants. Accordingly, some persons employ sadistic and/or sadomasochistic fantasies and acts *for the purpose of discharging anger*. According to this view, anger is *not* an erotic stimulus. To the contrary, it is "gotten out of the way" in order for a person to be able to experience sexual pleasure. Tenderness and affection are the normal emotional concomitants of erotic feelings, while aggression is an impediment which must be bypassed, or neutralized, or resolved. This view of the negative relationship between anger and sexual passion is in direct opposition to that of Stoller and others who believe that anger and aggression are the normal and universal aspects of erotic experience, that good sex requires the integration of angry and erotic impulses. While I believe that anger is commonly associated with sexual feelings because of the negative contingencies which permeate our early sexual development, most people can handle this sufficiently to be able to function. In fact, in the course of sex therapy patients who need help in dealing with disturbing hostile impulses might be encouraged to employ sadomasochistic fantasies in order to circumvent these, in the same way that patients are encouraged to use fantasy to bypass disturbing sexual *anxiety*.

According to this view, the need for a strongly hostile element in love-making occurs only in pathological conditions. For example, when a sadomasochistic system is operative, desire is interwoven with the anger created by submission and domination. Schizophrenic and borderline patients also may, as part of the ambivalence which is characteristic of this population, experience hatred and love/sex towards the same person in rapid oscillation. However, in persons who are free of major psychopathology, anger evokes defenses against openness, erotic feelings and sexual abandonment and usually serves as an obstacle to sexuality.

Masters and Johnson have reported that "partner rejection" is a significant factor in treatment failure. To the extent that "partner rejection" refers to anger at the partner, this observation is in agreement with the idea that anger is a "turn off" that cannot be bypassed with sensate focus. A couple must "make up" before they can make love; in the clinical situation, anger must be resolved, at least in part, before desire and erotic feelings can be expected to emerge. If this cannot be accomplished treatment will fail.

CASE 3   **DICK AND DORA**
> *Inhibited Sexual Desire*
> *Anger Towards Spouse*
> *Failure*

Chief Complaint

Dick was a 39-year-old surgeon with his own medical group firm. His wife, 35, was a physician on the faculty of a teaching hospital. The couple had been married ten years. They had one little girl.

The chief complaint was Dora's total lack of sexual desire and her partial avoidance of sex. Dick liked to make love in a slow, sensuous way. She found this objectionable, "creepy." She did not like any physical contact with him, even in nonsexual situations. She pulled away when he tried to hold her hand while walking, etc. When they did make love, she wanted to "get it over with" as quickly as possible. Dora was orgasmic; in fact, she reached orgasm very rapidly.

History

The couple met when he was at a prestigious medical school and she was attending a city college. When they first met he did not hide the fact that he considered her to be inferior to him in intellect and social position. She felt deeply attracted to him and pursued the relationship with an obsessive intensity. He tried to terminate the relationship several times, on the grounds that "he could do better," but she always persuaded him to continue. Despite his misgivings, they married and for a while both seemed content.

After the busy time of the birth of their child, her medical studies and his establishing himself professionally, the balance of the relationship shifted. Now she ceased to find him attractive while he pursued her.

The evaluation revealed that both were extremely competitive. She had never made a proper identification with her mother, and was still governed by immature competitive feelings towards her.

He came from a prominent family and also had a highly dominant mother. He, too, was basically immature and had never been able to fall and stay in love. He could only desire a woman who had no interest in him. When a woman wanted him, he became extremely critical and focused on her undesirable features.

Etiology

The immediate cause of Dora's lack of desire was her intense hostility towards her husband. She kept herself angry at him by dwelling on his shortcomings and on his past criticisms of her. These feelings became especially intense in sexual situations. In part this was consciously perceived by her and attributed to the real insults of the early phase of the relationship. This was correct, but there was also an unconscious component. This seemed to be due to unrecognized anger at men which had its genesis in an unresolved oedipal wish. Her husband's degradation and rejection of her, early in their relationship, evoked old feelings of rage at "the rejecting father," and she could not forgive him. Her current sexual block served both as a defense against further injury and as her revenge against all rejecting men.

Treatment

Not surprisingly, the pleasuring exercises evoked intensely negative feelings in Dora. The sigs were modified with the goal of reducing the negative impact of physical contact with her husband. The caresses were repeated but shortened in duration and she was placed in "control" of when and how the tasks were conducted. But even with these modifications, physical contact with Dick evoked feelings of discomfort and anger in her. She was simply too angry and had no wish to give up her anger.

The therapeutic exercises served to confront both husband and wife with the heretofore unacknowledged fact that she did not *want* to feel sexual desire for him, that she wanted to feel angry. In sessions alone with Dora, we explored the question of *why* she did not want to. She clearly understood that it was because she was too angry with him to give to or receive pleasure from him. An attempt was then made to resolve this couple's hostilities in conjoint therapy. This was unsuccessful and they terminated treatment.

Outcome

Shortly after termination, Dora found a relationship with an older, wealthy, powerful man. After a bitter divorce, she married her lover. Dora has an excellent sexual relationship with her new husband, who treats her in a protective, fatherly manner and does not object to her emotional demands. Dora still harbors intense resentment toward Dick, which she expresses by tormenting him whenever she has the opportunity—taunting him about her new successful marriage and great wealth, gloating about the success of her career, and generally acting in an insulting manner towards him.

Dick became depressed after the breakup of his marriage. He could not form another attachment, finding fault with each of the many women who found him attractive. He became obsessed with his failed marriage and preoccupied with the question of whether he has the capacity to love. He is currently in intensive psychotherapy with the objective of gaining insight into and resolving his relationship problems with women.

This case illustrates the inhibiting effect that anger at the partner can have on libido. Dora functions well sexually with her second husband for whom she feels no animosity. Her desire was inhibited with her first husband only after she began to feel openly hostile towards him. It may be argued, however, that her desire for and pleasure with her second husband derives, at least in part, from her feelings of vengeance for Dick, and perhaps symbolically for her father. By "setting up" the situation so that each sex act now becomes a symbolic punishment for the men she is angry at, she discharges her hostility and "gets it out of the way" so that she can be free to enjoy erotic pleasure. However, it is also important to note that Dora's new husband is kind and loving and meets her dependency needs, and on a reality basis gives her no cause for anger.

6

TREATMENT OF

DESIRE DYSFUNCTIONS

THE INHIBITION OF SEXUAL DESIRE is frequently associated with avoidance of physical contact, which may reach the intensity of a *phobic avoidance*. A pattern of avoidance of sexual experiences presents clinical problems, in that this precludes standard treatment. The assigned sexual tasks evoke intense anxiety in these patients which is therapeutically counterproductive; therefore, sexual avoidance must always be resolved before any other sexual problem can be addressed. Failure to recognize and deal with sexual avoidance has resulted in treatment failures.

MANAGEMENT OF PHOBIC AVOIDANCE

Clinically, phobias, even when they are severe, have a generally favorable prognosis and can often be managed successfully within the context of brief treatment. It is beyond the scope of this discussion to describe the various approaches to the treatment of phobic disorders in detail, but the clinician who undertakes the treatment of sexual dysfunctions should be cognizant of the fact that pharmacologic agents and various psychological methods, as well as procedures that combine both modalities, are available which can benefit a substantial number of phobic patients.

Medication

Sexual avoidance may be an isolated psychogenic symptom or it may be secondary to the phobic anxiety syndrome which is a drug responsive disorder described by Donald Klein. Phobically anxious patients should be detected because clinical experience indicates that they have a relatively poor prognosis with psychological treatments while they are intensely anxious. Their high anxiety level, their tendency to experience panic attacks, and the anticipatory anxiety which causes them to avoid any situation which may precipitate such painful panic attacks interfere with these patients' ability to benefit from the standard therapeutic process. They become so tense that they simply cannot do the structured sexual tasks and may, in fact, become even more anxious and phobic if they are confronted with feared erotic situations. Fortunately, several investigators have reported that a significant proportion of this patient population experiences substantial protection from panic attacks when given medication of the tricyclic and/or MAO inhibitor class.* Another group of psychoactive drugs, the diazepoxides,** protect many of these patients from anticipatory anxiety which was acquired as a consequence of the painful panics. When properly administered, these medications often have a long-lasting anxiety-reducing effect, which often persists after the drugs are discontinued.

It is our practice to medicate patients whose sexual avoidance appears to be secondary to the phobic anxiety syndrome, commencing sexual therapy only after the panic attacks have abated and the anxiety level has been reduced to a point where the patient can comfortably do and benefit from the prescribed sexual interactions.

It makes clinical sense to combine chemical anxiety reduction with in vivo desensitization to reduce sexual anxiety. This approach seems to be effective for patients suffering from a variety of phobias, including sexual phobias. Our approach does not substitute medication for psychosexual therapy, but rather employs these modalities in an integrated manner. The medication is employed chiefly to protect the patient against panic attacks. By itself it usually does not cure the symptom of sexual avoidance, which is primarily related to anticipatory anxiety. It does, however, create the conditions which make

---

* Commonly used tricyclic drugs are imipramine (Tofranil), amitriptyline (Elavil), desipramine (Norpramine).
** The most commonly used diazepoxide drug is chlordiazepoxide (Valium).

psychotherapy more effective. In my experience some phobic patients who have previously failed to benefit from sex therapy do well when they are first protected from panic attacks and their anxiety level is reduced to a therapeutically useful level with medication. We generally prescribe tricyclics for several weeks to months, until the patient is comfortable, before commencing sex therapy.

In our admittedly limited experience, patients *do not relapse* after medication is discontinued. This is usually attempted six to 18 months after termination of sex therapy.

Psychological Management

Not all patients who avoid sex fall into the phobic anxiety category, nor should all be given medication. Many patients who are not particularly anxious or phobic develop a specific sexual avoidance or an isolated sexual phobia. Such patients do not meet the criteria for medication and should be treated only with psychotherapeutic means.

Isolated and specific phobias have an excellent prognosis with brief therapy. Both behavioral and psychodynamic methods have been developed which are reported to be effective in treating phobias and the attendant avoidance of the phobic situations. We employ a psychodynamic variant of in vivo desensitization. The patient is encouraged to participate in progressive sexual experiences designed to desensitize the sexual anxiety. But we do not use a strictly behavioral approach, since, in our experience, resistances are diminished and insight and integration facilitated when the progressive sexual experiences are combined with psychotherapeutic methods.

For example, some patients, who have anticipatory anxiety about sex and have consequently developed an avoidance pattern, find that even the gentle, nondemanding sensate focus exercises evoke intense and intolerable anxiety. This happened in the case of Sam and Susie (see pp. 73-75). Their previous therapists had not taken her phobic avoidance pattern into account. When they prescribed sensate focus, she had a panic attack at the mere anticipation of physical contact. Then the therapists tried to demonstrate the pleasuring techniques (while they were properly clothed) during the therapy session. Again, Susie panicked at the thought that she would have to do the same thing at home.

If any task evokes negative feelings which are too intense to be therapeutically useful, it makes sense to devise a less anxiety-provoking one. I have employed such tasks as lying near each other, first clothed, then unclothed, for several weeks, until this becomes comfortable, before proceeding to more intimate behavior. Or I have assigned kissing for 15 seconds, stroking each other's hand, taking a bath or shower together, etc. Once, with a highly anxious couple, I had them both stroke their dog at the same time. This was as much intimacy as they could initially tolerate. Such tasks seem trivial for the conflict free person but may be very difficult for the phobic patient.

With each task, the patient is instructed to *stop* the task if the negative feelings become too intense. Then, in the next session with the therapist, these negative feelings are discussed in an accepting manner and their meaning explored. If the previous exercise evoked anxiety which was too high, a new one of lesser intensity, a smaller, more comfortable step, will be devised either by the therapist alone or by the therapist and patient together. The technique of enlisting the patient's help in structuring the therapeutic tasks fosters the patient's taking responsibility for moving treatment forward. He is taught to accept his feelings as a reality, and if he wants to change these, to work on this actively, but not to try too hard to "bully through" them.

THERAPIST: Having Sam touch your breasts was much too anxiety-producing. We'll have to think of a smaller step. What do you think you could do comfortably?

SUSIE: I don't know. I feel so ashamed—I couldn't even let him touch me for two minutes without getting hysterical.

THERAPIST: Being ashamed won't help. You are where you are. That's why you are here. If you don't like it we can change it. But it has to be done in comfortable steps. Usually you try to overdo it.

SUSIE: (*Anxiously turning to Sam*) I bet you are disgusted.

SAM: Look, as long as we are making progress, it's OK with me.

THERAPIST: I think Sam is better to you than you are to yourself—sure he wants sex—but he is willing to work on it. Now what do you think you can do next week? Sam, what do you think?

SAM: I don't know. (*turning to Susie*) Anything you want, honey—we'll get there.

SUSIE: Maybe if he lies still—and doesn't grab me. I could kiss him and touch him and lie on top of him.

THERAPIST: Don't you think that's a bit much? I think kissing and touching him is fine—you can stop if it gets to be too much. But lying on top of him and maybe feeling his erection seems a little intense to me. Let's save that for a while. Could you ride his hand on your breasts for a few seconds to see how it feels?

SUSIE: Oh yes, that sounds good!

THERAPIST: Sam?

SAM: Yeah, that's fine.

This dialogue also illustrates involvement of the partner. This is useful for many reasons. The partner of the sexually phobic patient can understandably become frustrated and discouraged; he gains a sense of hope if he is actively involved in his partner's treatment. It is not surprising if he feels threatened when he hears that his touch or kiss evokes anxiety or boredom or even disgust in the person he loves. For this reason, sexually inhibited patients often do not communicate clearly with their partners. They are afraid to hurt them and are also understandably worried about being rejected. This lack of communication then precludes resolution of the problem. It is helpful for the therapist to emphasize that the rejection of the partner is not personal, but a reflection of the patient's problem which has been evoked, but not caused, by the current situation. Understanding this psychic reality makes it easier for the partner to lend his crucial cooperation to the therapeutic enterprise.

Sometimes a partner is infinitely patient and cooperative while his spouse is inhibited but becomes resistant and sabotages therapy when he/she begins to experience sexual feelings. This is a familiar phenomenon whenever a system—be it family, marital, work or sexual—is changed and signifies that the partner's emotional needs must be dealt with.

If undue resistances emerge to the desensitization process, it is our practice to shift to a more psychotherapeutic mode and to try to resolve the deeper issues which may underlie such resistances. For example, in the case of Sam and Susie, material that might be regarded as oedipal emerged very clearly during the course of therapy. She found that Sam "smelled like her father" when she lay next to him, and this evoked memories of incestuous fantasies and experiences. This material was clarified and her guilt about having secretly enjoyed her father's sexual interest was worked through during the sessions. At the same time, she was instructed to "sniff" Sam and report any memories and dreams.

The integrated approach employed in this instance, i.e., the use of the behavioral olfactory tasks with the psychotherapeutic exploration of the material that these experiences evoked, was employed to foster insight into oedipal issues. In my experience, combined and integrated methods can accelerate the treatment process considerably in some clinical situations.

CASE 4   JIM AND JUDIE
Inhibited Sexual Desire with Phobic Avoidance
Loving Relationship
Partial Success

Chief Complaint

Judie, a 34-year-old woman, and Jim, her 29-year-old lover, had been living together for six years. She worked as a secretary and he as a high school English teacher. The couple had never had intercourse although they had enjoyed sex play to orgasm for both without coitus for the first year and a half of the relationship. The frequency of these contacts gradually decreased and for the last three years they have had no sexual contact at all. The reason for the asexualtiy in this relationship was Judie's lack of desire and her avoidance pattern. She avoided all physical contact because sexual activity made her feel anxious to the point of panic.

The psychosexual evaluation revealed that Jim had no difficulty in sexual functioning. He found Judie attractive and felt desire which he relieved by masturbation two or three times a week. He had good erections and pleasurable, well-controlled orgasms. Moreover, he was a gentle and patient lover, very sensitive to Judie's anxieties, sexual as well as in other spheres of experience.

Judie was orgastic on self-stimulation. In the past she had been orgastic on clitoral stimulation with partners but she was no longer able to relax sufficiently to have sex with a partner. She had never had intercourse because she was afraid of vaginal penetration. She claimed that she had completely lost her sexual desire in the past years although she and Jim loved each other, lived in harmony, and he was sexually skilled and considerate. She apparently had experienced some panic attacks during enjoyable sex play several years ago, and had developed severe anticipatory anxiety and a strong pattern of sexual avoidance.

Judie had a history of severe psychopathology. She had had a stormy childhood and adolescence, being the product of a great deal of stress within the family. She dropped out of a city college because of an acute psychotic reaction. She recovered, did not return to school, but took a series of secretarial jobs. She lost several jobs because she became too anxious to function. She had had approximately ten years of therapy with a very devoted and interested therapist. She was treated with appropriate medication and also with group and individual psychotherapy. The patient had developed a remarkable degree of insight into her vulnerabilities and conflicts and had done a marvelous job of rehabilitating herself.

Judie was referred by her doctor for sex therapy. At the time I saw her she did not project or deny or externalize her problems. She could identify and admit when she was being "crazy," i.e., irrational and overly emotional, and could correct her behavior. She was involved in an excellent supportive and intimate relationship and she was functioning well at her present job where she had been for 18 months. The sexual symptom, however, did not improve; in fact, it was getting worse despite the fact that Jim did not pressure her.

Etiology

The immediate cause of Judie's ISD was a phobic avoidance of sexual pleasure, especially in the presence of a partner. Deeper etiological factors were not clear at the time of the evaluation. The treatment plan was gradual in vivo desensitization.

Treatment

The pleasuring excercises were deemed to be too anxiety-provoking for this patient, so she was advised to stroke her own body, in the presence of her partner, while he also stroked himself.

This exercise was extremely pleasurable for the patient. However, she became somewhat depressed that week. The patient was confronted with the association of physical pleasure and depression. This confrontation evoked material that indicated that she had been raised by a severely disturbed mother, who had highly competitive and ambivalent feelings whenever she saw her daughter happy, exuberant and joyful. The shared self-pleasuring exercises were continued for several weeks. At the same time, during the sessions, the patient integrated her insights about the destructive effects on her ability to experience pleasure which resulted from her mother's negative and competitive attitudes.

At an appropriate level of anxiety, the couple advanced to ordinary, i.e., partner-induced, pleasuring. I continued to encourage her to have pleasure, contrary to what her mother had done, while confronting her with her resistances, which took the form of vague depressions and obsessive thoughts that she would never be able to experience sexual pleasure.

Jim was extremely cooperative and she worked diligently at her therapy. She continued to progress steadily in her ability to tolerate physical contact. Almost immediately her desire began to return. After 14 sessions Jim and Judie were again able to have enjoyable sex play to orgasm. They still did not have intercourse, but Judie felt that she was not ready for this; she had achieved her goals and wanted to end treatment.

I agreed and encouraged her to use her own judgment and good sense, which had proven so constructive in her life. Follow-up three years later revealed that her sexual desire has remained excellent, the couple has sex at least once a week, she still does not want penetration and this pattern of sexual adjustment has remained satisfying to them.

If the couple's sexual frequency and enjoyment of sex are low primarily because of a sexual avoidance based on a phobia, then in vivo desensitization will solve the problem, i.e., shortly after the patient is no longer uncomfortable with physical contact, he will begin to feel sexual desire and pleasure. This kind of outcome was illustrated in the foregoing case. If, however, desire is inhibited, apart from the sexual avoidance, then comfort with physical contact in itself will not produce an increase of the sexual appetite. The ISD syndrome requires specific intervention in addition to treating the avoidance component.

TREATMENT OF INHIBITED SEXUAL DESIRE

Traditionally, insight therapies have been employed for the treatment of disorders of libido. Both individual and couples psychotherapies are used for these problems. These are designed to foster resolution of unconscious intrapsychic conflicts and occult relationship problems which have presumably produced the inhibition of desire. These modalities rely on verbal methods and intervene on the level of remote and unconscious causes; however, the specific and immediate antecedents of the problem are often neglected within the context of the traditional psychotherapies. Outcome data are not available but no one has claimed impressive successes and the general impression is that some ISD patients are helped by insight therapy but treatment tends to be lengthy and outcome uncertain. It appears that for many patients, insight alone into either unconscious intrapsychic conflicts and/or hidden problems in the relationship is not enough.

Brief sex therapy has also been disappointing with respect to the desire disorders. The experiential techniques which intervene on the level of the symptom and its immediate antecedent often do not deal extensively enough with deeper conflicts which so often seem to play a crucial role in desire problems. It may be speculated that in the more serious dysfunctions, intervention on the immediate level is also not enough. Some insight into deeper causes is often required in order to cure the patient.

The method of psychosexual therapy for desire dysfunctions which we are exploring combines features of the traditional insight and the new sex therapies. It is lengthier and more flexible and more dynamically oriented than classical sex therapy, with greater emphasis on insight therapy. This approach utilizes the capability of sex therapy—of modifying the specific antecedent of the sexual symptom directly and specifically while, at the same time, relying more heavily on active, confrontive psychotherapeutic interventions to accommodate the more complex dynamics and more tenacious and more remote causes typically found in disorders of sexual desire.

PSYCHOSEXUAL THERAPY OF ISD

In the simplest terms, the objectives of treatment are to modify the patient's tendency to inhibit his erotic impulses, and to allow these feelings to emerge naturally and without effort as they will in the healthy, conflict-free person. The patient must learn not to fight his natural tendency to "turn on."

This outcome usually requires that the patient attain insight into the immediate antecedents of the symptom. For many of these patients this is the involuntary and automatic focus on negatively charged thoughts, which produces a suppression of sexual feelings. In addition, most of these patients also need to gain insight, to some extent at least, into the underlying causes of this mechanism.

To implement this objective a combination of experiential tasks and psychotherapeutic sessions is employed. The couple is usually seen once a week in the therapist's office, while doing specific, assigned, erotic tasks at home. The experiences with the sexual tasks are discussed in great detail during the therapeutic sessions. Meticulous attention is paid to the physical events as well as to the feelings evoked by these experiences in both partners. In addition, an attempt is made to determine the unconscious meaning of these structured erotic interactions by inquiring about dreams and fantasies and other forms of behavior which may be revealing in this respect. If resistances and conflicts are evoked, these are explored during the session and new tasks designed to advance treatment are assigned.

In the psychosexual therapy of desire phase disorders, behavioral experiences are employed together with psychotherapeutic exploration of resistances, just as in the treatment of the simpler genital phase dysfunctions. However, the balance between behavioral and insight modalities varies with the difficulty of the case.

The treatment of most orgasm phase disorders and of the simple excitement phase disorders relies heavily on the structured sexual experiences; psychotherapy is used mainly in the service of resolving resistances to doing the exercises, which are the active ingredients of treatment. Patients learn to recognize and modify the immediate antecedents, but insight into the underlying causes is often not necessary to obtain a cure, and the therapist's role mainly is to encourage and reassure the patient and his spouse.

But ISD patients will seldom improve unless they gain some measure of insight into underlying conflicts, into *why* they do not want sex, and so therapeutic exploration of emotional conflicts with the aim of fostering insight becomes the primary treatment modality. As the clinical problem becomes more complex, the structured sexual interactions are employed as much for their ability to evoke significant psychic material as for their intrinsic therapeutic value. The erotic tasks assigned to a dysfunctional couple are not mechanical exercises. If they are sensitively constructed, they are highly charged with emotion. They are designed to require a person to engage in experiences which he has avoided all of his life because they are threatening. They make him vulnerable; they open him up; they confront him dramatically with his problem; they evoke sensitive psychic material more rapidly and vividly than usually occurs in the course of therapies which rely solely on verbal interchange.

The objective of psychosexual therapy is to resolve the symptom as rapidly as possible and to obtain a stable cure. Intervention is kept at the minimum consistent with these objectives. The first maneuver is to attempt to modify the immediate antecedents of the symptom and deeper interventions are only executed if resistance is encountered. Intervention is then limited to the extent that it is necessary to resolve these resistances.

Initially ISD patients are usually assigned sensate focus or pleasuring exercises. A small percentage of patients responds favorably just to the reassuring, nonpressuring, sensual experiences which are so exquisitely designed to dispel fears of performance. The following case illustrates a positive outcome which resulted from traditional, symptom-oriented sex therapy. The patient in this case experienced an increase in desire without attaining insight.

CASE 5   **TONY AND TERESA**
         Inhibited Sexual Desire
         Mild Causes
         Successful Outcome with Brief Treatment

Tony was a 55-year-old restaurant owner married for five years to a woman who claimed to be 38, but who was probably ten years older than her stated age. He was obese, always had a cigar in his mouth, and was carelessly dressed. Teresa, on the other hand, was slim and carefully groomed. Her hair was dyed a uniform blond, she had long red nails, and she was dressed expensively and fashionably. This was the second marriage for both. He had been divorced, and she had been a widow.

Chief Complaint

Teresa complained that Tony had no sexual interest in her. He admitted this, and attributed it to the pressures of business. The couple had intercourse approximately once a month, during which time he tended to climax rapidly. Teresa was increasingly agitated and depressed about this situation. Tony's medical history was negative, and he reported that he had had a "strong sex drive" in his first marriage.

Etiology

The immediate cause of the problem appeared to be the interplay between his performance anxiety and her obsessive sexual demands. The more remote dynamics probably involved mutual parental transferences. To Teresa, Tony was not what he was in reality—a tired, rather shy man who needed her reassurance. Through transferential eyes he was the rejecting, powerful daddy. He saw her not as she actually was—insecure, afraid of aging, vulnerable—but as the insatiable, demanding mother. These deeper problems were noted, but they did not emerge specifically in therapy.

Treatment

Teresa was reassured about Tony's feelings for her and also confronted with the negative effects on his sexuality of her insistent demands. They were assigned nondemanding, pleasuring exercises. No resistances appeared. During the sessions I persistently emphasized the very real, positive elements of their relationship and this reduced her anxiety level greatly.

Tony revealed that he was upset because he required direct stimulation of his penis in order to have an erection. He believed he "should" erect instantly on looking at her and he had been ashamed to tell Teresa this. He was reassured as to the normalcy of his need for tactile penile stimulation and he soon learned that he could function well as long as she stimulated him. She loved to do this and his performance anxieties vanished. She learned to identify her sensations of anxiety and to express them verbally by asking for reassurance of his love instead of demanding sexual performance which set her up for feeling rejected. After ten once-a-week sessions, his desire had returned and the couple had intercourse every weekend, which was satisfactory to both. On follow-up one year later they were still doing well.

This case is unusual in that the ISD was produced by superficial causes—her obsessive demands and his performance anxiety—that yielded readily to brief intervention. More specifically, when they were about to make love, he would remind himself that he might not function and focus on anticipation of her anger and disappointment. These negative thoughts made him angry and anxious and served to suppress his desire. More often such mild underlying problems are associated with orgasm or excitement phase problems.

His desire improved when he gained sexual confidence and she became less demanding. He gained no insight into the fact that he conjured up negatives and certainly not into any unconscious forces that might have contributed to his sexual desire block. In my experience and in our population, only a small proportion of desire phase problems respond to such simple, symptom-oriented therapeutic intervention. Most often, resistances arise in the course of treatment of ISD. When this occurs, therapy becomes confronting and the patient is faced with the existence of his inhibition. The experience of not being able to respond to the gentle exchange of sensuous caresses, of feeling boredom or anxiety or discomfort instead of pleasure, can be employed as a vivid confrontation of his inhibition. At this point in treatment, if this dynamic is operative, it can be pointed out that the patient is actively, if unknowingly, "turning himself off." He is focusing his attention on negatives, on business pressures, on his partner's irritating qualities, or on performance fears. The negative affect which accompanies such thoughts—the anger, the tension—is incompatible with sexual feelings.

The patient is now confronted with the fact that this "negative thinking" is under his control, that he has a choice, and that it is up to him if he wants to change.

Some patients will respond to the crisis created by this confrontation with improvement. They will integrate this insight sufficiently to allow themselves to enjoy the sexual experience which they had previously fought against.

However, often the mere realization that he is blocking himself and he is depriving himself of pleasure is not sufficient to produce a cure. Further insight can then be fostered by confronting the patient with the consequences of his inhibition. The crisis created by his realization that his marriage is in jeopardy, that his spouse is suffering, that he himself is being deprived of a normal life, can sometimes be used to unblock desire without further insight. Case 6 later in this chapter illustrates this treatment course.

Confrontations and crises may still not produce a cure. Although the patient realizes that he could stop "turning himself off" and that the consequences are destructive to himself, he feels powerless to alter his behavior. Further insight and resolution are needed into the unconscious roots of the problem before the patient can allow himself to feel desire for and pleasure with the beloved person. In our experience, if the underlying conflicts operate on a "mid-level" of consciousness, such as a fear of success or pleasure, sufficient resolution can often be accomplished within the brief therapy framework or within 20 to 30 sessions. Cases 18 and 21 illustrate successful treatment of such patients.

Finally, there are some cases which will not respond to these methods. The underlying causes are too deep, too intense, too tenacious. Brief treatment, even when modified, will not produce a cure in such cases. Cases 9 and 11 are illustrative of such treatment failures.

Experiential or Behavioral Aspects of Treatment

Unless the evaluation reveals reasons to the contrary, the form and sequence of the behavioral tasks assigned for the treatment of ISD are like those employed for excitement phase disorders:

1) Sensate focus I,
2) Sensate focus II,
3) Sensate focus III,
4) Non-demanding coitus.

Treatment usually begins with sensate focus I or pleasuring. This consists of gentle caressing of the partner's body without touching the primary erotic area: the clitoris, nipples, vaginal entrance, or penis and scrotum. If this task evokes no resistances, i.e., if it is experienced as pleasurable by both, the couple goes on to sensate focus II. In this exercise the partners again take turns caressing each other's bodies and also caress the genitals gently and teasingly, without the rhythmic motion that produces orgasm. If genital caressing evokes pleasure in both, if they enjoy receiving as well as giving, then the next task is to stimulate each other's genitals to orgasm manually (after a period of bodily pleasuring) (sensate focus III). At this time coitus is still precluded. If this is a positive experience, the next task includes gentle penetration without orgasm until the experience of intravaginal containment is integrated by both partners. Finally, they proceed to penetration with orgasm for both.

The tasks are designed to provide a nondemanding, reassuring, nonthreatening and intimate ambience which will resolve such common obstacles to sexual pleasure as performance anxiety, anxieties and angers arising out of poor communications with the sexual partner, as well as out of disappointing, rapid, and mechanical sex, and unrealistic expectations due to sexual ignorance and inexperience. In those cases where such relatively mild problems and anxieties have caused the patient to suppress his sexual desire, these erotic and communicative behaviorally oriented methods will cure the problem. However, with ISD a positive response to the sensate focus exercises alone is the exception. Usually, the therapist must expect that, at some point in this sequence, obstacles to the experience of erotic arousal will be erected.

Most often resistances arise between tasks one and two. Often the gentle nondemanding caressing cannot be tolerated by these patients because this evokes sexual feelings which are threatening and so mobilize defenses against this experience. This is not the end of treatment but marks the beginning of insight therapy. The resistance creates the first therapeutic crisis and provides the opportunity to confront the patient with the existence of his block, with the inexplicable and involuntary suppression of erotic feelings, with his previously unrecognized tendency to focus on angry or frightening thoughts at the time of love-making.

HILDA: I started to feel good when he stroked me and then I had a rush of anger—I wanted to strangle him.

THERAPIST: Why? Was he doing something unpleasant?

HILDA: No—he was fine—he was trying hard to please. It's happened before. I get into a rage . . . It is involuntary and inexplicable . . . I feel very badly about that.

THERAPIST: Sounds like you manage to think of something that makes you angry when you two make love.

HILDA: I know, I've come to realize that. It's crazy . . . I don't know why I do that. I get furious. I thought it was because of his erections, but it happened anyhow. He is so good to me—it doesn't happen with other men. Why?

THERAPIST: That's a good question.

And so the crucial process of exploration has begun. The patient must now ask *why?* Why is this happening? Why don't I respond? She is faced with a puzzle which motivates her to explore and find an explanation.

First comes the recognition of the fact that the patient is not a victim of a mysterious loss of libido. Rather, if this dynamic is operative, she is confronted with the fact that she is actively, albeit unconsciously and involuntarily, evoking negative emotional responses in herself by focusing on negative aspects of her partner or the relationship or by remembering past injustices. She comes to recognize the fact that in this way she spoils her sexual pleasure or "protects" herself against the "dangers" of sexual openness. The therapist confronts her with the fact that it is impossible to feel sexual desire while she is making herself angry, that it is impossible to feel erotic while she "wants to strangle him," that she is depriving herself of sexual pleasure.

This again raises the question *why?* Why am I making myself so angry that I can't enjoy sex? The insight that, although she complains of the contrary, she on some level *does not want* to feel sexual emerges clearly. The irrationality, the paradox of the situation, creates a crisis which provides the opportunity for the rapid gaining of insight.

The therapist confronts her further with the effects of her sexual block. The patient must ask: What effect is this having on my life? My marriage? Is this to my advantage? Is sex the real problem?

The issues are dramatically illuminated by resistance to the tasks, by the muting of sexual feelings which occurs in ISD, and these issues can then be dealt with in the sessions. In this manner, negative responses to the behavioral exercises are employed to help the patient gain insight on progressively deeper levels.

Psychodynamic Aspects of Treatment

The therapist plays different roles as treatment proceeds through various stages and as progressively more difficult resistances unfold. The treatment of ISD usually begins with the exercises described in the previous section. During this phase of treatment the therapist is supportive and encouraging to both partners. When the couple experiences difficulty in doing the tasks, he reassures and encourages both to enjoy themselves. He is nonjudgmental and accepting, as well as sensitive to the couple's emerging anxieties and insecurities. If the tasks evoke too much anxiety, the therapist encourages the couple to repeat them or he devises tasks of lesser intensity that are modified to fit the specific dynamic requirements of the clinical situation. Interpretations at this time are limited to confronting the patients with resistances to doing their exercises.

If the patient responds to these behavioral methods with increased desire, the therapist helps the couple integrate this behavior and tries to foster sufficient insight to insure stability of the cure.

If, on the other hand, resistances arise and it becomes clear that the patient will not respond to the structural experiences alone, the therapist becomes more actively confrontive. He creates a series of mini-crises. For instance, he may create a crisis by confronting the patient with his resistance to pleasure, with his unconscious but active role in his lack of feelings, and with the fact that he evokes negative feelings to suppress his sexuality. Both direct confrontation and "joining the resistance," i.e. paradoxical confrontation, are useful at this point. The therapist now points out that the patient has a *choice* and that he has *chosen* to not feel sexual. This crisis usually moves the insight aspect of treatment forward.

It may also be useful to confront the patient with the consequences of his inhibition. He is depriving himself of sexual gratification and his relationship is suffering. The couples therapy format is often useful to confront the patient with the destructive effects of his problem on his spouse and on his relationship.

Suppressing sexual desire can be extremely self-destructive. Not only does it deprive the person of pleasure and sexual gratification, which can also diminish self-esteem, but it is often very destructive to the marital relationship. This is often denied by patients. When psychotherapeutic exploration reveals to the patient that his lack of interest is destructive to a valuable and precious romantic relationship, he often becomes highly motivated to resolve his desire problem in therapy. In fact, in mild cases confrontation leading to insight into self-destructive consequences may by itself result in the lifting of the inhibition.

CASE 6 **DONALD AND DONNA**
   Inhibited Sexual Desire
   Confrontation with Anger
   Successful Outcome

The couple consisted of Donald, age 74, a retired chairman of the board of a large mercantile company, and Donna, his wife of six years, who was 54. The couple had married shortly after his traumatic divorce from his first wife, to whom he had been married for 30 years. She had been widowed for two years at the time of the remarriage. He had three grown children by his first marriage and she had two by hers. He was intensely in love with his present wife.

Chief Complaint

The couple had a bilateral problem. Initially he complained about erectile difficulties, but the evaluation revealed that she too had a problem. She had little desire for sex.

She only consented to intercourse as an accommodation to him. She was passive during love-making and would not touch his penis or kiss him. She tried to hurry him and expressed relief when he managed to ejaculate.

He was an extremely sensitive man and responded to her lack of interest with distress and developed an erectile problem.

Etiology

The immediate and sole cause of his impotence was his wife's unresponsiveness. The etiology of her lack of desire was not clear at the time of evaluation.

Treatment

Treatment began with sensate focus exercises. She was obviously resistant. She admitted that he touched her with sensitivity and care, but stated that she did not enjoy touching his body. "He gets too eager."

She showed signs of hostility towards him in other ways. She demeaned the many material things he offered her: "I don't care for that money shit." She embarrassed him in front of business and social acquaintances; she was slovenly in her appearance at home, but dressed beautifully and stylishly

when she went out. She showed the family dog more respect and considera-
tion than she did her husband.

She was confronted with her refusal to give in to her sexual feelings and
also with her hostility towards him. She was made to face the fact that no
self-respecting man would put up with her outrageous behavior and that she
was in serious danger of losing her marriage.

At first she was furious and stomped out of the session. But she trusted the
therapist. The sessions had showed her that the therapist cared for her, that
she was not just attempting to make her into a better sex object for her
husband, and that her welfare was considered important.

So Donna came back. She came to realize that her behavior was self-
destructive and that she really wanted this marriage. She respected Donald
and appreciated the protection and love he offered her. She came to see that
she had been in conflict about accepting this marriage because she had not
yet worked through her anger at losing her first, dearly beloved husband.

As we worked on this material during the sessions, she changed dramatically. She seemed to come to an inner decision to accept her current
marriage. She became more loving to Donald and more giving, not simply to
appease him so he would not leave, but rather because she saw that it was
really in her interest to make the best of this marriage.

She now deliberately began to focus on the positive aspects of the marriage
and of her husband. When about to make love, she focused on his very real
intelligence and sensitivity and on the good life he offered her. At first it was
an effort, but gradually she began to give herself to the sexual situation in a
spontaneous manner. His impotence cleared rapidly and she began to
experience the best sexual response she had ever had in her life.

The patient saw that she was "doing it to herself" and that this was to her
disadvantage. With the realization, "I may lose him and I really don't want
to. I am depriving myself of pleasure," a crisis occurred. She learned in
therapy that she could control her "turn off" and she decided to do this.
Internal integration took place; she focused on the positives in this relationship and she felt desire again.

Such confrontation does not always result in an acceptance and
improvement of a relationship. There are times when a poor marital
relationship, which has been hiding behind a smoke screen of sexual
problems, is revealed by exploration of the underlying causes of the
lack of desire. In those cases, libido is unconsciously inhibited *in order*
to destroy a relationship which is noxious to the patient. This may
occur when a person does not accept a relationship, but has not, for a
variety of reasons, faced this on conscious level. In such cases, insight
may result in the decision to rupture the relationship.

CASE 7   HAROLD AND HILDA

Inhibited Sexual Desire
Confrontation with Anger
Failure

The couple consisted of Harold, a 62-year-old musician, and Hilda, his 55-year-old wife, who owned a successful jewelry business. Both were German-Jewish, and rather formal in style.

They had been married seven years. This was his second marriage; his first wife had died ten years before of cancer. It was Hilda's first marriage. Neither had children.

Chief Complaint

He was impotent, with a pattern of losing his erection when he entered the vagina. The couple had had sex therapy at an excellent clinic two years prior to their consultation with me. The treatment failed to improve his erectile ability. They were seeing me to try again.

The evaluation revealed that Hilda had no desire for Harold. She did not find him attractive. This issue had not been recognized or dealt with in their previous therapy, which focused on his genital symptom. When they attempted to make love, she felt no pleasure. In fact, she had an impulse to strangle Harold during love-making, which she falsely attributed to his loss of erection. She had no insight into the fact that she conjured up rejection and disappointment fantasies whenever they made love, and these were the source of her anger and lack of desire. She had a normal response with respect to desire, excitement and orgasm with other sexual partners.

During the sensate focus exercises, Hilda felt rage at Harold, even though he maintained his erection. This experience served to reveal and confront her with her active role in the suppression of desire. She had to admit that the problem did not stem only from Harold's erectile difficulty and that she selectively focused on negative aspects of this relationship when it was time for sex.

In the course of exploring the consequences of her resistance to feeling sexual desire, it became apparent to Hilda that she did not really *want* to feel sexual with Harold, that she did not *want* to give him pleasure or to receive pleasure from him. Finally, she realized that she did not want to be his wife. She really disliked Harold, but had not been able to admit this to herself. She felt anger at her husband and at herself for being "trapped" in this marriage. By suppressing her sexuality, she was creating an excuse to escape from her marriage, without having to face the real issues which were painful to her.

There was an attempt to resolve this couple's difficulties in conjoint treatment. She came to understand *why* she was angry at Harold, and also why she had not been able to face this on a conscious level. He was anxious and submissive, but subtly hostile and destructive to her. Whenever she was having a good time he managed to spoil it somehow. He sabotaged her self-esteem and pleasure, while maintaining a surface pleasantness and compliance. Her background was such that as long as he treated her with decency, at least on a surface level, her harsh conscience could not permit her to admit to herself how dissatisfied she was. Nevertheless, her rage at him and at herself was intolerable and blocked her sexual desire. In working with the husband, an attempt was made to foster his insight into his covert hostility to her but he was highly resistant and this was not successful.

Sex therapy terminated with no improvement of the sexual problem. She remained in individual therapy and gained a great deal of insight into her deeper problems with men, which had prevented her from finding and keeping a pleasurable romantic relationship all her life. However, she resolved these conflicts only partially.

Eventually she divorced Harold, which was an immense relief to her. Her long-standing depression lifted and she has led a happy and productive life for the past three years.

She now has a good sexual relationship, but with a man who lives in another country and is able to visit her only three or four times a year.

Levels of Intervention

Psychosexual therapy first attempts to help the patient by reducing sexual anxiety rapidly with behaviorally oriented methods. Case 5 with Tony and Teresa illustrated a successful outcome with this approach. But if behavioral strategies do not produce a cure, the next step is to attempt to foster insight into progressively deeper unconscious issues.

Insight into the immediate antecedents and into the consequences of the desire may be effective in relatively mild cases, as was illustrated in the case of Donald and Donna. In clinical practice this level of insight may not be enough to effect a cure in more serious cases. Even if the patient clearly understands that he has an active role in allowing negatives to intrude in his sexual pleasure, realizes that he can control this, and also faces the fact that he is destroying his highly valued marriage, his desire may not improve.

Patients often need to understand and resolve, on some level, the underlying reason—"*Why* am I doing this to myself?"—before the inhibition lifts. Patients almost never have insight into deeper issues of why they are afraid or why they do not want to feel sexual desire. Typically, patients are extremely puzzled by this question. The search for an answer and resolution or circumvention of the unconscious need that is served by the inhibition of desire become the main therapeutic tasks in the treatment of ISD.

Within the context of brief therapy it is often useful to attempt to foster the patient's insight on a "mid-level" of unconsciousness. If this is appropriate and/or feasible, the therapist goes beyond performance anxiety but not to the earliest and deepest levels of consciousness. In other words, the patient is confronted with self-destructive behavior without significant references to its earliest genesis. Unconscious fears of success and pleasure and fears of intimacy are highly prevalent in patients who suppress their desire. This level of pathology is not as accessible to conscious awareness as performance anxiety, but it is not as deeply threatening nor as intensely defended against as significant oedipal and preoedipal material. Interpretations on the level of unconscious success and intimacy fears are often accepted without mobilizing the intense resistances one would expect if deeper level interpretations, referring to oedipal and preoedipal material, were attempted within the context of brief or even moderately brief treatment. In other words, in psychosexual therapy the patient can accept and work with, "You are being self-defeating," or "When things get too good you sabotage yourself," or "The negative messages you received from your mother are hurting you"—*but usually not,* "You wanted to take your mother away from your father," or "You wanted to kill your mother because she was the queen, because she was the winner, you were the loser."

In some cases insight into and resolution of mid-level conflict, at least in part, allow the patient to give up his defensive suppression of sexual desire and produce a cure of the symptom. This may occur without intensive exploration of or insight into the earlier problems which have presumably produced these "mid-level" conflicts.

Usually the period of 10 to 14 sessions which typically comprises sex therapy for the genital dysfunctions is too brief to explore such mid-level conflicts and to enable the patient to integrate his new insights. This is true even if active, confrontational psychotherapeutic and psychosexual methods are employed. The objectives can, however, often be implemented within a moderate period of therapy, comprising 20 to 30 sessions.

Special Methodologic Considerations

Psychosexual therapy may be considered a form of brief therapy which uses an amalgam of behavioral and psychodynamic techniques. It is unique only in that it focuses on the rapid resolution of sexual problems, as opposed to other issues. It is a type of crisis intervention which exploits the crises produced by sexual inadequacy to foster reintegration on a more constructive level of functioning. Our own method is but one of a number of brief therapy styles or variations that can implement these objectives. It has the following features: flexibility, active intervention, and support.

Flexibility

The content of the sessions, i.e., the specific issues that are dealt with, is determined by the source of the resistance. When *intrapsychic* conflicts of either partner impede therapeutic progress, these become the focus during the therapy session. But when issues in the couple's relationship raise obstacles to treatment, the focus of intervention shifts to problems in the *marital system*. This method of dealing with intrapsychic and interactional issues in a fluid manner that is responsive to the constantly shifting patterns of the couples' resistance is illustrated in Cases 8 and 9 in the following chapter.

In psychosexual therapy it is important that treatment be tailored to fit the specific dimensions of individual problems. When resistances are encountered, when sensate focus does not work, one need not give up. One can shift to different behavioral strategies in the effort to reduce sexual anxiety, to provide specific corrective experience, and also to evoke and resolve the patient's or couple's specific underlying difficulty. There can be no blueprints or specific guides for this. The therapist uses his ingenuity and creativity, together with his knowledge of sexual pathology, to devise appropriate therapeutic tasks. The following tactics are often useful in the treatment of resistant problems.

Self-stimulation sigs are often useful when a patient cannot respond to the partner. This is especially true in two contexts: 1) when the patient is not comfortable with his sexual feelings and 2) when intimacy problems play a significant role in the clinical problem.

Masturbation guilt is endemic in our society. The origin of many persons' sexual guilt, fear and suppression lies in parental and cultural disapproval of childhood masturbation. The negative contingencies—the early and powerful associations of sexual arousal with fear and guilt—are often internalized and may burden the person all his life to the extent of impairing his ability to function sexually as an adult.

The therapist's encouragement and approval of all sexual pleasure, irrespective of whether it is attained by the partner's caresses or by the patient's own, are employed in an attempt to exorcise these negative attitudes. The combination of the experience of pleasure and the therapist's approval creates a powerful experience which can sometimes do a great deal within a brief time to undo the negative "messages" of the past. These messages, which have been incorporated by the patient and are still active, must be replaced with a more pleasure-oriented, rational system which will permit him to enjoy his sexuality—and not punish him for erotic pleasure.

There are males who suffer from such profound masturbatory guilt that they cannot touch their penis with their hand. They do not masturbate at all or they do so by rubbing against the bed. If the evaluation reveals this pattern, the patient is encouraged to masturbate manually; patients are often freed considerably by this experience. In addition to reducing sexual anxiety and guilt, this procedure can uncover psychodynamically valuable material. The intense feelings and memories that are frequently evoked by self-stimulation tasks provide the opportunity for attaining insight into the existence of the harsh and irrational conscience which treats this biologic function as though it were a sin and a hazard.

Self-stimulation is often important in the treatment of those female ISD patients who have never experienced orgasm. This is often a first and necessary step before any pleasure can be shared with a partner. It is easier to experiment, to feel, and to learn to be comfortable with sexual feelings and with orgasm when one is alone. The presence of a partner can be an inhibitory factor on many counts. The usual sequence in treatment is for the patient to learn to reach orgasm by herself and then to gradually share her sexual feelings with her partner.

In some clinical situations it is useful to incorporate shared autoerotic activities into the therapeutic program. There are some persons who can feel sexual desire when they are alone, but their inhibitions are evoked in the presence of the partner. She feels sexy all day long but as soon as her husband comes home she becomes cranky or tense or sleepy or enraged with him for trivial reasons. Such cases may be associated with the fear of intimacy; shared masturbation can help bring the partners together. Case 18 illustrates this method.

Masturbation in the approving presence of the partner can enhance the couple's intimacy as well as free the individual to experience sexual feelings. A man's confidence is increased if he knows he can help himself attain and maintain his erection by self-stimulation without risking rejection or ridicule. A woman becomes more secure if she knows that, should she fail to reach orgasm on coitus, she can count on giving herself an orgasm while she lies in the accepting arms of her lover. Those women who are inhibited by "clitoral guilt," i.e., the feeling that the only legitimate way to climax is during coitus and without clitoral "assistance," are especially benefited by these masturbatory exercises.

External erotic stimuli. If the pleasuring experiences fail to evoke desire, external erotic stimulation in the form of books or films may be employed. These experiences are employed to provide the patient with the opportunity to feel erotic pleasure within an approving context and also to broaden his fantasy life. In addition, these experiences may foster insight into previously unrecognized sexual issues. The patient learns 1) that he *can* have sexual desire in the right circumstances; 2) that his desires will be inhibited, i.e., that he will conjure up negative feelings, only when specific conflicts are evoked; 3) that the reasons for this pattern are a mystery to the patient, that they derive from some irrational source that can be explored in treatment; and 4) that he can identify what sorts of sexual situations are most arousing to him.

The sexually blocked couple might be advised to see a certain erotic film or read a book together which is consistent with their value system and their therapeutic objectives. They might be instructed not to attempt sexual behavior after that, but simply to talk about the feelings evoked by this experience. They might be surprised to learn that they feel desire when they are not expected to perform, but nothing when they feel the pressure of sexual demands—or that they can feel desire when viewing erotic material alone, but not in the presence of the partner. The experience of being able to feel desire, contrasted with not feeling desire in a different context, can be extremely instructive, illuminating the active role persons play in the control of their sexual feelings and highlighting specific points of inhibition. For example, a patient might feel unexpected sensations of anxiety or unexpected interest at certain scenes in a book or film. He might be startled to learn that, while he allows himself to enjoy an erotic book by himself, when he is about to share this with his partner he focuses his attention on her "stupidity" or poor complexion and, not surprisingly, feels only disappointment. He might learn that his partner enjoys his pleasure in erotica, and that he is excited by hers.

Patients are encouraged to view their own responses, both erotic and inhibited, and their partner's as well, with a nonjudgmental and positive attitude. These experiences are regarded as learning opportunities—not failures or successes. They can reduce anxiety and guilt and foster insight rapidly, especially if reactions and feelings are explored verbally and integrated during the therapeutic sessions.

Fantasy may be employed to *bypass* a tenacious conflict. If a patient remains blocked, if he continues to experience anxiety or to suppress his feelings, he might be instructed to imagine that he is in a different, less threatening erotic situation during sexual activity with his partner. This tactic can often diminish the anxiety and anger evoked by the real sexual experience sufficiently so that desire can emerge.

These experiences attain their maximum value when they are used to relieve guilt and anxiety about sexual pleasure and to foster insight into underlying conflicts during the therapeutic sessions. The patient is encouraged to use his fantasy in the service of his pleasure, without regard to its content. In this context, erotic imagery is viewed as a nonchemical tranquilizer which reduces anxiety sufficiently to permit the patient to function. However, in a different context, the content of the fantasy may be explored in order to gain insight into the unconscious sources of the inhibition.

The individualistic pattern of patients' anxieties make it impossible to devise a set and structured treatment plan that will fit the diverse needs of the ISD population. Following a structured treatment plan is more feasible for the genital dysfunctions with their narrower etiologies and less tenacious resistances. In the psychosexual treatment of the more difficult desire dysfunctions, considerable flexibility and creativity and art can and should be used to devise and select tasks which fit the specific requirements of individual clinical situations.

Active Intervention

In the sessions support is balanced with active confrontation in order to maintain a rapid therapeutic pace. This process may be threatening for the couple. They are asked to quickly engage in new kinds of sexual behavior which may evoke deep ancient fears and guilts. They are encouraged to do and feel things they may have regarded as wrong and dangerous all their lives. They are asked to be open about intimate matters with a stranger they have just met. Often they risk rejection and hurt.

When they resist they are actively confronted. They cannot be allowed to "get away" with any sabotage, with any evasion, with any self-destructive act, with any obsessive thought, with the slightest rationalization, with anything that does not make sense. If treatment is to be successful, any resistance or obstacle to therapeutic progress that cannot be bypassed must be resolved so that treatment can proceed.

Psychosexual therapy aims at rapid resolution of highly sensitive and deeply significant sexual conflict. This can occur only if resistances are actively and even aggressively addressed. Techniques for rapid resolution of resistances include repetition of the erotic task with reassurance. This will cause some anxiety reduction via the process of desensitization. If this is not sufficient, the exercise is restructured so that the resistance is circumvented or bypassed. Tenacious obstacles that cannot be resolved or bypassed without insight are dealt with by "joining the resistance," i.e., creating paradoxes which the patient must solve, and also by continuous and active confrontation and the creation of therapeutic crises. Active interpretation of unconscious conflict, usually on a "mid-level" of conscious awareness, on the level of self-destructiveness, is employed when desensitization and confrontation are not sufficient to resolve resistances. These techniques are described in greater detail in the following Area on *Strategies of Psychosexual Therapy.*

Support

A close and trusting bond between the therapist and the patient and between the therapist and both partners of a couple is crucial to sustain the rapid changes and high emotional tensions of psychosexual therapy. The patient must draw from the therapeutic relationship the confidence he needs to take the emotional risks entailed in the treatment process and to give up defenses. He must have sufficient respect and trust for the therapist to accept the active confrontations and not to walk away from the crises which often characterize the therapy of the more difficult cases. There must be enough caring and warmth so that the patient is able to discard his old cruel conscience and adopt the more rational, gentle value system offered by the therapist.

The therapist's warmth and acceptance, his nonjudgmental and encouraging attitudes, and his sensitivity to the vulnerabilities of both partners are essential ingredients in forming a strong therapeutic alliance rapidly. He is gentle but active; he supports and accepts but also confronts. But, while confrontations are at times intense and even audacious, they are never destructive. They are always clearly in the context of helping the couple to experience pleasure and love and intimacy. Interpretations and confrontations are mainly designed to help the patient gain insight into and control of his self-destructive behavior. He is confronted only with the fact that he is sabotaging his own pleasure in life, that he has a choice, that he does not *have* to continue to "do himself in."

The therapist becomes the "good parent." He is loving but firm. He is accepting of the patient but sets limits on self-destructiveness. He is caring but strong. He is a powerful advocate on the side of the couple's sexual and romantic success and their pleasure. In this he must be conflict-free. He wants them to be "winners." The therapeutic relationship must be strong enough so that they "get the positive message" and introject these loving attitudes, exchanging them for the irrational guilts and self-hatreds which have previously tortured them. When the therapeutic relationship is successful, the "enemy within" is exchanged for a friend.

WOMAN: Well, I had an orgasm, but it was sick. I had the fantasy I was with a little dog. I am disgusted with myself. I almost didn't tell you.

THERAPIST: I am so glad you had an orgasm. That's wonderful!

WOMAN: But dog fantasies, Jesus Christ!

THERAPIST: Hey, you had an orgasm—you let yourself have more pleasure than you ever had in your life. That's what is important. We'll get to the fantasy later. Do you think you are worrying about the fantasy to punish yourself—to spoil your pleasure?

WOMAN: Is it really OK? Am I setting myself up again? You are right—it did feel good. For some reason I did not stop it this time. It was really easy.

TREATMENT CHOICE

Only a small proportion of ISD patients responds favorably to standard, traditional, time-limited, behaviorally oriented sex therapy. Behaviorally oriented sex therapy focuses primarily on modifying the immediate antecedents of the symptom and deals only briefly and superficially with the unconscious forces that have produced these antecedents. This is often effective with the simpler genital phase dysfunctions, but is usually not sufficient to resolve desire inhibitions.

Unrecognized desire problems account for many of the failures of sex therapy. It has been our experience that the yield of successful outcome can be increased by working specifically with the immediate antecedent of the desire inhibition, the patient's involuntary but active tendency to evoke negative affect in the sexual situation, if that is operative, and at the same time employing a more flexible and more dynamically oriented therapeutic format. This usually requires a lengthier period of therapy than the 14 sessions which is the average time for treatment for the genital dysfunctions. Our sample is still too small to accurately determine the efficacy of this approach, but it makes sense from a theoretical perspective and it is our preliminary impression that these modified and more flexible techniques hold the promise of increased effectiveness for difficult cases over brief, behaviorally oriented sex therapy. Nevertheless, even with these lengthier, more complex techniques, which are capable of resolving, to some extent at least, the underlying conflicts which characterize this population, results are less impressive than when the sex therapy techniques are employed with a patient population selected for the genital phase dysfunctions.

Perhaps the greatest clinical advantage spawned by the recognition of a separate desire phase syndrome is that it has enabled us to select out the "pure" genital dysfunctions from the undifferentiated mass of functional sexual complaints. The rapid sex therapy techniques are indicated for these disorders and outcome with orgasm and excitement phase difficulties is excellent. Many treatment failures, frustrating to the clinician and discouraging to the patients, can be prevented by limiting traditional sex therapy to patients complaining of genital phase disorders.

These findings raise the question about the treatment of choice for ISD. Since clinical experience and, most particularly, studies of treatment failures indicate that the prognosis is poor with "classic" or symptom-focused sex therapy, it could be argued that these patients should be encouraged to seek other, more intensive forms of treatment, that ISD patients should be offered long-term marital and/or individual therapy which has the capability of resolving complex issues which are beyond the reach of brief treatment.

In view of the relatively poor prognosis of ISD with brief sex therapy and clinical evidence that indicates the severity of this syndrome, this argument makes sense.

However, an alternate point of view can be also be advanced. This is based on three considerations: 1) There are no outcome data available attesting to the efficacy of long-term individual and couples treatment for these disorders, so while common sense tells us that the deeper problems often seen with this population should be treated in depth, there is no actual proof of the usefulness of long-term individual and/or couples treatment. Indeed, it is the general impression that low libido patients have a guarded prognosis with all of the treatment modalities thus far employed.

The experience of treating ISD in persons who, in terms of the sexual symptom, have been treatment failures with prior long-term couples and individual therapy reveals that some patients fail to be cured of their sexual complaints even though the underlying conflicts appear to have been resolved. When treatment intervenes only on the level of underlying conflicts and does not deal with the immediate antecedents of the symptom, as is the style of therapies that rely solely on verbal exchanges, the resolution of such conflicts may effect symptom relief in some patients but not for others. This observation suggests that resolution of unconscious conflicts does not automatically insure that the symptom will be cured. Two cases in the next chapter illustrate this point. Winston's (Case 8) eight-year analysis fostered his insight into the early genesis of his self-destructiveness, but did not help him with the specific expression of the conflict in the sexual sphere of his life. Another example of resolution of underlying dynamics without symptom cure is that of Ruth and Roy (Case 10), who resolved many of their interactional problems in marital therapy to the extent of improving the quality of their life together without, however, relieving their sexual problem. Psychosexual therapy intervenes on the level of the immediate symptom via the experimental tasks, in addition to dealing with remoter conflicts. This combined focus can in some cases help patients who are not relieved of the sexual symptom when treatment focuses exclusively on the remoter causes.

2)It is not possible to predict with accuracy how ISD patients will respond to brief psychosexual therapy. When the underlying problems seem mild and situational, a fairly accurate guess can be made that sex therapy is a sensible alternative and can be successful. At the other extreme, when the problem is chronic and long-standing and seems to be a product of severe psychopathology or a severely disturbed relationship, then sex therapy even in its modified form is not likely to be effective. But in the "middle" group, outcome is not predictable with accuracy. Since brief therapy is less costly and time-consuming than lengthy therapy, it makes sense to try this first, provided that there is a reasonable chance of success.

Experience with employing the modified form of psychosexual therapy with this population in a flexible way and for varying lengths of time has indicated that some patients who have been treatment failures with brief sex therapy can be helped when they are able to resolve some of the remote causes of sexual inhibition, which are beyond the reach of the briefer, more symptom-focused methods. On the other hand, some patients who have not attained symptomatic relief with the lengthier verbal therapies have also been helped when the previously neglected immediate antecedents of their symptom are dealt with by the integrated approach.

3) A trial of a few sessions of sex therapy is not destructive. Indeed, this holds the opportunity for cure or insight, with minimal risk. Some patients are helped with their symptoms; those who are not may benefit in terms of increased understanding of their problem. This is especially true when the patient learns that he has more control over his sexual feelings and his pleasure in other spheres of life than he had previously realized. He has, if he chooses, considerable power to allow himself to feel desire or to prevent himself from feeling this. Outside reality is only one determinant of pleasure. Over those forces we have only limited control. But one's inner attitudes towards pleasure and sexual gratification are also important elements in the quality of one's experiences, and one can learn to master these to a very great extent.

The trial treatment experience can serve as a superb diagnostic instrument which can reveal both problems and assets which are not readily apparent on evaluation. Patients can gain insight into their underlying problem and are often motivated to seek further help if this is appropriate. We consider insight and engagement as legitimate treatment goals.

On the basis of these considerations, the following criteria govern my decision regarding the treatment of choice for sexual dysfunction associated with inhibited sexual desire.

1) Those few patients who show clear evidence that their desire inhibition stems from mild causes such as performance anxiety and who thus have an excellent probability of deriving help from brief treatment are accepted for sex therapy. We are, however, prepared to shift to the lengthier mode if resistances should arise.

2) When there is clear evidence that a patient's desire inhibition is associated with profound intrapsychic and/or marital pathology, appropriate long-term therapy is considered to be the treatment of choice. In such cases prognosis with the more rapid and economic sex therapy techniques is too poor to justify even a trial of sex therapy.

3) For those patients who fall in the middle group with respect to seriousness of etiology, or for those patients where the evaluation does not allow for a reasonably accurate prognosis, it makes sense to recommend a brief *trial* of psychosexual therapy.

4) Patients with sexual symptoms, including inhibited desire, who have been treatment failures in previous therapy, brief sex therapy or lengthy individual or couples therapy are suitable candidates for psychosexual therapy. Treatment is particularly worthwhile in such cases if the evaluation reveals that *either* the remote or the immediate causes of the inhibition have not been specifically or adequately dealt with in the prior therapy.

These criteria for the treatment choice of ISD are, of course, highly unsatisfactory because they are subjective and based solely on clinical experience and intuition rather than on solid outcome data. We are still in the learning stage. The therapeutic approach described above appears to offer hope for some of the patients who were failures with traditional sex therapy either because the patient did not gain insight into the specific antecedents of the desire suppression or because the underlying conflicts were not dealt with sufficiently. But the range of effectiveness has not been extended far enough. The most troubled patients—those who are in the greatest need of help—still carry a poor prognosis even with the new methods. It is hoped that more reliable criteria, as well as more effective methods of treatment, will be developed for this patient population.

7

CLINICAL ILLUSTRATIONS

THE FOLLOWING CASES illustrate various courses and outcomes with the modified and lengthened method of psychosexual therapy which has been described herein. The cases described below did not respond to the behavioral aspects of sex therapy. Neither insight into the superficial causes and immediate antecedents nor confrontation with the destructive consequences of the inhibition produced the kind of positive outcome that can be obtained when the underlying problems are mild. In these cases intervention into deeper levels, into unconscious conflicts about pleasure, intimacy and sexual success, was necessary. Sometimes earlier material was also dealt with, but not in depth, and more for the purpose of clarifying and integrating the "mid-level" conflicts than for intrinsic resolution.

Both cases which ended successfully and similar cases that were treatment failures are presented. The case material also illustrates some of the different kinds of underlying problems which may be associated with ISD. These may require an intrapsychic and/or an interactional focus of intervention. Since both relationship and intrapsychic issues may cause sexual inhibitions, and also mobilize resistances during the treatment process, couples oriented as well as individually oriented therapy is employed. Cases 8 and 9 illustrate the flexible use of intervention both on the intrapsychic level and also in conflicts in the couple's marital system. The therapeutic focus in Cases 10 and 11 was on problems in the relationship. The couples in Cases 12 and 13 were inhibited primarily because of underlying intrapsychic determinants of one partner, and treatment dealt mainly with those issues.

CASE 8   WILLA AND WINSTON
Inhibited Sexual Desire
Therapeutic Focus on Intrapsychic and Relationship Problems
Successful Outcome

The couple consisted of Willa, a 36-year-old successful dress designer, and Winston, her 38-year-old photographer husband. They had been married for five years. They had no children.

Chief Complaint

One year after their marriage Willa began to lose her desire for Winston. She now feels boredom or irritation when he touches her. Winston, on the other hand, is obsessed with his desire for her and is preoccupied by fears that she will leave him.

The couple experienced a crisis last year when she disclosed that she had been having an affair for half a year with a colleague. This had occurred shortly after an unsuccessful attempt at marital and sexual therapy at an excellent institute. At the time of consultation she had given up her lover and they were making a "last attempt to save their marriage."

History

Winston had been in psychoanalysis for seven years. He had a history of alcohol abuse. He was expelled from a fine university in his senior year for drunken driving and fighting in a tavern, despite his excellent academic record. He cured himself of his alcohol addiction and finished his studies at a less prestigious college. He gave up his plans to become a physician and took up a career in photography. He was enormously talented, but managed to mishandle the financial aspect of his photography studio; consequently, his income was much below his potential. Although he had improved greatly and developed a good understanding of early developmental issues in psychoanalysis, his self-defeating pattern was still operative in his relationship with Willa. He had virtually no insight into his destructive role in the marital problem.

The couple had been very much in love when they first married. Slowly she had lost sexual interest in him, but she still loved him and hoped to make the marriage work.

Etiology

The immediate cause of her sexual suppression and avoidance was his obsessive pressuring for sex. He had been behaving very destructively to this relationship which meant so much to him in many ways and his pressuring was only the "tip of the iceberg." His sabotage had its roots in deeper problems.

She was unconsciously afraid to commit herself to him emotionally and sexually because of her own conflicts about romantic success. In addition, she responded to his subtle sabotage which she sensed but had not perceived clearly.

Treatment

His pressuring created an obstacle to treatment. For this reason no physical tasks were assigned until he had attained enough insight into the destructive effects of his pressuring and manipulative behavior to be able to control this. At the same time, other interactions which were subtly destructive to this relationship were observed in the conjoint therapy sessions and were confronted and explored.

THERAPIST: What effect do you think your statement had on Willa, Win?

WINSTON: Well, I have a right to express myself! I just didn't believe that she enjoyed it.

WILLA: But I did—I said so.

WINSTON: You are just saying that to show the doctor that it's all my fault—I know you are here only to soothe your Jewish conscience. You don't love me.

THERAPIST: I thought she was trying to be closer to you—she said she enjoyed your kiss last night. I felt good about that. How did that make you feel?

WINSTON: Suspicious—tense.

THERAPIST: Can you see what you did when you got tense? You pushed her away. Do you want to do that? Suppose she *really* enjoyed it?

WINSTON: No . . . no. I want the opposite. . . . (*to Willa*) Did I really push you away?

Winston rapidly became aware of his self-defeating pattern. Whenever Willa expressed love and warmth, he reacted with tension and hostility. In the course of treatment he slowly learned to identify the tense sensations he felt when he experienced pleasure and closeness, and stopped, at least in part, acting these out. Willa was extremely relieved as she saw his growing insight. She admitted having been frightened when she learned, one and a half years after her marriage, of his alcoholic and self-destructive history. She felt less frightened now that she could understand it and saw him actively working on his fear of pleasure and success. As his insights grew, she felt more in control of her destiny.

Gradual stimulating and teasing erotic tasks were assigned the couple with intercourse prohibited until Willa began to feel desire. Initially she felt very little. She was upset and guilty about not being able to feel erotic even though her husband had made such positive changes. Gradually it became clear that she was silent and uncommunicative during sex. This made Winston, who needed a lot of reassurance, anxious and insensitive as a lover. A detailed examination of her experiences revealed that one reason for her unresponsiveness was that she blocked her sexual feelings and pleasure by focusing on his former alcoholism, on historic disappointments and also on her own feelings of inadequacy when she was with him. She never realized that she was doing this or that she could exert control. When she was first confronted with her active role in suppressing her desires and in contributing to Winston's tensions, she was overwhelmed with guilt: "It is all my fault." After this defensive guilt had been worked through, she was able to control her impulses to evoke or to permit the negative thoughts which had caused her to avoid sex with Winston.

At the same time, he learned not to engage in sabotage when she felt close and responded sexually.

The couple was seen for 21 sessions. During this time the focus was on his self-destructiveness in this highly valued relationship. An attractive, intelligent man, he had presented himself to her in the worst light as untrustworthy and "dense." He was constantly and subtly sabotaging their sexual relationship. He gained some insight into the existence of his unconscious success anxiety but we only touched upon, and did not work through, the genesis of this pattern, which seemed to have its roots in childhood adaptations to a highly ambivalent father and a seductive mother.

During the course of treatment, as he improved, she became resistant and depressed as she faced her own conflicts. These had previously been camouflaged by Winston's destructive behavior. But now her conflicts constituted the immediate obstacle to the couple's sexual improvement and became the focus of intervention.

In joint therapy sessions her past was explored. Willa's mother was a highly competitive woman, who dominated and abused her husband. She encouraged her three daughters to pursue educational and career goals, but was sabotaging and disparaging to their sexual and romantic development. Willa was left with a deep guilt about "having it all," i.e., attaining both a successful career and romantic fulfillment. The idea of enjoying sex purely for pleasure and not in the service of procreation mobilized additional guilt and also fears of retribution from mother. During the course of therapy she became aware of intense and previously unrecognized anger at her mother. These issues were clarified and resolved, at least to the extent that her desire returned in part.

On follow-up one year later, all their troubles were not over; he still tended to be destructive when he became really happy. Nevertheless, his tolerance for happiness had increased and the couple was alert to this dynamic and did not let it develop to a destructive level. They both reported that their sexual and emotional relationship was good.

CASE 9   **BILL AND BEULAH**
Inhibited Sexual Desire
Focus on Relationship and Intrapsychic Problems
Failure

The patient was a 36-year-old landscape gardener. His wife was 35 and a housewife. The couple had been married 14 years and had six children. Both are religious Southern Baptists.

Chief Complaint

The chief complaint was that Bill had shown no sexual interest in his wife for the last five years. Since that time, the couple had had no sexual contact. He avoided any sexual opportunity, falling asleep in front of the TV set in the basement den every night, and going to the marital bedroom only after she was sound asleep. The husband seemed indifferent to lack of sex in the marriage, but the wife, who had initiated treatment, was agitated and upset. The couple reported that they had enjoyed "a very good sex life" for the first nine years of marriage.

History

The sexual problem began five years ago after Bill sustained a serious head injury when a tree fell on him during his work. He was in a coma for several weeks and then began to have convulsions which necessitated his taking high doses of anticonvulsive medication. Because of the toxic effects of the medication and the disabilities caused by his head injury, this previously active, independent and "macho" man became completely dependent on his wife. Beulah became nurse, mother, and accountant. She had to bathe him, feed him, take care of the family finances, and, after he became ambulatory, chauffeur him around.

At the time of treatment he was fully recovered physically and back to work, but he had not desired sex with his wife since his accident. On one or two occasions during the past five years, in response to her urgings, they had attempted love-making, but he was unable to maintain his erection.

The couple was referred by a family therapist from a suburban clinic after one year of unsuccessful marital treatment.

Etiology

It was hypothesized (and hoped) that the immediate cause of his lack of desire was performance anxiety, resulting from the few unsuccessful attempts at intercourse which occurred prematurely before he was sufficiently recovered from his accident. The remote causes were not clear at the beginning of therapy.

Treatment

Sensate Focus I and II were performed by Bill in a mechanical and obviously bored manner which understandably upset his wife. She responded with vociferous complaints, which provoked one of the couple's chronically bitter and unproductive fights.

An attempt was made to deal with his resistance, i.e., the mechanical and unpleasant way in which he touched his wife, by sympathetically exploring his feelings. I confronted him with the pessimistic attitude with which he approached the tasks, which insured their lack of pleasure. Therapy was made difficult by his passive aggressive uncommunicativeness. He behaved towards me in the therapeutic sessions very much the way he behaved towards his wife in bed. He answered questions mechanically and did not speak spontaneously. Confrontation with this resistance created a small crisis, which I used to try to face him with the benefits he would experience if he could allow himself to feel sexual again. We talked about potential improvements in his self-esteem and pleasure if he could rehabilitate himself sexually the way he had rehabilitated himself medically.

Repetitions of the pleasuring exercises became progressively more enjoyable for both and within a few weeks he managed to have an erection and then an orgasm manually induced by his wife. He also was able to stimulate her to orgasm orally. He was still frustratingly uncommunicative during the sessions. Meanwhile, Beulah continued her chronic complaints and demands, even though I tried to confront her with the destructive effects of her behavior. She seemed to want him to be sexual, but only under her control.

The week after he had the erections and orgasm, he reported that his sexual desire had increased. He now thought about his wife during the work day and even had the impulse to come home during his lunch break and have sex. The couple now went to bed together every night.

However, the improvement was very short-lived. The couple began their bitter bickering again, and he retreated to his den.

Outcome

I attempted to work through the resistances for several more sessions, but was totally unsuccessful. She complained and he remained uncommunicative. When I finally shared with the couple my feelings of sadness and frustration because it looked like the therapy was not going to be successful, he surprised me by expressing concern about my feelings and also by showing insight into the underlying cause of his sexual inhibition. He said, "Don't feel bad, Doc. You tried hard and I appreciate it. It's just that since I've been ill she has taken over. And I can't get back control over my own house." This was authentic insight about the source of his sexual inhibition—their power struggle. He suppressed his sexual feelings because they had become a symbol of acquiescence in his power struggle with his wife. He did not *wish* to feel desire under those circumstances. He used his anger to "turn himself off." I felt that this couple's complex and deep-seated interactional problems could not be bypassed or resolved in the modified, but still too brief, treatment.

The couple was referred for a further course of long-term marital therapy, but they decided not to do this.

Comment

Even with the active, psychodynamically oriented methods, a negative outcome may occur when the desire problem is a manifestation of profound, deep conflict which precludes symptom removal or rapid conflict resolution. Even when the patient understands that one part of him does not *want* to feel desire, that he is being deprived of sexual pleasure, and that he has a choice, he may not be motivated to resolve this conflict because he is too angry. However, as was true in this case, even when the symptom fails to improve, there is often some benefit in terms of greater insight and self-awareness on the part of the couple. Sometimes this motivates them to seek further help and sometimes, unfortunately, it does not.

CASE 10 RUTH AND ROY
   Inhibited Sexual Desire
   Focus on Depression and Relationship Problems
   Successful Outcome

The husband was a successful 41-year-old publisher; his 35-year-old wife was active in charities and social events. They had been married for five years and had two sons aged four and three.

The chief complaint was lack of sexual activity for the past three years. Roy felt no sexual desire for his wife, but did have some erotic feelings which he expressed by masturbating. Ruth complained of a total lack of sexual desire.

The couple was extremely sophisticated and intellectually aware. Both had been in individual therapy, as well as in couples therapy, for many years.

History

The couple had a stormy history. When they met, he was immediately attracted to her and courted her intensely. She was initially not very interested, but eventually succumbed to his ardent pursuit. Their sons were born within the first two years of their marriage.

There was trouble immediately, which was due, at least in part, to her mood swings. Since her early twenties Ruth had suffered from moderately severe episodes of depression which alternated with hypomanic episodes. Her maternal family contained several members who also suffered from depressions. The affective disorder was not treated with medication by her previous therapist and was regarded as a neurotic problem by both the patient and her spouse.

Roy had grown up in a family which was dominated by his demanding mother, who was probably a borderline schizophrenic. He had felt responsible for the impossible task of making his mother happy when he was a boy, and had only emancipated himself with difficulty as a young man. His wife's depressions evoked a similar pattern: He felt responsible for her depressions and at the same time had hostile impulses towards her. His defensive and angry responses to her real appeals for his help caused her to see him as insensitive and uncaring and made her mistrustful and fearful of abandonment.

In addition to these emotional issues, on a purely technical basis, their love-making had never been very satisfactory. She had a moderate degree of orgasm inhibition which resulted in her needing lengthy stimulation before she could climax. He found this tedious and burdensome and became angry, perceiving her as demanding—just like his mother.

Despite these difficulties, the couple loved each other deeply. Nevertheless, they had a serious problem with closeness. When they moved (emotionally) too far apart, they both felt anxious and moved close again. But at a certain point of intimacy, both grew anxious, and one or the other provoked a distancing maneuver. This could take any number of forms: Fights about his weight, or about cleaning the family parrot's cage, or about the maid, or about money, were this couple's favorite devices for maintaining a distance which was "safe" or comfortable for them.

Etiology

One immediate cause of this couple's problem was clearly her untreated mood swings. Depression is one of the common causes of hypoactive sexual desire. The situation was complicated by their infantile transferential reactions to those mood swings. He felt put upon and trapped; she felt abandoned and misunderstood. In addition, both had a problem with intimacy which, again, seemed to have its origin in mutual unresolved parental transferences.

Treatment

Ruth's depression was treated with medication (desimipramine and lithium) and psychotherapy before sex therapy commenced. In eight weeks her mood was stabilized sufficiently and both were extremely pleased and relieved by this result. Her sexual desire returned to some degree, but she was still inhibited in his presence. He felt more relaxed with her but still had no feelings of desire.

Initially the prescribed sexual exercises evoked strong resistance in the husband which took the form of avoidance. He was still angry and mistrustful with his wife, and these feelings could not be bypassed. The confrontation that he was using the old resentments to suppress his sexual response did not free him to feel desire.

At this time sexual therapy was interrupted and therapy was focused on resolving the neurotic interacions.

It took six months of couples therapy to work through his anger and his mistrust of women. Initially he externalized his conflicts with women, blaming Ruth for overspending and for being demanding. He was confronted with the fact that he was endangering his marriage and also with his own sexual conflicts. His anger, and with it his need to suppress his sexuality, diminished only after we worked on its origin, his relationship with his mother. As he learned to assert himself appropriately, realistically, and in a more mature, effective manner with his wife, his anger began to diminish. Before this couple could enjoy sex and stop sabotaging their sex life together, they both had to resolve the anxiety they felt about closeness and intimacy.

When Roy indicated his readiness, sexual task assignment was resumed, focusing on the anxiety which was evoked in both partners when they felt intimate and sexual towards one another. He became aware that he could feel sexy when he was alone, but evoked negative thoughts when they were together. He also saw that it was to his advantage to try to stop doing this.

The initial sigs consisted of shared autoerotic activities which evoked less anxiety than mutual stimulation. The partners were instructed to kiss and caress each other. At a point of excitement which was still comfortable, each stimulated him/herself to orgasm. Gradually, the level of shared arousal which could be tolerated before they became anxious was increased. Proceeding in this gradual manner, they were eventually able to stimulate each other to orgasm. Initially, it was suggested that, while stimulation occurred, they immerse themselves in their own fantasy, which was not to include the other. This served to diminish the anxiety which was produced not by erotic feelings, but by their closeness to each other.

At the same time, the material evoked by these experiences was actively explored in the therapy sessions. The emphasis of the interpretations was on fears of intimacy and sexual success with some references to the genesis of these conflicts. As they attained insight into their fear of intimacy, it gradually diminished. They learned to share their fantasies and to use these to increase closeness rather than to create distance.

At one point in treatment, when the couple began to resume intercourse, Ruth's resistance rose. She became angry at Roy. She felt him to be clumsy and mechanical. She had dreams which indicated that old feelings of shame and guilt about sex were being aroused by her progressive sexual involvement with her husband and these evoked her old defenses. These resistances were worked through sufficiently for sexual progress to occur.

Outcome

On follow-up one year later, the couple enjoy a good sexual relationship. "We don't do it every day," but report that they both feel desire. They usually have intercourse once a week. Her orgasmic response is still rather slow, but now this does not seem to impair their pleasure. When he finds himself angry, he does not try to make love, but talks it through with her until he is calm again.

Comment

This case demonstrates the flexibility required to treat the more complex sexual dysfunction problems. This couple failed to be helped in couples therapy and in individual therapy, probably because treatment did not focus on the immediate antecedents of the problem. The stormy course of treatment suggests that they would also have failed to improve if sex therapy were limited to brief, time-limited, primarily behaviorally oriented techniques.

CASE 11   MANUEL AND MARY
Inhibited Sexual Desire with Avoidance
Focus on Intrapsychic Problems
Failure

The couple consisted of Manuel, a successful attorney, age 47, and Mary, a housewife, age 46. The couple had been married 24 years and had two children.

Chief Complaint

The chief complaint was the wife's severe avoidance of sex and complete lack of desire for her husband. This began on their honeymoon. During their courtship, Mary had enjoyed kissing and fondling with Manuel, but with the first intercourse she lost her desire, and sex became a nightmare for her. Mary had stoically endured sex for the first ten years of marriage, but finally, after the birth of their last child, she had expressed her distaste for sex with Manuel and had refused to have further physical contact with him. At the same time she complained about the lack of sex in her life. In fact, she had never had any sexual feelings except when she was anesthetized by narcotics.

She blamed her husband's "brutality and ignorance." In fact, he was a gentle, if inexperienced man, whose major crime had been his total insensitivity to his wife's distaste for sex.

Mary had a long history of severe emotional difficulties. She had been severely depressed and suicidal; she had also been addicted to narcotics, which were initially perscribed by a well-intentioned dentist for her complaint of chronic dental pain. After eight years of psychotherapy, the patient's depression improved and she was able to remain drug-free. She began to function well in some areas, becoming active in the community and extremely involved in bridge and golf. As she learned to express her chronic angry feelings, she became depressed and obsessed with her "deprivation of sex," pushing her husband to seek sex therapy at three reputable clinics. Each experience not only proved a failure, but also evoked even more profound rages and depressions. She was unable to tolerate any of the psychotropic medications which had been prescribed by various doctors. My diagnostic impression of her was borderline schizophrenia.

Etiology

The immediate cause of this woman's difficulty seemed to be that sexual feelings were invested with irrational meanings or fantasies. Sexual feelings therefore evoked very intense conflicts and ambivalences which were dangerous to the integration of this barely compensated patient.

Treatment

Joint therapy began with the strict admonition not to attempt any sexual interaction. We began to gently talk about sexual feelings and experiences. The mere mention of anything sexual brought tears to her eyes and evoked outbursts of rage, but any suggestion to the effect that if the pain was too great we might try to work towards an asexual adjustment evoked even more intense protests—"I'll kill myself."

Slowly, as she began to trust me, she came to understand that all sexual feelings, even those mild ones brought on by talking about sex, evoked in her intolerable rage and fear. No wonder she suppressed her sexual desires. With this insight, therapy shifted to individual treatment. Mary remained in therapy for only eight months. During this time she came to accept her psychic vulnerability and made peace with the possibility that she might never be able to dissociate the negative affect from sexual feelings. Sex might always be a dangerous emotional trigger for her. She decided that the cost of sex for her was too high and came to recognize that her obsession with her husband's inadequacy was a defense against admitting to herself the unacceptable sexual feelings or conflicts. She gained a modicum of peace.

She stopped therapy at this point with the request that if she ever felt ready to take the risk, she would work on her problem again. Her husband accepted an asexual relationship as preferable to a separation.

This case was not resolved successfully because of the severe psychopathology of the wife which could not be circumvented in treatment. However, this case illustration should not be taken to imply that only the sickest patients fail to respond to this method. Underlying problems may be intractable to brief therapy for many reasons, and there are many clinical situations where neither partner is schizophrenic and/or the relationship is not grossly disturbed, but treatment is still not successful.

CASE 12   **BENJAMIN AND BRITT**
 Inhibited Sexual Desire with Avoidance
 Focus on Relationship and Intrapsychic Problems
 Successful Outcome

Benjamin was a 64-year-old film producer and Nora was his 38-year-old wife, a former airline hostess. They had been married for eight years and had one child, a girl aged six. This was his third marriage and her first.

Chief Complaint

The wife had no desire for sex. In fact, she was repelled by the idea and could not tolerate any physical contact with her husband. He was desperate to the point of obsession about this.

History

The couple met ten years ago while she was a stewardess on a European airline and he was traveling on business. He pursued her ardently. Initially they had frequent sex. She remembers this as not having been very exciting. This angers him since he feels it was very good for both of them.

When they married, he insisted that she stop working and assume a traditional housewife role. He supplied her with a beautiful house, servants and a child, but allowed her little freedom. He was extremely jealous; he did not permit her to go skiing or to join a tennis club and instructed his chauffeur to report on all her moves.

Initially she seemed to accept this life-style. She loved her child and mothering absorbed a great deal of her energy. But she grew increasingly cold towards him.

Four years after they married, he learned that she was having an affair. He became enraged. The couple separated for one year.

After this period of time, he begged her to return to him. She agreed, but only on the condition that he would not press her sexually. He agreed to this, but defined her as "sick." She entered psychoanalytic therapy for the purpose of "curing" her sexual problem. In addition, the couple also commenced conjoint therapy.

She had not allowed him to touch her in the last three years since they had been reunited. He was depressed and obsessed about this. She stated that she would like to be able to have sex with Benjamin, but could not get herself to do this. When she tried, she was overcome by feelings of revulsion.

Etiology

The immediate cause of Britt's lack of desire and avoidance was the angry feelings she experienced whenever Benjamin approached her. Sexual avoidance was the only means she had of asserting herself. But she was not aware of this. Her rigid conscience would not allow her to "rebel" or to consciously withhold anything from her husband. She had no insight into the fact that she was actively conjuring up old memories and injustices when sex was contemplated.

On a deeper level, Britt was extremely angry at Benjamin. She felt helpless and overwhelmed by his strong personality and was unconsciously taking vengeance on him. Her intense anger was partially due to his controlling style and her real feelings of weakness vis-à-vis him. On a deeper level, the relationship evoked old angers at her father and at other men who had rejected her. She had gained insight into her father-related problems in the course of her analysis, but this did not affect her sexual avoidance of Benjamin.

Treatment

Before any sexual exercises could be assigned, treatment was first directed at getting Ben to stop pressuring and obsessing. This was no easy matter for this anxious and angry man, but in time, with support and confrontation of the destructive nature of his behavior, his behavior towards her became supportive and reasonable. He did continue to be overly generous and to shower her with unwelcome and excessive gifts, but his destructive jealousy diminished greatly. On her part, Britt became more gently assertive with him. In therapy we focused on her guilty conscience and on her right to feel angry. The relationship between them improved substantially and became more equal as a result of the insights they gained during this couples therapy phase of treatment.

She then had to face her own conflicts. She was puzzled as to why she could not tolerate sex with Benjamin. She attributed this to "lack of chemistry." She was confronted with the illogical nature of her construction and with the need to recognize her inner feelings.

She was supported in asserting herself with Ben. She was given understanding and support of her real complaints in this marriage. I told her, and I genuinely felt this, that unless she truly believed it to be to her advantage, I would not attempt to work on her desire inhibition. Her feelings and needs were not unreasonable and were just as important to me as Benjamin's.

She was adamant about wishing to have sex with Ben. She knew that the marriage would not last on its present basis. She understood that Ben could not tolerate an asexual relationship forever, and neither could she. She wanted to make this marriage work for her own sake.

She had very good insight into the deeper issues that lay beneath her symptom. She understood her ambivalence towards her father and how she had acquired her strict and relentless superego. But the crucial insight for this patient, the insight which served to resolve the impasse, was that she was actively evoking unpleasant thoughts, that she was making herself upset in order to block her sexual feelings. This recognition created a crisis. Her conscience would not allow her to continue this process once she recognized it. She went on to explore and resolve the conflict between her anger and her love for Ben which had evoked her defense against sex. She found that when she focused on the genuine positive elements of the relationship and on Ben's real attractive features, she felt much less resistance to sex.

At this time sex was still prohibited. Britt was instructed to "practice feeling good," i.e., to selectively focus on positive elements in nonsexual situations. She succeeded in doing this and found that she was having a very good time on trips, on weekends, and at social occasions. Her increasing pleasure was encouraged by the therapist.

When she indicated that she was ready, sex was resumed. They began with the pleasuring experiences. She became much more assertive and active in the sexual situation. She learned to set the time and pace and how to say, "not now" and "not yet" without guilt. More anxiety and resistances were evoked in both spouses, but these were dealt with successfully in the sessions.

At the time of termination, the couple was having sex regularly. For her it was now comfortable but not intensely passionate. He was much happier, but was still not completely satisfied. He wished she were more responsive.

In this case the obstacle to sexual desire was in the immediate, inhibition-evoking behavior of the patient which had persisted even though the deeper conflicts appeared to have been resolved in analytic treatment.

AREA III

STRATEGIES OF PSYCHOSEXUAL THERAPY

During the past five years an effort has been made to improve the effectiveness of treatment for the more difficult sexual dysfunctions, among which desire problems are heavily represented. This experience has yielded valuable theoretical insights and technical advances which promise to have wide application beyond the area of sexual problems. One of these involves the concept of multiple causal levels. *Accordingly, a single etiological factor is not regarded as producing a symptom. Rather, and/or more often, multiple levels of causes interact to produce the resultant clinical disorder. This construct opens the way for more discrete and elegant therapeutic interventions which can be aimed with great precision at the area of maximum vulnerability in the* defensive carapace which protects and maintains the patient's symptom.

The integrated treatment approach which consists of an amalgam of behavioral and psychodynamic and even pharmacologic forms of intervention is ideally suited for implementing such strategic specific attacks on the psychopathological symptom. The original method of sex therapy—a brief, active form of integrated treatment—has been refined and developed so that it has become more subtle, more complex and more precise, which has extended its range to more deeply troubled patients than was possible with the original techniques. Chapter 8 contains a discussion of the concept of remote and immediate causes, i.e. the concept of multiple causal levels, as it applies to sexual problems. Its relationship to the integrated treatment approach is also described in that chapter.

Another concept which is useful for organizing therapy, and most especially brief therapy, involves the range or level of anxiety which is optimum for therapeutic progress. *This concept derives from learning theory, where it was first employed in systematic desensitization. In this behavioral method the intensity of the patient's anxiety about a particular fear or phobia is the crucial indicator which the therapist uses to determine the speed and nature of therapeutic intervention. This concept has important applications to brief combined treatment, of which sex therapy is a prime example, and to brief psychodynamically oriented therapy as well. In Chapter 9 the concept of optimum therapeutic anxiety is discussed. Methods by which the therapist can apply this concept are also described. The therapist can raise the level of anxiety when resistances arise during the therapeutic process by confrontation and the creation of controlled crises. He can reduce the tension level when this is of counterproductive intensity by support and by fostering reassuring ambiance in the couple's sexual interactions. The balance of support and confrontation is employed to move treatment forward at the most rapid pace, which neither produces disruptive anxiety and distress nor mobilizes undue resistances.*

The concepts of the fear of sexual and romantic success *and the related* fear of pleasure and intimacy *are extremely important in understanding and treating the sexual dysfunctions, particularly desire phase dysfunctions. Until recently this area has been relatively neglected. Behaviorists were more interested in the immediate antecedents of sexual symptoms, while psychoanalysts and family and couple therapists tended to focus their attention on the most remote and deepest etiological factors. The importance of pleasure and intimacy fears, which may be thought of as falling somewhere in between the* **immediate and deepest causal levels, has not been sufficiently** *appreciated. Recently, however, there has been a growing recognition of the high prevalence of success fears. This concept is increasingly attracting the interest of clinicians of varied orientations. In my experience, intervention on the level of fear of success or of intimacy can be highly effective in the brief therapy of many kinds of problems that involve self-destructive patterns of behavior, including that monumental* *form of human self-sabotage, the destruction of one's love relationships and sexual pleasure. The fear of sexual success is discussed in Chapter 10, while Chapter 11 contains a discussion of intimacy problems.*

Chapter 12 deals with issues of termination. *Questions arise about discharging patients in those forms of brief treatment which do not have a predetermined time limit. Symptomatic cure is not sufficient. The probability of relapse is reduced when the patient and/or couple gain insight, at least to some degree, into the causes which have led to the original difficulties.*

CHAPTER

8

THE CONCEPT OF

MULTIPLE CAUSAL LEVELS

THE MULTILEVEL CONCEPT of the etiology of sexual dysfunctions, i.e., the division of the causes into different psychic levels, has proved to be very useful in organizing treatment strategies. According to this concept, sexual symptoms are produced by immediate antecedents which may or may not be the product of deeper and more unconscious conflicts, i.e., remote causes.

Within this theoretical framework, the initial and overriding objective of psychosexual therapy is to modify the immediate antecedent of the presenting symptom. If this immediate cause can be modified or controlled, the symptom will be cured. This can be done successfully even when the immediate cause is not ultimate, even when it is a reflection of deeper pathology. For example, if the premature ejaculator can be taught to focus his attention on the sensations associated with high levels of sexual arousal, he will learn ejaculatory control. If he concentrates, he can control his orgasms—irrespective of whether his distraction is simply a learned habit with no special psychic meaning, or whether it is a reflection of deeper sexual conflicts.

It is a basic strategy of sex therapy to attempt to modify the immediate antecedents of the sexual symptom and to deal with more remote underlying anxieties only if resistances arise in the course of

145

treatment. Resistances to the removal of a sexual symptom presumably are only mobilized if the symptom serves as a defense against deeper and unconscious conflict.

In order to implement these treatment objectives, psychosexual therapy employs an amalgam of behavioral and psychotherapeutic techniques. In general, the behavioral or experiential methods are used to modify the immediate causes, while psychotherapeutic techniques are employed for resolving deeper problems. The structured sexual interactions or behavioral prescriptions which are assigned to the couple as homework are designed to relieve performance anxieties and obsessive self-observations and desensitize other superficial or mild sexual tensions. The psychotherapeutic work, which contains elements of support of sexual pleasure, confrontations with resistances, and exploration of unconscious intrapsychic conflicts and marital difficulties, is aimed at clarifying and resolving those deeper causes which have shaped the sexual problem and which are responsible for the resistances mobilized by the process and the outcome of treatment.

Thus, psychosexual therapy employs an integration of techniques and, perhaps even more important, an integration of multiple levels of intervention. Clinical experience suggests that this strategy of focusing on both the immediate and also the remoter levels of causality, of aiming at a wide spectrum of targets, can sometimes broaden the range of therapeutic effectiveness over modalities that focus exclusively on any one causal level.

In individual and couples psychotherapies, intervention is primarily focused on the remote and underlying causes of the problem, with the hope that the symptom will be cured by resolution of these deep conflicts. Sometimes this happens, but there are also many instances where the patient or couple receives enormous benefits from long-term therapy and major conflicts are resolved, but the man still ejaculates prematurely or the woman is still anorgastic at the end of analysis. This is because these therapies tend to neglect the immediate antecedents of sexual symptoms, which may not change automatically when the deeper conflicts that may have spawned them are resolved. Often specific attention to the symptom is required in order to cure it. In fact, these immediate sensations and causes may not even be identified accurately in the course of long-term psychotherapy, since material relating to the sensations associated with specific sexual experiences is not likely to emerge in the free associations of analysis. Nor will the analyst question the patient directly about the physical and mental details of, for example, his masturbation. He knows about the patient's sexual experiences only as they emerge spontaneously in treatment. The same lack of focus on the immediate sexual experience is also characteristic of other types of insight therapies which intervene on the level of deep unconscious intrapsychic and marital conflict.

On the other hand, behavior therapies focus too narrowly on the immediate symptom antecedents and commit the opposite error—neglect of the deeper causes. Behavioral techniques are exquisitely designed to accurately identify the immediate antecedents of a symptom and to modify these. In behavior therapy, the therapist obtains a crystal clear and detailed picture of the contingencies and sensations experienced by the patient in the actual problem situation. He then uses this information to construct therapeutic experiences which are specifically designed to modify the contingencies which constitute the immediate causes of the symptom. Classical sex therapy has the characteristics of the behavioral approach. It relies on the detailed, two-day-long sexual history for a detailed assessment of the couple's sexual experiences and employs the structured sexual interactions to modify the behavioral antecedents of their difficulties.

Behaviorally oriented sex therapy is highly successful with the simpler problems, when the immediate antecedents are not associated with deeper roots. But when resistances, which grow out of unconscious conflict, arise, these techniques are relatively useless, because the constructs of unconscious motivation and of unconscious conflict have no place in the theory of behaviorism. This discipline constructs human behavior and psychopathology simply in terms of learned contingencies. Behavior therapists cannot delve "deeper," because in most learning theory models psychic "depth" does not exist.

The integrated psychosexual therapy approach extends the therapeutic range to both immediate and deeper causes, which often coexist in sexually dysfunctional patients. This broad spectrum approach is particularly useful with the more difficult sex therapy patients whose pathology is complex and who tend to be resistant to behaviorally oriented sex therapy.

The following cases illustrate the interplay between intervention at the immediate and more remote levels of causality, as well as the integrated use of behavioral and psychotherapeutic methods which is employed to implement this strategy. Although these broad spectrum, integrated techniques are particularly applicable to the more difficult desire inhibitions, they are illustrated here by four cases of female anorgasmia, primarily because the immediate causes of this syndrome are easily identified and so the theoretical issues emerge more clearly.

Anorgasmia in females is one of the simplest dysfunctions to treat and to cure. The immediate causes of the symptom include inadequate clitoral stimulation and "orgasm watching," i.e., an obsessive preoccupation with the orgasmic reflex during stimulation. These defenses are evoked at high levels of arousal. Often the superficial causes have no discernible deep roots; even if the orgasm block has deeper meanings, these can often be circumvented by working directly with the superficial causes. In fact, for many women, anorgasmia may be considered more of a learning disability than a psychopathological problem. Thus, many women who have never had an orgasm respond to written instructions about overcoming the immediate antecedents alone, or with the addition of some peer encouragement. However, in other cases, anorgasmia is associated with deeper underlying sexual anxiety. In these cases behavioral suggestions alone are not effective, and additional psychotherapeutic intervention is required in order to resolve resistances which will arise in response to attempts at direct symptom removal.

Therapeutic intervention usually entails encouragement and instruction about clitoral stimulation. If obsessive defenses interfere with orgastic release, distraction with fantasy is employed to circumvent the underlying conflicts. Sometimes mild underlying fears of losing control of anger as well as sex, guilt about sexual pleasure, and relationship problems emerge in the course of the exercises, and a certain degree of insight into these issues is necessary before the woman will be able to reach orgasm. But cure is generally rapid and becoming orgastic will essentially solve the patient's problem.

In some cases anorgasmia is associated with and represents a defense against more profound psychopathology. Then one of two clinical courses can occur: 1) The patient will not be cured with brief therapy. In my experience 10 percent of anorgastic women may be expected to be treatment failures. 2) The patient will learn to have an orgasm but will be left with a great deal of residual psychopathology.

In *The New Sex Therapy* two orgasm phase dysfunction treatment failures were described. One patient was a borderline schizophrenic. She had unrealistic fantasies associated with orgasm. With every step closer to the experience of orgasm, she became intensely anxious and delusional. She was obsessed with the thought that her husband would let her die if she became ill. She did not attain insight into the irrational symbolism with which orgasm was embellished and she did not learn to have an orgasm. Another patient who failed to become orgasmic was not basically psychotic; she was a rigid, obsessive woman who was unable to give up her excessive need to exert control over her feelings within the context of brief therapy. Although she attained some insight into the deeper meaning of her symptom, which involved fear of losing control over primitive angry and envious impulses, she did not improve.

However, these failures are exceptions. Most women, even those who harbor profound sexual anxiety, can eventually become orgastic. Nevertheless, such patients may prove highly resistant and treatment may be difficult and complicated, requiring the bypass or resolution of profound psychic conflict. It is frequently possible to circumvent deeper psychic problems by focusing directly on the symptom. Patients learn to have an orgasm even though the deeper layers of the sexual conflict remain untouched. If the patient needs additional help with these deeper problems, long-term psychotherapy is required after she has become orgastic in response to rapid treatment. Obviously, sex therapy or any other form of brief therapy is not an appropriate treatment modality for deeper, more pervasive or developmental problems.

I have had the opportunity to follow four anorgastic patients, whose symptom was associated with deeper and unconscious conflict, in long-term treatment after they learned to have orgasms in response to brief sexual therapy. These experiences illustrate the complex interrelationships between the symptom and the patient's psychodynamic system, and also the interactions between therapeutic interventions which are conducted on multiple levels of psychopathology.

CASE 13   ABBY

Anorgasmia
Obsessive Self-Observation with Unresolved Oedipal Conflict
Successful Outcome

Abby was a single, 34-year-old woman whose chief complaint was an inability to have an orgasm. She also had numerous other difficulties. She was out of work, which was the final resultant of a long history of work inhibition. She had been trained as a teacher but did not pursue this career, finding it "too fatiguing." She had worked as a travel agent and cocktail waitress and in an art gallery—but she did not find any of these jobs satisfying. She also had a history of serious difficulties with romantic relationships. She had been married briefly when she was 20 to a man considerably older than herself who turned out to be mentally ill. Since that time she had numerous ill-fated and destructive relationships with a variety of psychopaths and sadists who all exploited her financially, emotionally and sexually. She was depressed at the time of her initial consultation.

Etiology

The immediate cause of the anorgasmia was that at high levels of sexual arousal the patient would begin to obsessively observe herself and question whether she was going to reach orgasm.

On a deeper level, this patient's intense and unresolved oedipal problem made it unconsciously dangerous to have a full sexual experience. She experienced sex not in terms of pleasure, but in terms of competition, presumably with fantasy mother figures. In other words, the patient suffered from a fear of sexual and romantic success which may be regarded as having had its roots in an unresolved oedipal conflict.

Treatment

The patient's expressed concerns centered around her sexual symptom. Therefore, treatment first focused on her anorgasmia which was, admittedly, the least of her problems. She was encouraged to have pleasure and instructed in the usual way about clitoral stimulation and the use of fantasy. After 16 sessions of a rather stormy and complex treatment course, Abby learned to reach orgasm with a vibrator. She had learned this by "separating," i.e., dissociating her orgasm responses from her deeper sexual conflicts. Six sessions after she became orgastic on self-stimulation, she was able to climax on oral stimulation with her current partner.

This, of course, did not solve her characterologic problems. She suffered from chronic depression and anxiety; above all, her life-style was generally unsatisfying. Her existence was riddled by serious self-destructive tendencies.

She was encouraged by her success in sex therapy and entered long-term treatment with me. Her problems centered around unresolved oedipal issues. She was still deeply attached to her handsome father. She harbored intense and diffuse competitive attitudes towards other women. These were expressed in a stormy transference. It took almost five years after her anorgasmic syndrome was relieved for the resolution of her deeper conflicts and integration of these insights into her behavior. The eventual outcome was extremely successful. At the time of termination, she had finished graduate school, was teaching, which she now enjoyed, and had married a gentle, loving man. On follow-up two years later, the couple had a child.

Their sexual adjustment was satisfactory. She continued to be orgastic but she was not altogether free in her sexual response.

CASE 14 BARBARA
Anorgasmia
Obsessive Self-Observation with Obsessive-Compulsive Character Structure
Partial Success

Barbara was a 36-year-old lawyer. She had been married eight years to a successful businessman. The couple seldom had sex although they enjoyed a good relationship in other respects. Her chief complaint was anorgasmia, which had not been helped by four years of classical psychoanalysis.

The analysis had helped her in some areas, especially in work and in terms of her relationship with her family, but the issues of orgasms, masturbation, and her sexual interactions with her husband had not emerged in her former treatment.

Etiology

The immediate antecedent of the orgastic dysfunction was the patient's obsessive, controlling self-observation, which was evoked at low levels of sexual excitement. This was related to profound characterologic difficulties.

Treatment

Therapy was difficult because this obsessive-compulsive patient had a great deal of difficulty fantasizing. It was almost impossible for her to control her tendency to observe herself when she began to feel aroused. After 18 sessions, she had her first orgasm with a vibrator while she was reading a romantic passage in a novel.

This patient wanted to continue treatment with me mainly for her periodic depression. I saw her for one and a half years. Her depressions were controlled with a combination of medication and therapy designed to make her responsible for recognizing and avoiding those circumstances that triggered her depression. Apart from gaining good control of depression and the ability to reach orgasm with a vibrator, the quality of her life did not improve. She continued to be over-conscientious, rigid and pleasure-avoiding.

CASE 15 CHARLOTTE
Anorgasmia
Obsessive Self-Observation with Unresolved Sibling Rivalry
Partial Success

The patient was a 29-year-old housewife. She had been married for seven years to a loving and sensitive man. They had two children.

Chief Complaint

She was anxious and depressed and suffered from numerous psychosomatic symptoms, but her main concern was her inability to have an orgasm. She had been in analysis with a TA oriented therapist for two years. This therapy dealt exclusively with conflicts stemming from her childhood but did not identify or focus on the immediate antecedents. Orgasm and masturbation and the intimate details of her sexual experiences never came up during the course of therapy. During her treatment she showed considerable improvement in her general status, but she did not gain help for her sexual symptom.

Etiology

The immediate antecedent of the patient's orgasm inhibition had its roots in intense feelings of envy towards and anger at other women. This was a derivative of strong, unresolved feelings of rivalry for a younger sister. She was not consciously aware of this rivalry, which was still intensely operative, to the point of seriously impairing this patient's ability to socialize and to work. For her, sexual pleasure and competency were yet another in her ubiquitous competitions. It could be speculated that she was unconsciously afraid to have an orgasm because this would mean humiliating and destroying her symbolic sister.

She responded to sex therapy with moderate ease. With no insight into her underlying problems, it took her only eight sessions to become orgastic on self-stimulation. Resistance was evoked by her considerable fear of pleasure and success but it was possible to bypass this by focusing on modifying the immediate antecedents of the orgasm phase inhibition during brief treatment.

One of the strategies employed to circumvent the basic pleasure inhibition was to confront her with the fact that she was obsessing about orgasm to distract her from the other more threatening problems in her life. She recognized that she had made orgasm a symbol for success but that in reality attaining an orgasm would neither make her life perfect nor affect anyone else. This occupied the first three sessions. Five weeks after she had attained this insight, the patient was able to have an orgasm with her husband.

When she attained orgasm she faced the fact that she had extensive, nonsexually related problems. She entered long-term therapy with me in order to work on these. The treatment was stormy. Massive transference problems arose which centered around this patient's intense and deep ambivalence towards all women, including the therapist. Unresolved preoedipal and sibling problems were involved in her considerable psychopathology. Her fears of pleasure derived from guilt about hostile feelings towards her sister as well as from fears of losing her mother. The transference resistances diminished substantially but she never became completely at ease with me.

Four years of analytically oriented therapy were moderately but not entirely successful in improving this patient's life. Follow-up one year later revealed that she is still orgastic.

CASE 16   DORIS
> *Anorgasmia*
> *Inadequate Stimulation, Father Transference to Husband and Depression*
> *Successful Outcome*

Doris was a brilliant, 46-year-old married woman who had recently completed law school which she began after her son had left for school. She had a history of several severe depressions for which she had received brief psychiatric treatment, including electroconvulsive therapy. She and her husband, a successful businessman, were deeply attached to one another but quarreled bitterly and frequently throughout their 25-year marriage. Their sexual adjustment was poor. They had intercourse infrequently and only in the early morning when he found it easiest to function. At other times he was impotent. She had never had an orgasm. The couple had previously sought help at a traditional sex therapy program, but Doris terminated treatment after four sessions because she felt "misunderstood" by the female member of the therapy team.

Etiology

The immediate cause of anorgasmia was inadequate stimulation. The psychosexual evaluation revealed that love-making was constricted and rapid and did not provide her with enough stimulation to be able to become aroused and orgastic. Since she did not assert herself appropriately, her husband had no idea of this problem. On a deeper level, the patient was blocked sexually, probably because she had formed a father transference to her husband. She idealized him but felt constantly depressed and enraged at his distant and nonintimate behavior. She regarded this as a rejection and humiliation, and not, realistically, as his personality style. In addition, she was raised in a moralistic family environment and was taught to regard sex and pleasure as sinful.

Treatment

She became orgasmic on self-stimulation after four sessions of symptom-focused sexual therapy. Three sessions later, she had multiple orgasms together with her husband. The couple was very satisfied with the outcome of therapy which, apart from symptomatic cure, had given them some insight into their marital difficulties and relief from their quarreling. They enjoyed two years of a greatly improved sexual and marital adjustment.

Then Doris' husband began to spend more time at his business. This activated her old feelings of rejection and envy of other women whom she imagined were blessed with more attentive husbands. The couple began to quarrel again. Doris experienced another profound depression and returned to therapy. However, she remained orgastic. Deeply rooted and profound problems emerged in the course of the treatment. Numerous crises occurred, but the ultimate outcome was very successful. The key was the resolution of an intensely ambivalent transferential response to the therapist and insight into her lifelong problems with father figures. Three years later the patient was free of depression and her marriage had improved somewhat, at least to the degree that both spouses continued to function well sexually. She had also learned to handle her relationships with males more realistically and had been made a partner in a prestigious law firm.

Once the patient understands and learns to control the immediate antecedent of the symptom, symptomatic cure tends to remain stable—even when there is little insight into underlying factors, and even in the face of other pyschological problems. This is a generalization which holds true more often for orgasm phase dysfunctions than for desire and erectile difficulties. Once the premature ejaculator learns to concentrate on his sensations he will attain and retain control. Once a woman knows how to control her obsessive tendencies, she will, with rare exceptions, be able to reach a climax irrespective of other influences, including significant changes in her relationship or other aspects of her life. This relative independence of the orgasm function from other areas of psychopathology was illustrated by the four cases cited above.

Impotent patients will vary in this respect. Some patients who have learned how to manage their sexual anxieties will never fall victim to this again, especially if they have also gained some insight into the dynamics. But others relapse when relationship or intrapsychic problems increase.

Clinical experience suggests that for the desire phase dysfunctions the relationship between immediate and remote pathogenic factors is closer than it is for many genital phase dysfunctions. Even when the patient gains insight into how he "turns himself off" by selectively focusing on his partner's unattractive attributes or by evoking other unpleasant issues and even if he successfully learns to modify this in therapy, he may not want or be able to control this tendency if intrapsychic or relationship problems create more pressures later on. It seems to be more difficult to disassociate desire from the rest of the psychic and marital system than it is to encapsulate orgasm or excitement.

9

THE OPTIMUM RANGE

OF THERAPEUTIC ANXIETY

THERAPEUTIC PROGRESS may be construed as taking place at an optimum level of anxiety. A patient cannot be expected to modify his behavior without experiencing some anxiety. If treatment mobilizes no anxiety at all, he will not change, for it is more comfortable to stay in the old defended position than to take the risks of behaving more openly. But if the therapeutic process creates too much anxiety, no progress will occur either, because resistances will be mobilized to the extent that treatment comes to a standstill.

When sex therapy is practiced within a flexible format, the pace at which the behavioral exercises are conducted will vary with the emotional requirements of the patient. The tasks are assigned fast enough or in steps large enough and confrontations are sufficiently intense to move treatment forward. This will create a certain amount of anxiety. But the tasks are not given so rapidly, nor are the increments so big, nor are the confrontations and interpretations so threatening, that the patient or the couple is upset to a counterproductive degree.

For example, as soon as the couple is comfortable with the pleasuring exercises, the therapist will proceed to prescribe genital caressing; only when this can be done with comfort will the next task be assigned. The timing must, of necessity, be flexible, tailored to the specific anxiety level and to the tolerance of anxiety of each patient and couple. Sometimes, if the sexual anxiety is mild, one can consolidate several steps in one set of instructions. On the other hand, if the patient's anxiety is intense, each step of a standard exercise may have to be broken down into smaller, less-threatening components. Thus, it happens that some patients are cured in five sessions, while treatment of others with the same symptoms will take 24.

In sum, it is the therapist's task to conduct treatment at the most rapid and effective pace without mobilizing counterproductive anxieties and their attendant resistances. This requires an accurate assessment of the patient's emotional response to the therapeutic process, as well as of his capacity to deal with anxiety constructively.

Determining just how big each step or task should be, just how fast the couple should move, when an exercise should be repeated, or when the anxiety has come down sufficiently so that the next step can be integrated, requires fine therapeutic judgment and a "feel" for the patients' optimum anxiety level. In order to make this kind of judgment, it is necessary to assess the emotional reactions of both partners to the assigned erotic tasks. For this reason, it is important to obtain an accurate and highly detailed account of what transpired during the period, usually one week, between therapeutic sessions. Consequently, during the first part of each clinical session, the therapist reviews the experiences of both partners with respect to their physical as well as their emotional responses while they carried out the erotic tasks which were assigned during the previous therapy session. This information is required to design the next assignment rationally so that it evokes an appropriate level of anxiety. This can only be done after the sex therapist has a crystal clear picture of both partners' experiences, very much like the behavior therapist who constructs specific and systematic desensitization procedures for his patients.

Apart from the intensity of the patient's sexual problem, another determinant of the optimum level of anxiety at which to conduct treatment is the patient's and the partner's tolerance of anxiety. People vary enormously in their capacity to deal with and integrate anxiety. Thus, one person can be given rapid assignments and be confronted vigorously with his resistances because he can constructively deal with the intense anxiety and crisis which this evokes. Other patients, those who are more fragile and not as well integrated, can only accommodate a very low level of anxiety. For such a patient very small behavioral steps must be taken and confrontations must be gently and carefully executed; otherwise they will not improve and may in fact regress or become hostile to the treatment procedure.

The assessment of the patient's or couple's optimum anxiety level is, of course, highly subjective. In this active and rapid form of treatment it is not unusual to err and to confront too vigorously or to assign tasks which are too disturbing. However, if this should occur, if the therapist has assigned an exercise which has provoked too much anxiety, which has given rise to resistances, all is not lost. In fact, this may become a therapeutic opportunity:

THERAPIST: It really made you nervous to touch his penis, didn't it?

SUSIE: Sure did. I didn't sleep well that night and I couldn't do any more assignments the rest of the week. I feel awful about this. After all, I was the one who wanted this therapy and here I am wasting time.

THERAPIST: No, that was not your fault—it was mine. I didn't understand how frightened you were of the penis when I asked you to do that. It was too difficult. You were right not to repeat the assignment. Doing something that uncomfortable is counterproductive. Let's take a more comfortable step. How about if you looked at his penis this week. Do you think you could do that?

SUSIE: Well, he always sleeps with his underwear. I never look at his penis. But I think I could do it. Yes, I think so. What if I get upset?

THERAPIST: Well, what if you do get upset?

SUSIE: I guess I could stop looking and ask him to put his pants on again.

THERAPIST: Yes, that's right. Don't do anything even if I suggest it that is really uncomfortable. But you will have to force yourself a little if you want to get over your penis phobia. You will have to endure a little discomfort while you look—your anxiety will not mount—it will go down if you can stay with it. If it gets really frightening, stop. We'll get it done slowly but surely.

This tactic creates several opportunities. The therapist models an accepting attitude towards her own "error." The structured experiences become a learning opportunity and there is no risk of failure. The examples set by the therapist of not needing to maintain a posture of perfection may be of benefit to patients burdened by performance pressures and perfectionistic attitudes. In addition the patient is given the responsibility for monitoring her own anxiety and for making an effort to keep it at a level at which she can progress comfortably, i.e., her own therapeutic optimum. Finally, the crisis created by her inability to do the task serves to confront the patient with the existence and magnitude of her sexually disruptive anxiety more vividly and effectively than verbal interpretation alone could have done.

REGULATING THE ANXIETY LEVEL

The therapist has at his disposal behavioral and psychodynamic tactics that can reduce his patient's anxiety level when this is too high to be therapeutically useful; he also has means of evoking anxiety if treatment is at an impasse, if the patient has retreated to a defended or resistant position by which he avoids anxiety. The experiential tasks and the psychotherapeutic interventions both have the power to reduce or increase a patient's level of anxiety. In psychosexual therapy these modalities are employed in an integrated manner to keep the process within the patient's therapeutically effective zone of anxiety.

The Tasks

The gradually increasing sexual tasks provide the patient with the opportunity for in vivo desensitization which will reduce his sexual anxiety. Assignments can be finely adjusted with respect to the amount of anxiety they evoke. When the task is only a small step away from the patient's current level of functioning, then the patient's anxiety diminishes. However, if a task is large enough to flood the patient with anxiety, desensitization will usually not occur and the patient will fail to carry out the task successfully.* The resulting crisis may be then used to confront the patient with his anxiety, as was illustrated in the aforementioned dialogue with Susie.

The Sessions

A number of psychotherapeutic styles can be successfully employed in the psychotherapeutic aspects of psychosexual therapy. The therapists in our program have evolved treatment styles that differ with their diverse personalities and theoretical orientations. As long as the essential strategies of psychosexual therapy govern the treat-

---

* "Flooding" or the assignment of an intensely feared task may, in fact, effectively reduce anxiety but only in highly specific situations.

ment procedure, there is room for a wide range of stylistic variations and each therapist should develop a mode that is comfortable for him.

I use a method that is characterized by an active interplay between *support* which calms the patient and *confrontation* which may create anxiety, to keep treatment moving at the optimum level of anxiety that the patient can handle. The active support, encouragement of pleasure, and sensitivity to and empathy with the patient's emotional needs facilitate the rapid formation of trust and confidence, i.e., a positive transference. This is an important ingredient in this kind of treatment.

A strong "good parent" transference endows the therapist with powers which enable him to encourage the patient to persist with his exercises even when these are difficult. It makes his praise of the patient's efforts and his acceptance of the patient's conflicts extremely valuable and effectively enables him to reduce anxiety. This kind of supportive relationship also makes it possible to be actively confronting, to rapidly face the patient with his resistances, that is, to create therapeutic crises when obstacles arise.

Creation of Crises

If the patient or his spouse is resistant, if nothing moves, if he will not do the tasks that evoke his anxiety, if she will not cooperate, the therapist can create a crisis to propel treatment forward. In one sense, each therapeutic confrontation and each new behavioral assignment create a "mini-crisis" because the patient must think and/or behave in ways he has previously avoided because they evoke anxiety. A crisis always contains an element of risk as well as an opportunity for growth and change. A crisis disrupts old defensive behavior patterns and the risk is that the patient cannot deal with this constructively and may leave treatment or even deteriorate. At the same time, if he *can* accommodate the emotional upheaval, then there is the opportunity for rapid integration at a higher level of functioning.

The therapist must plan the series of therapeutic crises meticulously and maintain very fine control over them. An uncontrolled crisis is dangerous and may produce negative results, but a controlled crisis is a powerful instrument for propelling therapy forward.

Crises are sometimes created by the patient himself, or by his spouse, with similar risks and opportunities.

THE OPTIMUM ANXIETY LEVEL
AND TREATMENT OUTCOME

Treatment failures can result from therapeutic errors in both directions—when too much anxiety is created or when treatment comes to a standstill because too little anxiety is mobilized.

Case 2 of Sam and Susie illustrates the first treatment error. The previous therapy failed because anxiety of counterproductive intensity was provoked by the sensate focus exercises. This is not unusual when the sexual problem is associated with phobias and intense avoidance of sexual feelings. The patient improved in our program because her anxiety was diminished by medication and by a strong, reassuring relationship with the therapist, as well as by breaking the standard tasks down into small, manageable steps.

The following case would have been a failure in standard sex therapy for different reasons. The tasks did not modify the symptom. The provocation of a crisis was needed to break down the patient's resistances.

CASE 17   **FRANK AND FRANCES**
            Premature Ejaculation and Lack of Desire
            Crisis Provoking Tactics
            Improvement

The couple, a law student, age 26, and his wife, also age 26, a fashion buyer, had been married for three years. Their chief complaints were his premature ejaculations and her lack of desire. The evaluation revealed that Frances was suffering from a high anxiety level and had a long history of severe agoraphobia. Frank played the role of nurse-doctor in the relationship. Both had been in individual psychoanalytically-oriented therapy for many years—he for six, she for four—with many benefits, but no relief of his prematurity or of her phobic state. Frances' high anxiety level impaired her ability to cooperate in sex treatment.

She was first treated with tricyclic drugs. Her desire did not increase in response to medication, but within two months her anxiety abated sufficiently so that sex therapy could begin. Both spouses were delighted about the dramatic improvement of her anxiety and phobic state which now permitted her to travel by herself and even drive a car for the first time in her life. This endowed them with a sense of optimism about improving their sexual difficulties.

Treatment

Rapport was established rapidly and easily with both spouses. Both had problems experiencing pleasure, and this issue was emphasized in the therapy sessions. It was clear that he became anxious when sexual pleasure was intense and prolonged, and this contributed to his inadequate ejaculatory control.

Treatment started with the stop-start exercises to improve his control. The couple was very cooperative but he failed to progress to intravaginal control. He learned excellent concentration and control on manual stimulation but continued to become distracted and to ejaculate rapidly on vaginal penetration. We worked for 18 sessions to analyze and resolve his resistances to modifying the superficial causes of his prematurity. He produced dreams and fantasies and both spouses were, at least on a conscious level, highly motivated. Although they worked diligently at the exercises, their effort was to no avail. He continued to ejaculate on five or six strokes after entry. Neither I nor the patients had insight into the underlying cause of this resistance.

I then created a crisis by sharing with them my honest concern that he would be one of the exceptional patients who failed to learn control in sex therapy. I said this with compassion but also with scientific detachment. I stated that I did not understand why he was not successful and also that I was very interested in studying failures. They reacted with understandable distress. His anxiety level rose but some process of integration seemed to take place.

In the next session he produced a dream. He dreamt that he dropped a burning cigarette into his aunt's boot and hurt her. According to a psychoanalytical frame of reference, this could be interpreted to signify that ejaculation inside a woman unconsciously held a hostile symbolic meaning for him. Whether this view is correct or not is, of course, beyond scientific validation. But interpretations were made on this assumption. During the sessions we discussed the oedipal implications of the dream: Aunt equals mother. We spoke of his previously denied anger at his mother and towards women in general. It may be speculated that by my disclosure of his poor prognosis I had joined his resistance and created a crisis, thereby propelling therapy forward.

The sig for the next week included the use of angry and sadistic fantasies during love-making. That week he reported excellent intravaginal control. This improvement was, however, only transient. Treatment was interrupted at this point because he had to take a law clerkship in another city.

When he returned three months later he had relapsed somewhat and his control was uneven. During the next 15 sessions, we worked both on his concentration in the specific sexual situation and also on his insight into his previously unrecognized feelings of anger at his mother and at his wife. He came to understand an unresolved competitive component in his relationship with his former analyst and with his father. He obtained good ejaculatory control which he lost only occasionally when he was under stress.

Treatment was terminated at this time because the couple moved to another city. They planned to seek further help for her difficulties, which improved only slightly during the course of therapy.

10

THE FEAR OF

ROMANTIC SUCCESS

THE EXPERIENCE of treating patients with sexual dysfunctions has made it increasingly clear that, although they tend to complain bitterly about their sexual *failures*, many are in reality, on an unconscious level, fearful of sexual and romantic *success*. This is especially true of the more difficult patients, many of whom suffer from desire disorders.

The theoretical construct of unconscious success anxiety is extremely useful in understanding and treating many of the patients who are resistant to the traditional sex therapy strategies. This is not surprising because sex therapy is basically designed to modify fears of sexual failure but does not cure success fears.

GENESIS

Freud recognized the existence of success anxiety early on. In 1915 he wrote a paper describing two persons who were "wrecked by success." They had both fallen ill and essentially ruined their lives shortly after having fulfilled a deeply wished for goal.

According to psychoanalytic theory, the unconscious fear of success has its roots in the oedipal situation. In patients who are afflicted with this problem, success is symbolically equated with a dangerous and immoral competition with the same gender parent for sex and power. "Winning" in adult life, that is, romantic success and intimacy, is symbolically and unconsciously equated with "winning" in the oedipal situation. More recent extensions of psychoanalytic theory include unresolved sibling rivalries as etiologic factors in success anxiety. Again, the unconscious equation of success with competition results in conflict about, as well as fear and avoidance of, success. More specifically, if a patient fails to resolve early conflicts about competition with his siblings, his world may forever be symbolically populated with sibling rivals and "winning" may forever mean the destruction of and possible retaliation from a brother or sister. In clinical practice, many, but not all, persons who suffer from success problems show evidence of unresolved oedipal and/or sibling problems.

According to Sullivanian theory, which does not subscribe to the notion of psychosexual stages and the oedipal crisis, conflicts about success and pleasure and intimacy are engendered in early childhood by the negative emotional reactions of "significant others" to success and competition. Sullivan considered the emotional responses of loved ones to be the most important determinant of acquired behavior. In other words, if the child's happiness and success and sexual pleasure evoke anxiety, anger or conflict in his parents, he will acquire a negative internal response to his own success which may burden him all his life. Clinical experience supports this notion. Irrational and self-destructive fears of success are common in individuals who were reared by psychotic or borderline parents, or by parents who are pathologically competitive to the extent of not being able to identify with their own children sufficiently to inhibit their competitive impulses towards them. These parents express this competition with their own children in a nonverbal manner which is very difficult for the child to identify and defend against. Children reared in such a pathological structure may unconsciously equate "winning" with the loss of mother or the loss of her love.

TA therapists, who place a great deal of emphasis on the fear of success in their theoretical concepts, have created a synthesis of the Freudian and Sullivanian concepts which makes good sense. Accordingly, transactional analysis has conceptualized the dynamic genesis of success anxiety in terms of nonverbal messages, injunctions and scripts, which program the youngster while he is in a vulnerable development stage when he is open to such input. According to this theory, early injunctions like "Don't have fun," "She is not trustworthy," "Don't do it," "You're a loser," etc. may produce sexual and other problems in later life. The messages and scripts, although they are not consciously recognized, shape the person's destiny all his life. Patients tend to act out the *scripts* they are assigned as youngsters. "Heros" and "princesses" have few problems in romantic relationships, but those relegated to the roles of the "understudy" by the competitive mommas or "bit players" by fathers who can tolerate no other star may experience anxiety and may engage in self-sabotaging behavior if they try to deviate from their assigned losing role, or from a role designed to adhere strictly to the support of the winning roles of other family members.

The fear of success may be conceptualized as the product of faulty superego development. The superego or conscience normally organizes our behavior according to ethical principles. It is programmed in early childhood to reward us with feelings of satisfaction if we do "the right thing" and to punish us with painful guilt and fear if we "do wrong." The conscience is passively acquired during childhood as a result of family interactions. In the course of normal development it should be reevaluated and adjusted in terms of the young adult's more rational ethical system, which is built on his own real experience. If he is taught at age five that masturbation is harmful, a young man should be able to reconsider that dictum when he is 15 and has discussed this issue with his peers and finds that "everyone does it," and no one seems hurt. If a girl is told by mother that boys don't respect promiscuous girls when she is 12, at 18 her own experiences ought to show her that in fact some boys fall in love with girls with whom they share sexual pleasure. This should allow her to reappraise the validity of her mother's judgment.

Patients who suffer from unconscious fears of success and pleasure behave as if they have not reevaluated the dictates of their immature and/or distorted consciences. They have not allowed themselves to question the values they were taught. They behave like helpless victims of the original maladaptive programming whereby pleasure and success are regarded as evil and sinful. Whenever such persons experience success, instead of the sweet feelings of satisfaction which are normally evoked, negative feelings are experienced—feelings of guilt and shame and fear, just as though they had committed a crime. As in sufferers from autoimmune diseases, these patients' normal defenses turn upon themselves and destroy them when things get too good.

Some of the reasons why a person may develop a harsh and irrational conscience have already been discussed. To a child, "good" equals parental pleasure and approval and "bad" equals parental anger or disapproval. Parents who are pathologically competitive with their children will react with discomfort at their successes and pleasures. Mother will not beam when her little girl flirts with daddy in a cute manner, but rather will act in a hostile and competitive way and her child "gets the message" that there is room for only one attractive female in this world.

Another factor in the development of an irrational punishing conscience derives from the prevailing cultural ethic that equates sexual pleasure with sin. Parents whose own conscience is so programmed will, of course, react with anxiety and embarrassment when their children show an interest in sex and have sexual feelings and pleasure. These negative attitudes about sexuality are transmitted to and absorbed by the child just as surely as his parent's language. And the discomfort with and avoidance of sexual pleasure automatically become part of his emotional vocabulary.

Within the framework of the concept of immediate and remote causes, the fears of success and intimacy fall into an intermediate category. These fears are not specific antecedents of sexual dysfunctions. They do not per se result in a loss of erection or block orgasm or inhibit desire. A person whose fears of success are activated by an impending successful love or sexual relationship can then destroy his sexual response by evoking the thought, "I wonder if I will be able to function tonight"—thereby losing his erection. Or the woman who fears success will not say to herself, "Oh, oh, I am going to be successful, I better watch out!" But she might obsessively focus her attention on her orgasm, which inhibits the orgasm reflex, or dwell on some injustice perpetrated by her lover in the past so that her desire for sex vanishes. In other words, a deeper cause such as the unconscious fear of success can use as its tools more immediate antecedents which can impair the sexual response.

The unconscious fear of success will typically be mobilized when a patient nears his sexual and romantic goal. Before this time he is conflict-free in his pursuit of sexual pleasure. But when his goal is about to be reached, when the prize is in his hand, at the last inch, he will sabotage himself in any one of many possible ways—by provoking his partner, by conjuring up fears of failure or other negative thoughts during the sexual act, by merely getting anxious, by neglecting his appearance, by avoiding sex, etc., etc., etc.

CLINICAL FEATURES OF THE FEAR OF SUCCESS AND PLEASURE

Usually the patient is not consciously aware that he is afraid of success and pleasure. His conscious experience is usually the opposite. He is aware only of striving for happiness, success, and pleasure. In fact, he is aware of a fear of failure and will not believe that he is afraid of succeeding. But the fear of success operates on an unconscious level and motivates the patient to sabotage the very success and pleasure he strives for with so much energy.

The fear of success varies with respect to the areas of life that are affected, as well as in its intensity and timing. The fear of success can be global and can affect all aspects of life: career, romantic relationships, social position etc. Such persons are "losers" in all areas of life. Or the success inhibition may affect only one function: love or career or social life or athletic competitions. Such persons behave as though it is dangerous to have all things go well at the same time. They "trade off" success in one area for failure in another. They become "lop-sided" in their development. For example, he may be a highly successful businessman but never manage to achieve a happy love relationship. Or he is blessed with a wonderful romantic relationship and family life but he repeatedly loses jobs or cannot obtain an appropriate promotion. If he should somehow make a little money, he has an accident, wrecks his car, or has a fight with his wife.

Sometimes the fear of success is mild or has "shrunk" and is confined to trivial areas of life which have only symbolic significance. Such people are successful in the important areas of love and career but may lose every tennis game, even to an inferior partner—and especially when they are ahead. Or a highly successful person may reveal his success problem by avoiding (i.e. being unable) to engage in competitive social games such as bridge or chess.

The fear of success also varies in intensity. Some people cannot tolerate any kind of happiness even for a very brief time. They will "overdose" on pleasure just from "passing the course." Others overdose and sabotage themselves only when things are really wonderful, when they are getting "A+s."

The life of persons with success phobias displays a characteristic pattern of fluctuation in the inhibited function. Typically, the individual will make a great effort to attain the desired goal. When he is far away he is conflict-free and highly effective. But when he is about to reach it, at the "last inch," he will sabotage himself in some manner. Or he may, indeed, attain his cherished objective, but quickly manage to become ill or disinterested or obsessed about losing it, i.e., he spoils his enjoyment in some way. After success is lost, the effort to regain it will commence again. The patient has an unacceptable level of failure, at which he will make an effort to succeed, and an unacceptable level of success, at which point he will sabotage himself.

The dimensions of these fluctuations are highly specific. They are related only to symbolic, rather than real, dangers. These symbolic dangers are so specific that they can be quantified and predicted with great accuracy for a given individual and a specific situation. For example, persons who suffer from weight problems are often unconsciously afraid of being beautiful and sexually desirable, i.e., "successful" in terms of appearance. This success anxiety arises at specific levels of weight. Thus, a patient may consciously feel distressed, like a "fat failure," when her weight reaches over 145 pounds. At that weight she becomes visibly upset and makes a great effort to reach a level of weight which is acceptable to her. She diets vigorously and effectively until she reaches 125 pounds. But then things get "too good." She begins to look "too sexy"—and that is too dangerous, perhaps too competitive with other women. She never reaches her ideal weight of 115 pounds. When she gets "too close for comfort" at 125 pounds, she begins to get uneasy, sabotages herself and overeats again. And she diets again when she reaches 145 pounds. Such patients may gain and lose thousands of pounds in a lifetime while gaining no insight into this dynamic.

The unconscious fear of success operates like the classic approach-avoidance conflict of animal experiments. The rat is hungry. He has been shocked near his feeding place. When he is far away he will approach, moved by his need for food. But at a certain distance he will withdraw, frightened by the anticipation of shock. At a certain point he is stationary, pulled equally in both directions. This is his "comfort zone."

People, too, behave as though they were governed by an invisible, powerful, psychic "comfort zone" about failure and success. When functioning falls below a certain line, anxieties are aroused and an effort is made to bring performance up. But when things get too good, self-sabotage soon brings it down to a psychically comfortable level again. Like the experimental rat, people are imprisoned between the barriers created by their desire for and fear of success. It is important to remember that the level at which success becomes dangerous never constitutes a real hazard. The danger is symbolic only and is born of past events of which the person has no memory.

Conscious awareness of success anxiety is not a critical variable. Insight does not insure change of the self-destructive pattern. Some persons are keenly aware that their irrational fears hold success forever in sight but perpetually unattainable. They are, however, unable to overcome this. More commonly, such persons are not aware of this pattern. They consider themselves victims of bad luck or persecution. Although they are aware of their fears of failure, they have no insight into their success anxiety.

The Fear of Success and Sexual Problems

The unconscious fear of sexual pleasure is an extremely common etiologic factor in the pathogenesis of the sexual dysfunctions. All phases of the sexual response may be affected by the unconscious fear of success. In clinical practice it is common to see patients who wreck their romances, who sabotage their orgasms, cause trouble with their erections, and manage to create conditions incompatible with sexual desire. When success anxiety is mild, the orgasm phase tends to be disturbed, while impotence is usually impaired by moderate fears of sexual success. Patients with severe fears of love, sex and intimacy are often unable to feel desire for appropriate and attractive partners.

Insight is usually, but not always, lacking; patients tend to complain of the opposite—that they are afraid of sexual failure. And this is truly their experience. The actual fear, which is seldom recognized, can be inferred from their histories, which clearly indicate that they are afraid of sexual and romantic success. This, of course, does not hold for all cases. For many patients, a genuine, simple fear of failure is responsible for sexual difficulties, and there is nothing else beneath this performance anxiety. However, often the manifest fear of failure really hides an unconscious fear of success, and patients actively, if unknowingly, conjure up destructive fears and thoughts of failure in the service of the opposite, of their underlying fears of success in pleasure, sex and intimacy.

The gentle, nondemanding sensate focus exercises are beautifully designed to dispel real performance anxieties or fears of sexual failure. These tasks do not, however, diminish the fear of success. When resistances arise in treatment, especially as improvement becomes evident, the clinician should consider the possibility that the consciously perceived fear of failure is merely a veneer that covers the patient's real terror—sexual success and pleasure.

Clues that this dynamic may be operative are evidenced not only by resistances and failure to improve during treatment but also by a history of characteristic fluctuations in sexual and romantic functioning. These fluctuations serve to preserve the erotic comfort zone— bordered on one side by depression about failure and fears of loneliness, and on the other by unconscious anxiety about success in the romantic and sexual spheres of experience. Such a patient perhaps can have erections with an unattractive or lower class woman who is "safe," but performance anxiety sets in , i.e., he conjures up obsessions about the hardness or performance of his penis, when he is in bed with a woman who is his ideal. Or a woman can feel sexual desire and excitement with any number of uncaring partners who are not interested in sharing her life. But on the day she marries the kind, giving man who will meet her dependency needs, i.e., makes a "successful" marriage, her sexual desire disappears.

Sometimes sexual difficulty represents a "trade off" for success in another area. The couple have achieved everything: Their careers have advanced splendidly; they are healthy and beautiful; their children are problem-free; they move into a great, new house. He begins to have erectile difficulty or she loses her ability to have an orgasm. Life is frighteningly successful. The sexual symptom protects against the evil eye of the harsh and irrational conscience which is evoked by this success. The unconscious injunction—"you are not entitled," "something will happen if things get too good," "who do you think you are," "you can't have everything"—may be the underlying cause of sexual difficulties in such cases.

Treatment

The resistances that protect the patient's "safe" position of failure are handled in psychosexual therapy exactly like any other resistance that may arise in the course of treatment. First, an effort is made to bypass this without any attempt at confrontation or interpretation. In other words, even if the evaluation reveals that the patient has an underlying success phobia, treatment is always first geared towards modifying the immediate cause of the clinical problem.

Success fears, depending on their severity and on the patient's personality structure, can produce disruption of any of the phases of the sexual response. Thus the orgasm, excitement, or desire phase can be impaired by fear of success. Therefore, a variety of immediate antecedents may be involved in the service of the fear of sexual success. Our strategy is to direct treatment first at modifying these immediate antecedents. For example, if the success phobic woman is anorgastic, treatment is directed at teaching her clitoral stimulation concomitant with distraction by means of fantasy. In other words, the modification of the immediate cause of the inhibition of her orgasm reflex is the first target of treatment. Or if a man who harbors unconscious fears of erotic pleasure develops erectile difficulty, therapy proceeds with nondemanding sensate focus exercises and the opening of communication between partners which so often effectively modifies the performance anxiety which is the immediate cause of impotence. As another example, consider the woman who has unconsciously been avoiding romantic success by "turning herself off," which she accomplishes by dwelling on her husband's age or pot belly. In therapy, fostering insight into this immediate pathogenic mechanism becomes the first goal.

When success anxiety is mild, treatment directed at modifying the immediate antecedent of the dysfunction may bypass or resolve it sufficiently so that this issue does not come up in treatment at all. The mere experience of pleasure in the encouraging ambience provided by the therapist may resolve the anxieties sufficiently to allow the patient to function. The experience of enjoying pleasure without the anticipated negative consequences may in itself free the patient.

If resistances emerge, repetition of the exercise is usually the first maneuver employed. Sometimes the patient merely needs more time and encouragement before he can integrate the new pleasurable behavior. But if the resistances are unyielding, even after repetition of the exercises and a reasonable period of time, as well as reassurance and encouragement, the fostering of insight into his fear of sexual success is a sensible next step. This is first implemented by confronting the patient with the existence of his success anxiety. Initially the unconscious dynamics of this pattern are not dealt with. The exercises are employed to raise the patient's level of consciousness to the anxiety evoked by his progress and his increasing pleasure.

PATIENT: We couldn't do the pleasuring this week, I had to take work home and by the time we got to bed she did not feel like it.

WIFE: Honey, it was after two o'clock each night. I was tired.

PATIENT: Well, my job is important.

THERAPIST: I am sorry you have to work so hard. Perhaps this is not a good time for treatment. Do you think we should postpone it? (*Joining the resistance is often an effective confrontation method.*)

PATIENT: No, this is very important. Two weeks ago I had such good erections; I was so encouraged.

THERAPIST: Yes you did, and since then you "haven't found the time" to do the exercises. Do you really think that is the true reason or do you think that your success was a little scary?

PATIENT: No, that is ridiculous. That's why I am here, to be successful.

WIFE: Honey, it always happens when we have had good sex. You always disappear afterwards for weeks.

THERAPIST: It is not unusual for a person to have some anxiety when he starts improving. Let's talk about the week it worked so well. (*Giving the patient "permission" to have success anxiety may help his gaining insight.*)

The exploration of the patient's experiences continues until he becomes clearly aware of the existence of his pattern of avoidance of sexual success and he has recognized the sensations of anxiety he experiences when he has a good time. The genesis of this pattern has not been discussed at this phase of therapy.

Two sessions later:

PATIENT: You were right, I felt some anxiety just before we were going to do the exercises, especially the second time.

THERAPIST: How did it go the first time?

WIFE: It was great. He had the best erection yet and he really enjoyed it and so did I.

PATIENT: I thought it wouldn't be as good next time.

THERAPIST: Worrying about possible future failures is a great way to ruin your pleasures.

PATIENT: You are right, I do that a lot. I am a worrier.

THERAPIST: Do you do that especially when things go well?

PATIENT: Maybe I do, I think you are right. Why do I do that?

THERAPIST: Let's not worry about *why* right now. I just want you to become aware of *what* you do. You sabotage your own success.

The objective at this level of treatment is to foster the patient's recognition of the sensations of anxiety which he feels when "things get good," so he can learn to control his impulses to sabotage himself at these times. Employing the sexual exercises, together with confrontation by the therapist, is a useful strategy for implementing this objective.

Supplementing and reinforcing the experiential confrontations with verbal interpretations to the effect that the patient is governed by an unrecognized underlying success anxiety is very helpful now. An interpretation on this level is not threatening to most patients and is easily accepted, usually within a few sessions.

THERAPIST: Can you see that trying to function when you are nervous can get you into trouble?
PATIENT: Yes, I really can and I always get that little jolt of tension when it gets really good. I can stand pleasure for about five minutes—then I overdose.
THERAPIST: Let's try to increase your tolerance.

In fact, the objective of treatment is to increase the patient's tolerance for the intensity and duration of the experience of pleasure and success. For some patients, those whose anxiety is mild, the mere identification of success anxiety and the therapist's encouragement may be all that are needed for a cure of the sexual problem.

THERAPIST: How did it go this week?
PATIENT: Wonderful! I started to get that little jolt of anxiety. I found myself obsessing and then I stopped and I talked it over with Jane. I was very relaxed—not the old up-tightness.
WIFE: Yes, he didn't get all upset, we talked about it and we both felt better. We made love and it was absolutely beautiful.
THERAPIST: Oh, I am so glad. What did this teach you?

Sometimes, however, the more recognition of success anxiety is not enough to cure the symptom. It is necessary to resolve some of the underlying issues, the origins of the patient's fear of success, before he will be able to function. But there are limits to what can be expected of brief treatment in this respect. Therapeutic exploration within the framework of psychosexual therapy is usually not capable of dealing with highly neurotic patients who are suffering from conflicts that were acquired very early and are pervasive and intense. Exploration of such material tends to mobilize intense resistances and is usually done more fruitfully and appropriately in long-term reconstructive types of therapy. There are, however, exceptions. Sometimes when oedipal and preoedipal issues are mild, confrontation and active exploration in therapy can be accepted and integrated by the patient within the context of brief treatment.

It is often possible and effective to explore some early issues in a less threatening manner. Interpretations designed to foster insight into the patient's harsh and punishing conscience, as well as exploration of its origin, are appropriate in brief treatment. The existence of negative family messages and injunctions can also be explored with comfort in this context. Other suitable material includes the competitiveness, guilt and envy which are the residue of sibling rivalry.

Of special importance in treating success phobic patients is the fostering of insight into the previously *unrecognized competitive feeling*. A significant number of patients symbolically equate sexual functioning with a competition. This may rob them of enjoyment and/or impair their ability to function because of the negative emotional currents which are so often associated with competition in our competitive society, or perhaps in any society which raises its young within a nuclear family, with its inevitable competitions for emotional gratification. The competitive meanings of sex are often beyond conscious awareness because of the guilt and fear that are long-acting consequences of the earliest competitions for and also with the parents and siblings. There is usually great relief, as well as improvement in functioning, when sexual pleasure and romantic success are seen as the sources of happiness to which one is entitled, rather than in terms of competition with and vengeance against ancient and symbolic rivals.

We have been describing success anxiety in the symptomatic partner. But sometimes it is the spouse's unconscious fear of enjoying a successful sexual relationship or intimacy that constitutes the crucial block to the resolution of sexual difficulty. As with other resistances, the fear of success may arise in both the symptomatic patient and his partner, and must be dealt with in both for a successful resolution of the case.

In sum, success anxiety is a useful construct for dealing with some of the more resistant sexually dysfunctional patients. This "mid-level" intervention is often effective within the context of brief psychosexual therapy, especially when success anxiety is moderate to mild. These methods are not capable, however, of dealing with the more severe success problems.

The following two cases of ISD associated with the fear of success illustrate successful outcomes. A similar case which failed to be helped by this approach is also described.

CASE 18　**ROBERT AND ROBERTA**
　　　　　Inhibited Sexual Desire with Avoidance
　　　　　Sexual Success Anxiety
　　　　　Successful Outcome

Robert, age 34, was a successful physician and his wife Roberta, age 32, was just starting a career in social work. The couple had been married for 10 years and had one child. The chief complaint was Roberta's lack of sexual desire and sporadic avoidance of sex.

Etiology

The evaluation revealed that Robert functioned well sexually long as Roberta was receptive. He tended to lose interest in sex and develop erectile difficulties when his wife rejected him.

Roberta reported that she experienced sporadic periods of intense sexual desire and frustration, which disappeared when she had the opportunity to make love to Robert. She lubricated and often felt sexual pleasure, but she had never had an orgasm. In all other spheres both spouses were highly successful.

Treatment

Treatment first focused on Roberta's anorgasmia. When a woman with inhibited sexual desire has not experienced orgasm, it usually makes sense to begin treatment with this because a frequent cause of inhibition in these patients is the repetitive disappointment and anger they feel during love-making which produces a climax only for the husband.

She experienced a great deal of anxiety and resistance to this phase of treatment. Often she avoided self-stimulation. She could not concentrate on sexual fantasies or images, and she began to promote fights with her husband. She wanted to shift the focus of treatment to her marital quarrels.

The patient was confronted with her anxiety about sexual pleasure. She was supported by the therapist and encouraged to enjoy herself. Identification with the therapist was facilitated by her self-revelation and appropriate sharing of experiences. The sessions revealed that she was phobic of pleasure and guilty about her marriage to an attractive and highly successful man. She came to see that she became anxious and "turned herself off" at high levels of sexual pleasure by obsessing about reaching an orgasm. With a combination of encouragement and the repetition of the stimulating exercises, she began to have orgasms after 16 sessions, a relatively lengthy period of treatment for anorgasmia.

After she began to experience orgasm, she quickly integrated this new-found pleasure and felt exhilarated. Her orgasms rapidly became comfortable and increasingly enjoyable. Sex with Robert also became more pleasurable but she did not yet attempt to climax during intercourse on the advice of the therapist.

The next step in treatment was for her to have an orgasm together with Robert. This mobilized considerably more anxiety than the solo pleasuring exercises.

The behavioral aspect of treatment consisted of structuring a gradually increasing level of intimacy. Specifically, first Robert, who was most cooperative and sensitive, masturbated in her presence. This made her feel more comfortable about her own self-stimulation. Then, after making love, he turned his back while she stimulated herself to orgasm. After she had become comfortable with this, which took several weeks, he held her in his arms while she came to climax. Finally, she was able to reach orgasm in response to his stimulating her. Her sexual desire had greatly increased.

During this time, in the sessions, which were conducted alternately— Roberta alone and then the couple together—we worked on her avoidance of romantic and sexual success. She gained insight into the mechanism she had employed to inhibit her sexual desire. She found Robert's sensitivity and support as threatening as her sexual pleasure. Lacking insight into these fears, she had "protected" herself from sexual intimacy with him by focusing on some trivial unpleasant personal habits. Thus she would become enraged if he stirred his tea too vigorously or ate rapidly. These angers effectively precluded her sexual enjoyment.

She came to see that her conscience was harsh and irrational. She gained insight into her tendency to sabotage herself when things became "too good."

The therapist was consistently reassuring and encouraging both of the relationship and of her sexuality. It was speculated that the root of this patient's success anxiety lay both in guilt over competing with mother and also in intense jealousy of her younger brother, who was the overwhelming favorite of her father. She gained some insight into the sibling rivalry issue, but no attempt was made to deal with the oedipal conflict during the 20 weeks of treatment.

Outcome

At the termination of treatment, the couple was enjoying frequent sexual intercourse, which was enjoyable for both. She was orgasic on clitoral stimulation and had a high level of sexual desire. The couple was much closer and the quality of their life together had improved greatly. She had insight into the mechanism which she used to "turn herself off," i.e., focusing on his eating habits, and also, to some extent at least, into her fears of romantic success.

CASE 19   JOHN AND JOAN
Inhibited Sexual Desire with Avoidance
Anger with Sexual Success Anxiety
Successful Outcome

John was a 36-year-old biologist and his wife Joan, age 35, was a successful writer. The couple had been married for six years. They had no children.

Chief Complaint

The couple's chief complaint was her lack of desire for and avoidance of sex. This had commenced shortly after their marriage. During their 18-month courtship, they had had an excellent sexual relationship. Joan was very distressed about her lack of desire and her asexual life. She was also dissatisfied with her husband on many other counts. She was contemplating divorce at the time of treatment. Joan had been in therapy prior to seeking my help. Her former therapist had advised her to leave her husband.

Etiology

The immediate cause of the problem was Joan's anger at her husband. This led to the active suppression of her sexual feeling. Whenever they were alone together she would dwell on something unpleasant about him and keep herself in a perpetual state of anger. But her conflict about and avoidance of romantic and sexual success were the underlying significant etiological factors.

It turned out that Joan's anger and disappointment in her marriage were largely self-induced and not realistic. In fact, while he had some problems, John was an attractive and sexually adequate man. She, however, perceived him as ugly, rejecting and hostile. She was full of complaints about him and presented him to her former therapist in such a negative light that he felt that to stay married to John represented an expression of masochism.

When Joan was with John she focused only on his negative attributes and ignored his attractive ones. She was confronted with this at one point in treatment when she told of having admired the appearance and manner of a literary agent—only to be startled by the realization that he bore a striking resemblance to John.

Treatment

Treatment began with gentle nonpressuring caresses. Joan began to enjoy this but then ruined her pleasure by becoming extremely angry at John. During the sessions, she continuously "set him up" by causing him to behave in an anxiety-ridden, insensitive manner which he was likely to do when she rejected him. Then she provoked him further by blaming him for her rejections of him. The unconscious aim of this behavior was to convince the therapist that John was indeed an unsuitable husband for her. In fact, this represented an externalization of her inner conflict about sexual happiness.

She was confronted with her self-destructive behavior. This increased her tenderness for John, but she became depressed. We then focused on her inner conflicts about romantic pleasure and success. She came to see the striking difference in her conflict-free functioning in the career area. She was a highly creative and successful writer and experienced no difficulty in this area. On the other hand, she had a history of self-sabotage in the area of sex and romance. She had never in her life allowed herself to have a successful sexual relationship.

Insight into this dynamic was not sufficient to release her desire or cure her depression. We then began to explore the genesis of her difficulties, which seemed to have their roots in her relationship with her mother. The mother was a borderline schizophrenic, whose relationships with others were marred by intense envy and ambivalence. Unfortunately, the patient reminded her mother of a younger, more beautiful sister who was the family favorite. The patient's mother still harbored intense unabated hatred towards this sister. The patient was encouraged by her mother to succeed as a writer but was given highly negative messages about sex and men.

The patient was extremely suspicious of me, especially when during the course of treatment I was encouraging about her marriage and her sexual pleasure. This represented a transferential distortion—she projected her mother's ambivalence to me.

After a few months of treatment, Joan began to see John in a much more favorable light. She began to regard him as the attractive and suitable husband which he was in reality and was able to accept this. Her depression lifted and she began to feel desire and erotic pleasure again. Concomitantly, the couple's sexual life together improved.

She then entered long-term therapy in order to resolve her problems still further.

CASE 20   **GEORGE AND GEORGIA**
Inhibited Sexual Desire with Avoidance
Sexual Success Anxiety
Failure

George, age 52, held a high executive position in a large industrial company and Georgia, age 48, worked for a drug detoxification agency in an inner-city slum. They had three children aged 15, 19, and 21.

Chief Complaint

The chief complaint was Georgia's avoidance of sex and her lack of attraction for George and George's erectile dysfunction. The couple had had no sexual contact at all for four years.

History

During the first part of their marriage they had intercourse two or three times a week. George functioned well and enjoyed sex. Georgia at times felt some arousal but never reached orgasm. The couple did not discuss their sexual interaction. Georgia did not tell George that she found sex unsatisfactory, and he never suspected this.

Five years ago Georgia began to work at the agency, which she greatly enjoyed. At the same time she began to complain about George's poor lovemaking. She threatened to leave him. He became depressed and impotent. He loved her very much and did not wish to lose her.

The couple sought help at an excellent sex therapy program where they failed to respond to treatment.

Etiology

The immediate cause of the couple's problem was the wife's anger at her husband. She focused only on his shortcomings and kept herself at a constant level of anger, which precluded any feelings of tenderness or desire. Her anger also prevented her from cooperating in sexual therapy for his impotence. His erectile difficulty was originally a reaction to her anger and lack of responsiveness; by this time he had also developed considerable performance anxiety.

On a deeper level, Georgia had a typical pattern of success anxiety. She dropped out of college in her senior year after having been elected to Phi Beta Kappa. She entered into a conventional marriage with a successful man, whom she resented. When she finally was able to accept some creative and satisfying work again, she promptly created problems in her marriage. She blamed her husband for her lack of responsiveness but refused to have any physical contact with him unless he approached her with a full erection.

Not surprisingly, this happened very infrequently. She set him up to fail, and he permitted this. She had no insight into her own sexual anxiety and blamed their sexual problems entirely on his erectile failure.

Treatment

Good rapport was attained with both spouses rapidly and easily. She was confronted with her resistance to sexual pleasure. She admitted this half-heartedly, but stated that if he would learn to become a better lover she would respond. However, she also maintained that she did not have the patience to work with him and that he should visit a surrogate. She was confronted with the irrational nature of her construction, but she gained only limited insight.

He was eager and willing to do anything to improve the situation and did, in fact, find himself a skillful and willing partner with whom he could soon function.

Not surprisingly, she found other rationalizations for avoiding sex with him. The aim of treatment was focused on fostering insight into her anger; into her underlying fear of success; into her tradeoff of career for marriage; into her sabotaging of her sexual and romantic fulfillment.

Outcome

She never attained insight. She ended treatment and the couple continue to live together in an asexual manner.

When unconscious fears of romantic success are an issue, the goals in psychosexual therapy are quite ambitious. The patient is to gain insight into his unconscious fear of sexual success, to integrate this material and to be able to accept and be comfortable with new and higher levels of pleasure and love within the context of brief therapy, i.e., within 15 to 30 sessions. This cannot occur on the basis of behavior modification alone. The patient must modify his previous negative attitudes about himself. He must learn to accept himself and his desires; he must feel that he has a right to have pleasure and learn to view his anxieties and conflicts with compassion. It is surprising how often these complex goals can be successfully implemented in moderately brief treatment.

The therapist's active intervention in promoting the couple's pleasure and success is probably one of the keys to successful treatment. In a sense, he must transmit positive messages, which neutralize—which are an antidote for the negative ones that govern the patient's self-destructive behavior. He must facilitate the introjection of a mature and gentle conscience to replace the patient's primitive and punitive one. If the patient's family fostered sexual guilt and fear, the therapist encourages sexual pleasure and enjoyment. If the patient's superego moves him to "lose," the therapist "roots" for him to be a "winner."

These attitudes are expressed verbally, as well as nonverbally. The therapist's obvious pleasure when the couple improves, becomes more open or has fun is a powerful message. In addition, active interpretations are made, with the attempt to dissociate sexual pleasure from the competitive symbolism with which it has become contaminated in the fantasies of many of these patients.

The patient and his partner are encouraged to take an active role in working to insure their own success and pleasure in sex and apart from sex. They are encouraged to use their ingenuity and energy to actively work towards improving the quality of their lives.

The active confrontations with self-destructive behavior and attitudes and the rapid introjection of new and more constructive value systems which are characteristic of this treatment mode are effective only if there is a strong and trusting therapeutic relationship. This is facilitated by the therapist's sensitive support and his active siding with the pleasure- and success-seeking aspects of the patient and his spouse.

Clinical experience with treating patients and also of supervising and training others suggests that the therapist's own insights into and freedom from conflict about success and pleasure, as well as his ability to be truly giving and to take genuine pleasure from his patient's success, are important determinants of the effectiveness of these methods.

11

THE FEAR OF INTIMACY

INTIMACY DESCRIBES a special quality of emotional closeness between two people. It is an affectionate bond, the strands of which are composed of mutual caring, responsibility, trust, open communication of feelings and sensations, as well as the non-defended interchange of information about significant emotional events.

The prototype of intimacy is the maternal-infant bond, wherein the caring mother is constantly alert and responsive to the infant's feeling tone, to the fluctuations of the emotional currents of her baby.

Intimacy is an important ingredient in the quality of love and of life. A high degree of intimacy between two lovers or spouses contributes to the happiness and emotional stability of both. All activities are more enjoyable and life is richer and more colorful when shared with an intimate partner.

Sexual experiences are more pleasurable if your partner knows you intimately, when he or she is completely open and vulnerable, when you can trust him/her not to reject, not to disappoint, to care about your feelings and to take pleasure in your pleasure. Sex becomes less risky, the reflexes are more likely to work and abandonment is easier if you can be yourself and can discard your defenses in the bedroom.

An intimate relationship acts as a buffer, providing shelter from the pressures and tensions of daily life. We are social animals and without intimate relationships we tend to get lonely and become depressed. The availability of intimate relationships is an important determinant of how well we master life's crises.

The fear of intimacy is highly prevalent in our society and may produce problems that extend beyond sexual dysfunctions. We tend to spectator rather to participate together, watch TV, play cards and video games rather than engage in intimate conversation. It sometimes seems that people are more afraid of intimacy than they are of sex. They find it easier to masturbate than to make love, to buy impersonal sex than to share love with a lover, to blot out the partner with drugs than to experience him/her fully.

Persons who are made guilty or anxious by closeness or intimacy behave like the success-avoiding personality, i.e., as if they are governed by an invisible "comfort zone," one involving the parameter of emotional closeness. They will show characteristic fluctuations in emotional distance. If a single person has an intimacy problem he will get to a certain point of closeness with a new partner and then he will lose interest. When he first meets her, she is wonderful, but when the relationship reaches a certain point of closeness, he will focus on her shortcomings and become disenchanted or he will act in such a way as to provoke her to end the relationship. Such persons have an endless series of relationships which always end at a similar point of closeness.

Even if intimacy fears do not lead to termination of relationships, they are extremely destructive. The spouse who longs for intimacy is always striving for closeness. He tries to bring up emotional issues, share feelings, spend time together. The one who is afraid of intimacy is always ducking. She is on the telephone; she does the housework when he is at home; she will only talk about trivia; she will cook his dinner but she is unresponsive to his feelings. One always tries; the other resists. One feels rejected, puzzled—What am I doing wrong? He finally gives up, becomes angry, becomes depressed, or has an affair. The other feels invaded, pressed, confused—What does he want? He is a bottomless pit. She withdraws further and becomes angry.

Sometimes both partners in a relationship are afflicted with intimacy conflicts. Such couples long for closeness with each other, but when they achieve a certain point of contact they become anxious. Then one or the other will behave in such a manner as to create distance. When distance reaches a certain point, anxiety and longing for closeness will be evoked in the couple. They miss each other and will forgive each other and move closer to each other again—but not too close. Then the see-saw will move in the other direction.

Both the degree and the duration of closeness that can be tolerated vary, although the pattern is highly consistent for a specific couple. It is possible to predict at what level of intimacy and after what duration of closeness and warmth the couple will again engage in distancing behavior. The precise mechanisms of distance behavior are highly individual and specific. Thus, when things get too close, one person will characteristically provoke a fight; the next will become absorbed in golf, or business, or politics; another will become ill or gain weight or drink; and still another will act destructively with money or focus on a business crisis, or even have an extramarital affair. Typically, neither spouse is aware of this dynamic. Partners often blame each other for their turbulent life together.

A couple's sexuality often suffers in the stormy wake of intimacy problems. If these are only mild, they can be reduced and circumvented in treatment by promoting physical intimacies with the pleasuring exercises and by focusing on the erotic aspects of their relationship. Often, however, insight into and resolution of intimacy problems, at least to some degree, are necessary before a couple can begin to enjoy a sexual relationship.

GENESIS

The fear of intimacy, like the fear of sexual success, falls midway on the continuum of causal intensity or depth. Intimacy fears are usually less accessible to conscious awareness than performance anxieties. Persons fearing intimacy typically protest that they are lonely and consciously strive for closeness. Intimacy problems are acquired early in childhood, earlier than concerns about sexual performance. According to psychoanalytic theory, conflicts about intimacy are derivative of preoedipal and oedipal problems. More specifically, an intimate romantic attachment to a stranger may be threatening because it symbolically means separating from mother. In other cases, intimacy in adult life is unconsciously equated with the childhood wish for intimacy with the oedipal object, and is therefore avoided.

Another point of view holds that intimacy problems are intrinsic products of a developmental deficit. Accordingly, people develop fears of intimacy in adult life because of negative and disappointing experiences with intimate relationships in early childhood. They never develop what Erikson has called "basic trust" towards their parents, their first intimates, during their critical childhood period and thus lack a basic ingredient that is required for the capacity to trust and become intimate in later life.

TREATMENT

Conflicts about intimacy are handled in psychosexual therapy like other success fears. When resistances and obstacles are evoked in the course of sex therapy by underlying intimacy fears, interpretations on this level are often effective. This may be done in the context of brief therapy without necessarily delving into the earlier derivatives of this problem.

CASE 21   **PETER AND PEGGY**
        Inhibited Sexual Desire with Avoidance
        Intimacy Problems in Both Partners
        Successful Outcome

The couple consisted of a 40-year-old lawyer and his 38-year-old wife, an advertising executive. They had one child, a nine-year-old girl.

Chief Complaint

The couple had not had sex together for three years. Both contributed to the celibacy of the marriage. The wife usually had no desire for sex, but on those rare occasions when she did, he was impotent.

History

The couple married 16 years ago. Initially they met each other's needs exquisitely. She worked to support him through law school and he was always supportive of her through her many emotional crises. Nevertheless, their relationship was marked by bickering and fighting. After his graduation from law school and the birth of their child, their hostilities worsened and they separated for five years. During this time they both had numerous sexual relationships in which they functioned fairly well.

During the period of separation they missed each other very much. They reconciled four years ago. Since then their economic circumstances improved dramatically, both being extremely gifted and highly successful in their careers. They realized that they really loved each other but their life together was still marked by bitter and recurrent crises.

Both had been in individual as well as couples therapy for the last four years in an attempt to resolve their difficulties. The therapeutic experiences had been quite valuable in terms of their individual growth and had also improved their relationship; however, they and their therapist agreed that they had gone as far as they could and would need special help for their sexual problems.

Etiology

The immediate cause of the sexual problem on her part was an instant and involuntary suppression of sexual feeling. She would conjure up memories of his untrustworthiness and of her disappointments and proceed to get herself into a rage on those few occasions when the couple managed to create some privacy and sexual opportunities for themselves.

He, on the other hand, at those rare times when she was receptive, would plague himself with anxiety-laden thoughts: "I will disappoint her. She will complain about my love-making, etc." The anticipation of rejection effectively ruined any chance of erections.

These immediate reactions were employed in the service of deeper fears of romantic success and intimacy. Neither was anxious or conflicted about erotic pleasure in non-intimate situations. With distant or unsuitable partners both functioned well and could enjoy sexual pleasure. It was only when their shared sexual pleasure brought them into intimate emotional contact, "too close for comfort," that the defenses against sexuality were evoked.

The remote causes of this couple's sexual and marital problems seemed to involve unconscious fears of intimacy and romantic success in both partners. Originally, both spouses had suffered from success fears in work, as well as in the romantic spheres of experience. Both had been self-destructive to their careers. After graduating from law school, Peter managed to involve himself in a partnership with an unscrupulous older attorney and worked for coolie wages. At the same time, he spent excessive amounts of money and accumulated considerable debts, which included one to the government, to which he owed three years of back taxes. On her part, Peggy created a scandal just as she was advancing brilliantly in her first agency job. She had an affair with an important and married client. In addition, she blatantly neglected her work. Not surprisingly, she was fired and it took years of effort to rebuild her blemished career.

Both resolved their work-related success anxiety in individual therapy: She changed to a different agency where she rapidly rose to the position of vice-president; he extracted himself from the partnership and started his own law firm, developing a practice which was both lucrative and fascinating. At the time of treatment they were on a firm financial basis consistent with their talents and education. However, their fear of intimacy and success was still operative and they sabotaged the quality of their lives with their incessant quarrels.

The husband's success and intimacy fears had their roots in a pathological relationship with his mother. Peter was raised by a widowed mother who moved in and out of psychosis during his formative years. She was highly ambivalent and whenever he had pleasure or fun she would punish him sadistically. Not surprisingly, he developed a distrust for women and was afraid to be close to Peggy. He anticipated rejection and aggression if he should allow himself to trust her or to expose his vulnerability.

The roots of Peggy's success and intimacy problem were related to her defenses against her sadistic and controlling father, towards whom she was highly ambivalent.

Neither had insight into their fear of closeness. In fact, their experience was the opposite: They both yearned for intimacy and sexual pleasure with each other.

Treatment

Initially, pleasuring and nondemanding genital stimulation tasks were assigned. These met with success but this lasted for only a brief period of time. With every improvement one or the other became resistant and created obstacles. He was "too busy" with cases to spend the necessary two or three leisurely evenings a week devoted to closeness and sexual pleasure. When they managed to arrange a weekend away, she became preoccupied to the point of obsession with her job. On one occasion, when the couple enjoyed some peace and pleasure, she became obsessed about an insult from a casual acquaintance. Her agitated emotional state naturally precluded sex for that weekend. Their resistances persisted despite repetition of the pleasuring exercises and the therapist's encouragement.

At this point they were confronted for the first time with existence of an intimacy and pleasure problem. The behavioral aspects of therapy, i.e., the homework assignments, were interrupted while they worked to gain insight. Therapy sessions were conducted both with the couple together and with each individually.

After nine months, she seemed to have resolved her fear of sexual success and intimacy to the point where she began to feel a good deal of sexual desire again. Interpretations had been aimed at fostering her insight about her intimacy and success fears, but did not deal with the deeper genesis or those conflicts. Dreams of fantasies which contained material which might be considered to reflect unresolved issues about her relationship with her father were interpreted on the level of self-destructiveness but not on an oedipal level. For example, Peggy had a masturbatory fantasy that she was having intercourse with someone on the kitchen table and her father walked in and was very upset. She was very much ashamed of this fantasy and resistant to disclosing it. The interpretation of this material was aimed at fostering insight into her self-destructive behavior. She was confronted with her tendency to summon up unpleasant, punishing thoughts at the very moment that she experienced pleasure.

Some work, but only as much as was necessary to foster the patient's insight into and resolution of her success anxiety, was done on her relationship with her mother. The therapist played a "good mother" role and supported her in her efforts to enjoy her life. Peggy was quite receptive to the concept of success anxiety and gained insight into her tendency to self-sabotage her pleasure. She also came to recognize the part she played in the repetitive ebb and flow of closeness in the marital relationship. The concept of a comfort zone of intimacy was particularly useful in this case. It mobilized little resistance. She became aware of her anxiety and of her acting-out tendencies in this respect.

It took Peter somewhat longer, but eventually he also gained insight into his problem with intimacy and pleasure. Whenever the couple came closer and had a good time, he would obsess about her spending too much money or about her deceiving him about something. Gradually he became capable of tolerating increasing periods and amounts of intimacy and closeness with Peggy.

Peter needed more understanding of the deeper genesis of his problem than did Peggy before he could progress. He had to understand his mother's psychotic ambivalence, and his frustrating yearning for her love, and his childhood depression, before he could integrate the material about intimacy.

When the couple had gained enough insight so that their relationship became more tranquil and intimate and when they learned to monitor their anxiety about closeness and to control their sabotaging, the behavioral aspect of sexual therapy was resumed. Again, they engaged in mutual pleasuring and stimulation. The intimacy of these exercises evoked more anxiety than the erotic aspects. For this reason the exercises were modified. Initially they achieved orgasm by masturbation in each other's presence. This enabled them to keep a certain distance but provided the opportunity to gradually move close. After they could do this comfortably, the shared component of the erotic experiences was gradually increased. Some mild resistances were evoked as the couple became more intimate and close in the sexual situation. These were handled by confrontations together with support in the sessions.

Outcome

This case ended successfully. The couple now have sex together with reasonable frequency. When anxiety about closeness arises, as it still does occasionally, they have the insight and the psychic tools to deal with this in a constructive manner.

This case was a failure in conventional, time-limited sex therapy. By dealing with underlying issues on a "mid-level"—on the level of success and intimacy anxiety—and by allowing them time to integrate these insights, the case was brought to a successful conclusion. In this case experiential and psychotherapeutic methods were used in a flexible way. First behavioral tasks were used to ferret out resistances. Then the emphasis was shifted to insight therapy, and finally, when the blocks were sufficiently resolved, the structured experiences were employed again—this time for their intrinsic therapeutic value. This method of shifting modalities is often an effective strategy in such cases. However, this lengthier and more psychodynamically oriented type of intervention is by no means always successful. In the following case one of the couple had a severe intimacy problem which was not resolved in treatment.

CASE 22   NORMAN AND NORMA
Inhibited Sexual Desire with Avoidance
Wife's Intimacy Problem
Failure

The husband was a 42-year-old postal worker; his wife was a dietician, age 35. They had been married for five years and had no children because the wife felt she did not want to bring children into this world which she saw as full of pain and danger.

Chief Complaint

The chief complaint was absence of sex. The couple had had no sex for the past three years due to the wife's sexual avoidance and lack of desire. The consultation was initiated by the husband who was frustrated and agitated by the lack of sex in the marriage.

History

In their courtship of six months the couple had good sex and Norma seemed to be responsive at that time. However, when the couple returned from their honeymoon, things changed dramatically. Norma refused to have sex, claiming she had no desire, found sexual contact repulsive, and accused him of being a poor and inconsiderate lover. He pressured her for sex, threatening to dissolve their marriage unless they could develop a normal sex life. Occasionally she acquiesced during the first two years of their marriage. She was grudging in this and clearly let him know that she found him repulsive. He "gave up," and unhappily endured an asexual relationship for the last three years.

She had become increasingly withdrawn from him apart from sex. She engaged in compulsive housework and gardening which left little room for intimacy and time together. He had adapted by becoming absorbed in his old hobby—building wooden objects in his basement workshop. He also played cards for many hours with a group of men friends.

Both came from strict Catholic homes. Norman's family was warm and expressive. Norma's father was also a warm outgoing man; however, her mother was a rather withdrawn, compulsively neat and overly polite person. The wife's family history revealed schizophrenia. Her mother's only sister, Norma's maternal aunt, had been hospitalized several times with a diagnosis of paranoid schizophrenia and one of her maternal cousins was also schizophrenic.

Etiology

The immediate cause of this couple's problem was Norma's avoidance of sexual contact. This was aggravated by Norman's pressuring. It appeared that Norma was not afraid of sexual feelings or of penetration because she had functioned well briefly with Norman before their marriage. She also masturbated to orgasm with no difficulty. Sexual contact appeared to evoke her anxieties because of the feelings of intimacy and the vulnerability this evoked. In other words, in an impersonal situation, Norma did not seem to experience anxiety. It may be inferred that Norma was afraid of intimacy and closeness, especially in a family situation where she played the mother role. Norma was extremely uncommunicative in the sessions, and the deeper roots of this problem were not clarified.

Treatment

The sensate focus exercises evoked a negative response. She found "excuses" not to do these exercises for three weeks. Norman was very hurt about this. The possibility that pleasuring was too anxiety-provoking for her was explored in the therapy sessions. He gained some insight that her avoidance did not constitute a personal rejection, but was a reflection of her inner problems. The pleasuring prescription was repeated but with a lower level of intensity. Specifically, once a week, at her initiation, and for five minutes only, the couple was instructed to caress each other. After several repetitions she was able to do this. Slowly, the amount and duration of physical contact increased.

Apart from sex she literally avoided contact with him whenever she could: She watched TV during their dinner, went to bed hours after he was asleep, and spent the weekends in compulsive house and garden activities; she never spoke to him. Therefore, communication tasks were also suggested. The couple was instructed to talk together and share the events of the day during one half hour before dinner. She found this exceedingly difficult. Some progress was made, but it was slow and any gain was so small and temporary that the quality of this couple's relationship was not altered. During one of the sessions she admitted that the pleasuring and communication assignment did increase her desire for sex. But she did not tell Norman about this and she relieved her frustration by masturbating.

An attempt was made to try to resolve her intense and tenacious avoidance of intimacy by means of psychotherapy. She refused to come to the sessions alone, claiming it was a joint problem. I attempted to work with her within the couples therapy framework. The positives in the relationship were emphasized, and the destructive effects of her problem on this relationship, which gave her many positive things, were also discussed. He became more accepting of the situation as he realized that her behavior was not really a rejection of him, and that he could not do anything to change it. It was recognized by both that her detachment was the product of massive anxiety about commitment and intimacy which would probably be evoked in any permanent relationship.

Outcome

She was not able to gain any insight into the sources of her intimacy problem. Her behavior has not changed. He has accepted this because on some level he, too, has a pleasure problem. The couple has a distant asexual relationship which does, however, have secure and peaceful components.

In this case, the wife gained no insight and the intimacy problem did not improve. However, the husband, because of his own problems, accommodated this. Of course, a partner does not always accept an asexual or non-intimate relationship and may want to dissolve the marriage when it becomes clear that the situation will probably not change. In a similar case, the husband was asexual and emotionally detached to the point of using his home as a hotel. He never sought the company of others and came home on all evenings and weekends only to eat, sleep and change his clothes. He did not communicate, did not share his feelings, and did not seem interested in his wife's feelings. The couple never went out or took trips or shared any pleasurable activity. He did not discuss any personal matter. He gained no insight in the course of treatment; in fact, he did not admit that anything was wrong or odd about the marriage. Confrontations to this effect were simply not received.

During the course of therapy, the wife faced the reality of the lack of intimacy and sexuality in her marriage. First she became angry. Then she decided that she did not want to accept this kind of emotional deprivation and she eventually took steps to dissolve the marriage.

12

TERMINATION

IN TIME-LIMITED SEX THERAPY, termination of treatment occurs after a predetermined period of time. Thus, in the Masters and Johnson model programs, the couple is seen daily for two weeks, after which time treatment ends, regardless of outcome. Presumably, this method is based on the rationale that, if the couple's problem is amenable to sex therapy, they will have responded after 14 sessions; if they have not, extending the treatment will not help. When a more individual and flexible treatment format is employed, such as the one described here, termination becomes a matter for clinical judgment. Clinicians vary somewhat in the criteria they employ to decide when treatment should be ended. So far no one has devised an ideal set of criteria. Different points of view have their advantages and disadvantages. My own views are no exception.

Different considerations govern termination when treatment is successful and when patients fail to respond to sexual therapy.

TERMINATION: SUCCESSFUL OUTCOME

A case is closed when:

1) The symptom has been cured; 2) the immediate causes of the symptom have been modified and the patient and/or couple has attained insight into these immediate causes; 3) the patient and the

couple have integrated the new sexual behavior. If these criteria are met, a reasonably good probability exists that the cure will be stable.

Cure of the Symptom

Expectations regarding symptom cure will vary with the syndrome, and with the patient's own goals and capacities.

Premature ejaculators can expect normal voluntary control over ejaculation in the majority of cases. However, at the end of treatment, some men still need to "slow," i.e., decrease the velocity and force of their thrusting when they become highly aroused. In such cases therapy may be interrupted, while the patient and/or couple work to improve the man's control on their own, following the principles they have learned during therapy. They are then seen again in four to six weeks to reevaluate their status. In most cases ejaculatory control is by this time satisfactory. If control remains only fair or the symptom has relapsed, the couple may need more therapy sessions before the case can be successfully terminated. Premature ejaculation has such an excellent prognosis that it is worthwhile to persist in treatment beyond the standard 14 sessions if necessary; termination without cure is the exception when this attitude is adopted.

With *retarded ejaculation,* one can expect the patient to learn to ejaculate inside the vagina, but the prognosis is not as favorable as for premature ejaculation. Even in successful cases it is not unusual for patients to continue to experience some orgastic delay or some unevenness in intravaginal ejaculation at the termination of therapy. Only in mild cases is the goal of completely uninhibited ejaculation usually reached with brief therapy.

The termination point for *female orgasm inhibition* varies with the specific goal. The great majority of anorgasmic women can expect to learn to achieve orgasm by self-stimulation. Therefore, with rare exceptions, treatment is not terminated until this goal is achieved. Most women can then proceed to orgasm on clitoral stimulation in the presence of a partner. But this usually requires an additional period of treatment, the length of which is contingent on the severity of the woman's partner-related anxiety, on the partner's characteristics and on the quality of their relationship. Coital orgasm has a different prognosis. This pattern of sexual release is achieved by a much lower percentage of women. For coital anorgasmia treatment is continued until the obstacles to comfortable intercourse seem to have been resolved, or it becomes apparent that the woman cannot change her response pattern even though she experiences no manifest anxiety about penetration and can have orgasms on clitoral stimulation.

Treatment is terminated as a success in female anorgasmia when the patient has reached that level of orgasmic response that meets her own objectives or the objectives of the couple. Thus, I would call a case successful if a woman learns to have and enjoy orgasm, and learns to have an orgasm comfortably together with her partner, even if she fails to learn to have orgasm on intercourse without clitoral assistance, provided this is satisfying to the couple.

Excitement phase disorder of the male is deemed cured when the man can reliably have an erection which is maintained to the point of intravaginal ejaculation. This outcome can be expected for the majority of patients, but the extent of erectile security that is achieved will vary with individual patients. In some very favorable cases, potency is restored to pre-impotency levels or to complete erectile security. In such cases there is no question about outcome. Anxiety simply disappears.

In less favorable cases, there is a residual of sexual anxiety. However, in the course of treatment the man learns to compensate for this and manages his delicate erectile response successfully. In other words, he attains insight into his vulnerability in this area and learns to avoid anxiety-provoking circumstances while he is making love. He learns to use fantasy to diminish his anxieties or to employ more vigorous penile stimulation or self-stimulation to insure an erection if some anxiety emerges during love-making. He may also learn to help himself by communicating his emotional state to his partner. Termination is appropriate in such cases when it appears that the patient's sexually related anxiety will not be materially further reduced in brief treatment. A follow-up visit for reevaluation and possible further treatment in six months to one year is a sensible procedure.

Termination of treatment for *female excitement phase disorders* follows similar principles. The case is usually closed when the patient is satisfied that she experiences increased erotic feelings and pleasure and lubricates sufficiently for comfortable intercourse. Success is somewhat more subjective in this syndrome and depends more on her and her partner's judgments than on objective criteria.

The goals for the treatment of the *desire phase disorders* are the most flexible and subjective. In exceptionally favorable cases desire returns or emerges with full passion. But this is not a realistic goal for brief therapy in most cases. In the most usual course of treatment there is some improvement. The patient feels erotic desire some of the time and can allow himself to enjoy sex on a reasonably frequent basis. But a full return of desire is exceptional.

Treatment is ended when there is sufficient improvement to satisfy the patient, and she has insight into what she does to turn herself off and is no longer moved to do this, and when the underlying sexual anxiety and anger at the partner have been resolved as much as they can be in brief treatment. In my experience, follow-up of ISD cases which have been terminated according to these criteria six months to one year later reveals that for some desire has continued to improve in quality and frequency after termination of therapy. Such an outcome confirms the clinical judgment which led to termination. In other cases, however, desire has diminished again or has not improved further, indicating that therapy was not complete at the time of termination, and that criteria for termination of ISD need to be improved.

Vaginismus. The goal of the brief treatment of vaginismus is the comfortable opening to penile penetration of the vaginal introitus. This goal should be successfully accomplished in all cases which are not associated with physical problems. Apart from this the treatment objectives vary with different couples. Some want and can achieve a complete sexual relationship. But I have treated some who merely want to be able to consummate their marriage and whose primary goal is to have children. They are not interested in improving their sexual response in other respects; it is my feeling that treatment should end when the couple's—not the doctor's—objectives have been met.

When the vaginal muscles spasms are mild enough to allow penetration but severe enough to produce dyspareunia, the goal of painless intercourse can be expected in all psychogenic cases.

Ejaculatory pain due to genital muscle spasm. The preliminary impression based on the small number of patients I have treated is that the prognosis of this syndrome is excellent. Pain will disappear when treatment is directed at the immediate cause of the symptom, the involuntary and painful muscle spasm.

Sexual phobias and sexual avoidances have an excellent prognosis and treatment should in most cases be continued until the patient is comfortable with his sexual feelings and all reasonable erotic activities. However, individual patients vary considerably with respect to the length of treatment that is required to relieve the phobic symptoms, and to reduce the anticipatory anxiety to the point where sexual pleasure is no longer avoided.

Insight

Treatment should not end as soon as the symptom is cured or improved. There would be far too many relapses if the therapist did not insure that the patient and his partner gained some insight. At a minimum, the patient should recognize the immediate antecedents of the symptom, and these should be modified before the couple is discharged. The patient should understand that performance anxiety impairs his erections; treatment is not ended before the anxiety has abated or the patient and his partner have learned to manage it.

A premature patient should not be discharged until he understands the importance of focusing on his premonitory orgastic sensations, and he has learned to concentrate comfortably on his pleasure. And treatment is continued until the woman clearly understands that she is "turning herself off" and learns to identify and control the anxiety sensations which occur when she is in a sexual situation.

The process of insight and resolution of immediate causes may require at least partial resolution of the remoter causes. The extent to which such deeper insight and conflict resolution are necessary is extremely variable and a matter of clinical judgment.

Integration

Finally, the patient and the couple must be given the opportunity to integrate their new insights, their new levels of sexual enjoyment and their capacity for deepened intimacy. These kinds of experiences had been previously avoided because they were threatening. It takes time, encouragement and a certain degree of self-love to accept the fact that "I am an adequate sexual being," or to integrate the perception, "We have a great sexual relationship. I am happy," when the opposite has been true for such a long period of time.

The therapist can actively facilitate and accelerate the integration of the new pleasurable sexual and romantic behavior. When in the course of treatment he supports pleasure, encourages free sexual expression, and validates the patient's right to have enjoyment and experience love, he transmits a new value system which is necessary to insure a stable cure. In a sense a "superego transplant" occurs. The aim of therapy is to supplant the harsh antipleasure injunctions of childhood, to replace the primitive, punitive former conscience with a new set of values that contain within them permission to have pleasure. To the extent that the patient can introject the therapist's more rational, more permissive and more loving ethical or "superego" system, integration of the new forms will occur, and this will insure against the kind of relapse that is produced by the guilt and anxiety born of old taboos about success in love and sex.

TERMINATION: TREATMENT FAILURES

When a sexual symptom fails to respond to sexual therapy, the judgment of when to stop is even more individual and subjective than it is when the symptom is cured. Clinicians vary with respect to their tenacity in working with the sexual symptom. I tend to be on the tenacious end of the spectrum. I will try the traditional tactics and strategies; if these do not work, I will attempt to devise new ones that seem to fit the particular needs of the patient. Each difficult case is a new challenge which presents the opportunity to innovate, to try to create new methods and strategies in the course of attempting to understand, resolve or bypass a particularly difficult resistance.

But there comes a time when it becomes apparent to even the most persistent therapist, as well as to the patient and the spouse, that the problem is not amenable to rapid resolution, at least not by these techniques and by this therapist. At that point the course of treatment is reviewed and reevaluated and a decision is made, together with the couple, either to accept the failure and terminate therapy or to shift to a different therapist or to a different modality of treatment.

COUNTERTRANSFERENCE FACTORS IN TERMINATION

Termination tends to evoke countertransference ractions or unconscious motivational conflicts in some therapists. These lead to errors in two directions: premature termination and retarded termination.

When a patient or a couple shows rapid improvement and feels very positively towards the therapist, some therapists tend to become anxious. Perhaps they are afraid to disappoint the patients. Perhaps they do not want to give up their omnipotent position of having produced a rapid, miraculous cure. Perhaps some suffer from success anxiety; perhaps the anxiety represents a reaction formation against competitive feelings towards colleagues. Whatever the unconscious motivation, there is a tendency to reduce one's discomfort by terminating such rapidly successful cases prematurely, that is, before there has been a significant degree of insight into the antecedents which had produced the symptom or enough time for the patients to have integrated these changes.

The other kind of error is perhaps a reaction formation against the tendency to "quit while you are ahead." It may be born out of the therapist's insecurities or his disbelief that rapid treatment can be effective. Patients are sometimes kept in therapy long after reasonable treatment objectives have been met.

The best instrument thus far devised to help us to steer a safe therapeutic course between the Scylla of premature termination and the Charybdis of retarded termination is insight on the part of the therapist into the fact that we are not "treatment machines." We are involved in the treatment process in highly personal ways, and complex sensations and feelings are evoked in us, both when our patients get well rapidly and almost miraculously and also, and very differently of course, when even our best efforts fail to help them.

APPENDIX

TABLE 1: *Effects of Drugs on the Sexual Response*[1]

Drug	Medical Indications	Possible Mechanism of Action	Phase of Sexual Response Affected		
			Desire	*Excitement*	*Orgasm*
I. DRUGS WHICH ACT ON THE BRAIN (i.e., CNS)					
A. *Sedative-Hypnotics* Alcohol and non-toxic doses of: barbiturates and other similar agents (e.g., ethchlorvynol, chloral hydrate, and methaqualone)	Insomnia and anxiety states	General CNS depression. Effects are dose-related. In general, the higher the dose the more interference with sexual performance. All of these drugs affect the central state. Set and setting are very important. Expectation can override or alter pharmacologic effect. Most of these drugs potentiate one another. Alcohol with CNS depressants leads to greater CNS depression. In low doses, desire may be increased by reducing inhibition (anecdotal reports of methaqualone acting as an aphrodisiac have been described). In higher doses all phases of sexual response are inhibited. Chronic alcoholism may result in permanent neurologic damage and consequent impaired genital functioning.	Increased(?) in low doses in presence of inhibition. Expectation may play a major role on this parameter. Decreased in high doses.	With low doses excitement may be prolonged due to decreased sensitivity or to intimacy and shared feelings. Impotence with high chronic intake of alcohol and barbiturates.	Delayed in high doses.
B. *Anti-anxiety Drugs* Diazepines; Valium; Librium; Tranxene; Meprobamate	Anxiety states; muscle tension; convulsive states	Action on limbic system, and on interuncial neurons in the spinal cord.	May enhance desire slightly if inhibited or avoided due to anxiety. Diminished in high doses.	None reported	No effect in usual doses. In very high doses orgasm may be delayed.

[1] The table on Effects of Drugs on the Sexual Response was prepared in collaboration with David Benjamin, Ph.D.

TABLE 1 (*continued*)

Drug	Medical Indications	Possible Mechanism of Action	Phase of Sexual Response Affected		
			Desire	Excitement	Orgasm
C. *Narcotics* Morphine, codeine paragoric, d-propoxyphene and methadone	Analgesia (pain relief); control of: diarrhea, coughing, and narcotic withdrawal (methadone)	General depression of CNS and possible direct depression of sex centers; alteration of normal balance of biogenic amines in CNS.	Absent in high doses.	Impotence in high doses.	Inhibited by high doses.
D. *Antipsychotic agents*	Psychosis	Probably have no direct effect on the brain's sex center (with the possible exception of haloperidol, which may affect the sexual response directly). These drugs may affect sexuality indirectly because of their favorable effects on the psychic state. In addition, some agents infrequently are reported to cause erectile and ejaculatory difficulties probably because of their mild anti-adrenergic and/or anticholinergic or antidopamine effects.			
Phenothiazines: Stelazine, Mellaril, Thorazine	Psychiatric disorders; anti-emetic	Sexual response may be improved as by-product of recovery from mental illness. "Dry" ejaculation may be caused by effects on internal vesical sphincter paralysis, causing semen to empty into bladder; often seen with Mellaril.	Decreased desire reported, only in very high doses.	Impotence reported with some agents (rare).	Inhibition of ejaculation reported with Mellaril.
Butyrophenones: Haldol	Gilles de la Tourette syndrome, schizophrenia	Reported to reduce libido and potency and cause retarded ejaculations in some patients; mechanism unknown—may involve central or peripheral antiadrenergic and/or antidopamine activity.	May be decreased.	Impotence reported with some agents (rare).	None reported.

Drug	Medical Indications	Possible Mechanism of Action	Phase of Sexual Response Affected		
			Desire	Excitement	Orgasm
E. *Antidepressants* (e.g., tricyclics, MAO inhibitors)	Depression	No direct effects on sexuality; sex drive and performance may improve as depression lifts. The antidepressants have some peripheral autonomic effects which rarely cause some potency and ejaculatory problems in men.	Probably none	None	Some females report delay of orgasm.
Tricyclics (Elavil, Tofranil)		Anticholinergic side-effects	Probably none	None	
MAO inhibitors (e.g., Nardil, Marplan, Norpramine)					
Lithium Carbonate	Manic states and possible prevention of depression in bipolar illness	No reported effects on the sexual response, except that sexual urgency may diminish manic activities.	Urgency or desire may be reduced.	None	None
F. *Stimulants* Cocaine	Local anesthetic	General CNS stimulant; augments sympathetic NS function.	Reported to be enhanced.	Reported to be enhanced; high doses may cause impotence.	May be enhanced; high doses may interfere with orgasm, more so in females.

TABLE 1 (*continued*)

Drug	Medical Indications	Possible Mechanism of Action	Phase of Sexual Response Affected		
			Desire	Excitement	Orgasm
Amphetamines	Stimulant, appetite suppressants, minimal brain damage in children; narcolepsy	General brain stimulation. In acute doses, reported to enhance libido; in chronic doses, diminishes libido and sexual functioning as well as causing general debility.	Reported to be enhanced at low doses; diminished at high doses.	Decreased in chronic doses.	May be enhanced; high doses may interfere with orgasm, more so in females.
G. *Hallucinogens*					
LSD (lysergic acid diethylamide)	methysergide (LSD analog) used in prophylaxis of migraine headaches; no medical use for LSD except for experimental purposes.	Vasoconstrictor; may be a central inhibitor of (5-HT) 5-hydroxytryptamine; serotonin.	Mixed effects reported.	None	Physiologically none. Altered experience reported.
DMT (dimethyl tryptamine) Mescaline (trimethoxyphenethylamine)		Disrupt neurotransmission in limbic system and RAS. Reported by some to enhance libido and orgasm, by others to have no effect, while some users report impaired sexuality	Mixed effects reported.	None	Mixed effects reported.
THC (tetrahydrocannabinol)		May have some effects on muscle contractions; some reports of enhanced erotic feelings (?)	Mixed effects reported.	Mixed effects reported.	Enhanced orgasm reported (?).

Drug	Medical Indications	Possible Mechanism of Action	Phase of Sexual Response Affected		
			Desire	Excitement	Orgasm
H. *Miscellaneous CNS Agents*					
L-DOPA (dihydroxyphenylalanine)	Parkinson's disease	Increased levels of dopamine centrally	Reports of increased desire in elderly male patients	None	None
p-CPA (parachlorophenylalanine)	Carcinoid syndrome	Inhibitor of serotonin synthesis	Reports of increased desire.		
		These drugs presumably stimulate the sex centers of the CNS and so increase the libido and the genital response. Also maintain the genital organs in a functional state.			
II. HORMONES					
Androgens (e.g., testosterone)	Impotence, as replacement therapy; anabolic agent; low libido states	Stimulates sex centers of both genders. Fetal androgen causes gender differentiation of behavior. Androgens also act on periphery to enhance the growth, development, and functioning of the male genitals and of the clitoris.	Stimulates sexual desire in both sexes.	In males, may increase ability to have an erection in testosterone-deficient states.	In males, volume of ejaculate may be increased.

Table 1 (*continued*)

Drug	Medical Indications	Possible Mechanism of Action	Phase of Sexual Response Affected		
			Desire	*Excitement*	*Orgasm*
Estrogens (e.g., Estriol, Estradiol, Estrone)	Oral contraceptive; replacement therapy in postmenopausal women; prostatic cancer	Do not increase libido, in fact, may decrease sexual interest; act on the cells of the female genitalia to enhance their growth, development and functioning.	In men, may decrease desire; in women, variable response reported; increased desire may be due to decreased fear of pregnancy.	May cause impotence in males.	Ejaculatory delay; volume of ejaculate decreased.
Progesterones (Physiological precursor to testosterone)	Endometriosis; component of some oral contraceptives		Probably none	Probably none	Probably none
Thryoxine	Hypothyroid states; depression	Increased motor activity and augmented sympathetic nervous system activity. May decrease depression.	Enhanced desire reported.		
Cyproterone acetate	Experimental; employed in treatment of compulsive sexual disorders	Antagonizes testosterone	Loss of libido in both genders.	Impotence in males.	In males, volume of ejaculate may decrease; ejaculatory delay.

Drug	Medical Indications	Possible Mechanism of Action	Desire	Excitement	Orgasm
			Phase of Sexual Response Affected		
Adrenal Steroids	Addison's disease; allergic and inflammatory disorders	Mechanism unknown	May decrease libido in high doses.		
Spironolactone	Edema, hypertension and hypokalemia	May block the binding of testosterone to the androgen receptor; gynecomastia due to action on breast tissue.	Occasional loss of libido.	May cause impotence in males.	None
III. ANTIHYPERTENSIVES					
A. Centrally Acting (e.g., Responsive alpha-methyl dopa)	Hypertension	Block adrenergic nerves and innervated structures in periphery causing disturbances in the hemodynamics of erection by various mechanisms; occasional inhibition of emission.	Decreased	Decreased; impotence is major problem.	May be inhibited.
B. Diuretics Thiazides	Hypertension	Dilate blood vessel walls; decreases circulating fluid volume. Disturbs penile blood pressure.	None	May cause impotence.	None
Spironolactone	Hypertension, edema, hypokalemia	May block binding of testosterone at receptor site; gynecomastia due to action on breast tissue.	Occasional loss of libido.	May cause impotence.	None
C. Ganglionic Blockers Quaternary ammonium compounds	Hypertension	Block post-ganglionic nerves and innervated structures; disturb penile blood pressure; may inhibit sympathetic mediation of emission.	None	Often causes impotence.	May be inhibited.

TABLE 1 (*continued*)

Drug	Medical Indications	Possible Mechanism of Action	Desire	Excitement	Orgasm
D. General Antiadrenergic Drugs					
phentolamine; phenoxybenzamine; ergot alkaloids	pheochromocytoma; migraine headaches				
alpha-blockers: clonidine	Hypertension; narcotic withdrawal	Blocks alpha-adrenergic receptors—central and peripheral action	None	None	Blocks emission in males—dose-related.
Sympathoplegic drugs: Guanethidine, Bretylium		Deplete adrenergic nerves of norepinephrine		Often cause impotence.	May be inhibited.
beta-blockers: propranol	Hypertension; angina; mitral prolapse	Blockade of beta-adrenergic receptors of heart—central and peripheral action	Sometimes decreased.	Sometimes decreased.	None reported.
IV. ANTICHOLINERGIC DRUGS					
Banthine, probanthine, atropine, scopolamine; cogentin	Peptic acid disease; GI irritability; alleviation of extrapyramidal effects of phenothiazines	These drugs block the nerves controlling the smooth muscles and blood vessels of the genital organs which are involved in the sexual responses. They inhibit the action of acetylcholine on structures innervated by post-ganglionic parasympathetic nerves. Also has central anticholinergic action.	None	May rarely cause impotence.	None

| | | | Phase of Sexual Response Affected | | |
Drug	Medical Indications	Possible Mechanism of Action	Desire	Excitement	Orgasm
V. "APHRODISIACS"					
Spanish Fly (Cantharides), amyl nitrite	Poisonous—no medical indications; vasodilator, angina pectoris	Irritates GU tract—causes priapism. Enhances vascular response of genitals (?) and reported to improve orgasm (?).	None	Priapism, organic impotence.	None
VI. MISCELLANEOUS DRUGS					
Disulfiram (Antabuse)	Alcohol Abuse		None	Occasional impotence reported	Delay of ejaculation.
Tryptophan		Increased CNS concentration of serotonin	Decreased	Decreased	
Ephedrine	Antiasthmatic agent	Alpha-adrenergic stimulator			Treatment of failure to ejaculate
Amantadine	Peptic ulcer	Inhibits H_2 receptors, may cause lowered sperm count			
VII. NEURO-TOXIC AGENTS					
Halogenated aromatic hydrocarbons	No medical indications; agricultural fungicides	Neuropathy	Decreased	Decreased	
Carbon disulfide	No medical indications; industrial exposure	Neuropathy and premature arteriosclerotic changes due to hyperlipidemia.	Decreased	Decreased	
Mangan intoxication	Industrial exposure	Degeneration of the ganglion cells.		Decreased	
Lathyrism	Ingestion of seeds of genus Lathyrus	Sclerotic changes of spinal cord		Decreased	

TABLE II: *Effects of Illness on the Sexual Response*[1]

Disorder	Libido	Excitement	Orgasm	Pathogenic Mechanism
I. NEUROGENIC DISORDERS				
A. Disorders Affecting the Sex Centers of the Brain	Usually decreased; very rarely increased in hypothalamic lesions	Not usually affected or decreased secondarily	Not usually affected	
1. Head trauma; cardiovascular accident	May be disturbed	Sensations may be disturbed—may be decreased	Sensations may be disturbed—may be decreased	Injury to the sex centers and/or limbic system and/or parietal lobe.
2. Arnold-Chiari malfunction	Sometimes increased as initial symptom			Pressure on cerebral structures
3. Hypothalamic lesions, Chranio-pharyngioma	Variable, usually decreased			
4. Chomophobe adenoma (pituitary tumor)	Decreased	Decreased	May be delayed	Pressure on sex circuits and/or limbic system and elevation of prolactin which may persist after surgical removal of tumor
5. Psychomotor epilepsy	May be decreased	May be decreased	May be decreased	Disturbance of limbic sexual circuits
6. Encephalitis	Variable	Variable	Variable	Disturbance of sexual circuits

[1] The table on Effects of Illness on the Sexual Response was prepared with the assistance of Dr. Damir Velceck of the Department of Urology, New York Hospital.

Disorder	Libido	Excitement	Orgasm	Pathogenic Mechanism
B. Disorders Affecting the Lower Neural Structures that Serve the Genital Reflexes				
1. *Neurologic conditions*	Not affected	May be decreased or absent	May be decreased or absent	These disorders cause irregular lesions in the spinal cord. If these affect the erection or orgasm centers, corresponding genital reflexes are disturbed.
a. *Conditions injuring the spinal cord* combined system disease; malnutrition and vitamin deficiencies; tabes dorals; amyotropic lateral sclerosis; *multiple sclerosis; *alcoholic neuropathy; syringomeylia; myelitis				
b. *Conditions injuring the peripheral nerves:* Alcoholic neuropathy; herniated lumbar disc; lumbar canal stenosis	Not affected	Decreased or absent	May be impaired	Injury to somatic and autonomic nerves subserving erection and orgasm (may be associated with pain and/or bladder and rectal problems).
Primary autonomic degeneration—Shay-Drager syndrome.		Decreased or absent	May be impaired	Disorder of autonomic nerves subserving erection and/or ejaculation.

* Frequent cause of sexual difficulties.

TABLE II (*continued*)

Disorder	Libido	Excitement	Orgasm	Pathogenic Mechanism
*Diabetes Mellitus	Not affected	Impotence may be early sign (most common medical cause of impotence)	*Male:* retrograde ejaculation *Female:* absence or decrease in orgasm	*Male:* Peripheral neuropathy destroys the autonomic fibers that mediate the erectile reflexes. There may also be diabetic lesions in the penile blood vessels. Ejaculation can be impaired because of paresis of internal vesicle sphincter. *Female:* Neuropathy of the sensory nerves of the clitoris can impair orgasm.
2. *Surgical injuries to the spinal cord and peripheral nerves subserving erection and orgasm*				Operations which interfere with or disrupt the sacral nerves will impair erection.
Surgical thoraco-lumbar or lumbar sympathectomy;	Not affected		Impaired	Operations which interfere with or disrupt the sympathetic nerves will impair ejaculation.
Retroperitoneal lymphadenectomy	Not affected		Impaired	Operations which interfere or disrupt sacral somatic nerves will impair orgasm because of paralysis of the perineal muscles.
Aorto-iliac surgery	Not affected	Diminished if dissection is distal to iliac bifurcation	Impaired	

* Frequent cause of sexual difficulties.

Disorder	Libido	Excitement	Orgasm	Pathogenic Mechanism
Radical pelvic surgery (sacral resections, operations for rectal, bladder and extensive prostrate cancer (*not* trans-urethral or suprapubic prostate surgery))	Not affected	Diminished or absent	Diminished or absent	These radical procedures may disrupt the parasympathetic, sympathetic and sensory fibers that are necessary for excitement and orgasm.
3. *Traumatic injuries to the peripheral nerves and spinal cord serving erection and orgasm*				
Paraplegia (transection of spinal cord)				
a. low lesion	Not affected	Only psychogenic erection; no sensation.	Some reflex ejaculation; no sensation.	Sensory pathways interrupted. Poor expulsion due to paralysis of perineal muscles.
b. high lesion	Not affected	Reflex erections; no sensation.	Rare reflex ejaculation; no sensation.	Sympathetic fibers may be disrupted.
Posterior urethral rupture	Not affected	Diminished		Injury to sympathetic fibers and vascular injury

Table II (*continued*)

Disorder	Libido	Excitement	Orgasm	Pathogenic Mechanism
II. VASCULAR CAUSES OF SEXUAL DYSFUNCTION	Vascular disorders do not affect desire.	Vascular disorders may disrupt the penile hemodynamic system.	Vascular disorders do not affect orgasm.	Vascular disorders disrupt erection in the male. The effect of local circulatory problems has not been studied in the female because they seem far less disabled by disorders of the genital blood vessels.
A. Local—Disorders of the Penile Blood Vessels				
Large vessel disease—Lariche syndrome		Diminished or absent		Arteriosclerotic changes in pelvic and penile blood vessels impede the blood flow needed for erection or alter the outflow mechanism.
*Small vessel disease—i.e., pelvic vascular insufficiency		Diminished or absent		
B. Systemic Vascular Disorders Leukemia; sickle cell disease	Not affected	May be diminished or absent	Not affected	Thrombotic injury and occlusion of penile and pelvic blood vessels.
Cardiac disease, coronary artery disease; post-coronary syndrome; hypertension	May be diminished due to depression, antihypertensive drugs	May be diminished due to anxiety about sudden death, antihypertensive drugs	May be diminished due to anxiety about sudden death	Pelvic blood vessels may also be affected.

* Frequent cause of sexual difficulties.

Disorder	Libido	Excitement	Orgasm	Pathogenic Mechanism
III. ENDOCRINE AND META-BOLIC DISORDERS				
*A. Diabetes Mellitus (see above)	Not affected	Diminished or absent	Retrograde ejaculation in the male; orgasm impaired in the female.	See above.
*B. Testosterone Deficiency States	Variable, but both genders lose libido when testosterone is totally absent	Erection and lubrication may be diminished.	Orgasm and ejaculation may be retarded. Reduced volume of ejaculate.	Sex centers require testosterone. Neural transmission and cellular response of genitals may be impaired
In males: old age, disease of the testicles, disease of the pituitary, surgical or traumatic injury to the testicles, pituitary stress, antiandrogen medication (cyproterone, Provera), Kleinfelder's Syndrome, hyperprolactonemia states, bilaterally undescended testicles, hydrocoele, varicocele.				
In females: surgical removal of adrenals, ovaries, or pituitary for treatment of estrogen sensitive breast cancer.				

* Frequent cause of sexual difficulties.

TABLE II (*continued*)

Disorder	Libido	Excitement	Orgasm	Pathogenic Mechanism
*C. Thyroid Deficiency States surgery, trauma, infection of thyroid gland, iodine deficiency.	Variable, may be diminished	May be diminished	May be retarded	Not understood
D. Other Endocrine Disorders Addison's disease; Cushing's disease; acromegali; hypopituitarism	Usually diminished			These diseases produce various endocrine deficiencies which affect the sexual circuits of the brain and/or cellular response of the genital organs.
E. Other Medical Diseases				
1. Carcinoid syndrome	Decreased	May be diminished		Elevated serotonin levels depress brain sex centers.
2. Hemochromatosis	May be decreased	May be diminished		Hemosiderin deposits in the anterior pituitary produce endocrine deficiency.
3. Liver Problems: Hepatitis; hepatic failure due to alcoholic cirrhosis; post-mononucleosis hepatitis	May be decreased	May be diminished	May be retarded	Compromised liver does not conjugate estrogen sufficiently with the result that androgens are neutralized.
4. Kidney Problems: Nephritis; renal failure; dialysis	May be decreased	May be diminished	May be retarded	Depression may play a role. Premature arteriosclerotic changes in pelvis and penis

* Frequent cause of sexual difficulties.

Disorder	Libido	Excitement	Orgasm	Pathogenic Mechanism
IV. DEBILITATING DISEASES Advanced malignancies Degenerative diseases Pulmonary Diseases Some infections	Decreased or absent			General ill health, depression (in some advanced kinds of illness, such as, for instance, tuberculosis, libido is preserved until the end).
V. GENITAL DISORDERS OF THE FEMALE				Diseases of the female genitals do not affect desire but may result in a secondary avoidance of sex
Clitoral adhesions	Not affected	No effect	Anorgasmia or difficult orgasm	Interfere with clitoral stimulation
Clitoral phymosis	Not affected	Not affected	Anorgasmia	Stimulation of the clitoris is painful
Atrophic vaginitis	Not affected	Lubrication is reduced or absent	Not affected	Estrogen withdrawal, as in age-related or surgical menopause; coitus may be painful
*Atrophy, fibrosis, degeneration and/or weakness of the pubococcygeal muscles	Not affected	Not affected	Orgasm is absent or feeble	Age, injury during birth, poor muscle tone

* Frequent cause of sexual difficulties.

TABLE III: *Physical Causes of Dyspareunia in the Male***

1—*Spasm of the Genital Muscles*—cremasteric muscle spasm and spasm of the smooth muscles of the internal reproductive organs can result in pain on or after ejaculation

2—*Infections and Irritation of the Penile Skin*—pain on contact and friction

   A. Herpes genitalis
   B. Dermatides and dermatoses, shingles, etc.

3—*Cancer of the Penis*

4—*Disorders which Disturb the Penile Anatomy*

   A. Chordee, Peyrone's disease—pain on penetration
   B. Fracture of the penis, sickle cell disease—pain on erection

5—*Prostate Infections, Prostate Enlargement*—pain after arousal, ejaculatory and post-ejaculatory pain

6—*Infections of the Seminal Vesicles*—ejaculatory pain

7—*Testicular Disease*—ejaculatory pain, pain on penetration and touching

   A. Orchitis
   B. Tumors
   C. Trauma

8—*Torsion of the Spermatic Cord*—hernia

9—*Musculoskeletal Disorders of the Pelvis and Lower Back*—make thrusting painful or difficult

   A. Low back pain, spasm of the back muscles, discs
   B. Arthritis of the hip

10—*Cardiovascular and Respiratory Disorders*—angina and respiratory distress in intercourse

11—*Post-ejaculatory Headache*—reflex reaction of blood vessels of head and face(?)

   * Pain on intercourse or sexual activity can produce a secondary loss of desire and/or sexual avoidance

TABLE IV: *Physical Causes of Dyspareunia in the Female**

1—*Vaginismus or Spasm of the Vaginal Muscles*—spasm of the perivaginal muscles causes pain on entry

2—*Infections and Irritations of the External Genitals*—pain on contact and with friction.

    A. Infections: herpes genitalis, infected labial cysts, feruncles
    B. Bartholin cyst infections

3—*Clitoral phymosis*—pain on clitoral stimulation

4—*Infections and Irritations of the Vagina*—pain in vagina on intercourse

    A. Infections vaginitis: herpes genitalis, candida albicans, etc.
    B. Chemical dematoses caused by douches and contraceptives
    C. Allergic reactions to douches, contraceptives and semen
    D. Atrophic vaginitis
    E. Irritations caused by rough intercourse, intercourse with insufficient lubrication, insertion of foreign objects, hypersensitive spots

5—*Imperforate Hymen, Rigid Hymen, Tender Hymenal Tags*—pain on entry and on penetration

6—*Agenesis of the Vagina*—pain on attempts at entry

7—*Injuries to the Genitals and Reproductive Organs due to Birth Trauma*—pain depending on location

    A. Tender episiotomy scars
    B. Tears
    C. Uterine prolapse, etc.

8—*Surgical Trauma to the Reproductive Organs*—pain depending on location

    A. Post hysterectomy scarring
    B. Ovarian approximation to vagina after hysterectomy
    C. Shortened vagina

9—*Pelvic Pathology*—pain on deep thrusting

    A. PID
    B. Ectopic pregnancy
    C. Endometriosis
    D. Ovarian cysts and tumors
    E. Other pelvic tumors

10—*IUD Complications*—pain on deep thrusting and cramping, perforation, infection

11—*Uterine Cramps due to Estrogen Deficiency*—cramping on orgasm, painful vaginal reaction to friction

12—*Bladder Disorders*—pain on intercourse

    A. Cystitis
    B. Urethritis
    C. Urethral prolapse
    D. "Honeymoon cystitis" (pressure on urethra during coitus in certain positions)

*Pain or discomfort on intercourse can produce a secondary loss of sexual desire and/or sexual avoidance.

TABLE IV *(continued)*

13—*Musculoskeletal Disorders of the Pelvis and Lower Back*—make sexual activity and intercourse painful or difficult

    A. Arthritis of the hip
    B. Lower back pain, disc, muscle spasm

14—*Cardiovascular and Respiratory Disorders*—angina and respiratory distress on effort

15—*Post Orgasmic Headache*—reflex reaction of blood vessels of head and face

BIBLIOGRAPHY

I. PHYSIOLOGY

The physiology of the male and the female sexual response is described in *The Human Sexual Response* by Masters and Johnson (Boston: Little, Brown, 1966). This material is reviewed from a biphasic perspective in *The New Sex Therapy* by H. S. Kaplan (New York: Brunner/Mazel, 1974).

A. The following references contain recent information about the physiology of ejaculation:

1. Marberger, H.: The Mechanism of Ejaculation. In *Basic Life Sciences*, Vol. 4, Hollaender, A. (Ed.) Part B. *Physiology and Genetics of Reproduction.* New York. Plenum Press, 1974.
2. Kedia, K. and Markland, C.: The Effect of Pharmacologic Agents on Ejaculation *J. of Urol.* 114, 1975.
3. Beach, F. A. et al.: Comparisons of Ejaculatory Response in Men and Animals. *Psychosom. Med.* 28: 749-763, 1966.
4. Kinura, Y. et al.: On the Brain Monoaminergic Systems Relating to Ejaculation: 1. Brain Dopamine and Ejaculation. *Andrologia*, 8 (4), 1976.
5. Kinura, Y.: Studies of Ejaculation *Jap J Urology* V 67, 1976
6. McLean, D. et al.: Cerebral Localization for Scratching and Seminal Discharge. *Arch. Neurol.* 9: 485-497, 1963.
7. Robinson, B.W. and Mishkin, M.: Ejaculation Evoked by Stimulation of the Pre-optic Area in Monkey. *Physiol. Behav.* 1: 269-272, 1966.
8. Erection, Emission, Ejaculation (illustrated) *Medical Aspects of Human Sexuality.* Sept. 1978, p. 77.

9. Beach, F. A. et al.: Comparison of the Ejaculatory Response of Man and Animals. *Psychosom Med.* 28: 749-763, 1966.

10. Van Dis, H. and Larsson, K.: Seminal Discharge Following Intracranial Electrical Stimulation. *Brain Res.* 23: 381-386, 1970.

B. The following references contain recent information about the physiology of erection:

11. Weiss, H.D.: The Physiology of Human Erection. *Am. Internal Med.* 76: 793-799, 1972.

12. Conti, G.: L'Erection du Pénis Human et ses Bases Morphologico-Vascularis. *Acta Anatomica* 14: 217-262, 1952.

13. MacLean, P. D. and Phloog, D. M.: Cerebral Representation of Penile Erection. *J. Neurophysiol.* 25: 29-55, 1952.

14. MacLean, P. D. et al.: Further Studies on Cerebral Representation of Erection: Caudal Thalamus, Midbrain and Pons. *J. Neurophysiol.* 26: 273-292, 1963.

15. Muro, D. M. et al.: The Effect of Injury to the Spinal Cord and Couda Equina on the Sexual Potency of Men. *New England J. Med.* 239: 903-911, 1948.

16. Whitelow, G. P. and Smithwick, R.H.: Some Secondary Effects of Sympathectomy with Particular Reference to Disturbance in Sexual Functioning. *New England J. Med:* 245: 121-130, 1951.

17. Dail, W. G., Jr. and Evan, A. P., Jr.: Experimental Evidence Indicating that the Penis of the Rat is Innervated by Short Adrenergic Neurons. *Am. J. Anat.* 141: 203-209, 1974.

18. Dick, H.C. et al.: Pudendal Sexual Reflexes: Electrophysiologic Investigations. *Urol.* 3(1): 376-379, 1974.

19. Fitzpatrick, T.J.: Venography of the Deep Dorsal Venous and Cavernous Systems. *J. Urol.* III: 518-520, 1974.

20. Fitzpatrick, T.J.: The Corpus Cavernosum Intercommunicating Venous Drainage System. *J. Urol.* 113: 494-496, 1975.

21. Jupimotas, and Takeshige, Y.: The Wall Structure of the Arteries of the Corpora Cavernosa Penis of the Rabbit: Light and Electron Microscopy, *Anat. Records* 181: 641-657, 1975.

22. Gunterberg, B. and Petersen, I.: Sexual Functioning After Resections of the Sacrum with Bilateral or Unilateral Sacrifice of the Sacral Nerves. *Fertility and Sterility* 27: 1146-1153, 1976.

23. Wagner, G. and Brindley, G.S.: The Effect of Atropine, Anxiety and Beta Adrenergic Blockers upon Human Penile Erection. In press.

24. Ebbehoj, J. and Wagner, G.: Abnormal Drainage of the Corpus Cavernosum Causing Erectile Dysfunction. In press.

25. Ebbehoj, J., Uhrenholdt, A. and Wagner, G.: Infusion Cavernosography in the Human in the Unstimulated and Stimulated Situations and its Diagnostic Value. In press.

26. Wagner, G. and Uhrenholdt, A.: Blood Flow Measurements by the Clearance Method in the Human Corpus Cavernosum in the Flaccid and Erect States. In press.

C. The following contain recent information on female excitement and orgasm.

27. Wagner, G., and Levin, R.J.: Vaginal Fluid. In: *The Human Vagina*. Hafezes, E.S. and Evan, T.N.(Eds.) Amsterdam: North Holland Publishing Co.; New York: Oxford, 1978.

28. Levin, R.J., and Wagner, G.: Hemodynamic Changes of the Human Vagina during Sexual Arousal Assessed by a Heated Oxygen Electrode. From the Proceedings of the Physiol. Society 4-5 Nov. 1977. *J. of Physiol*. 275: 23-24, 1978.

29. Levin, R.J. and Wagner, G.: Mechanisms for Vaginal Movements in Women. From the Proceedings of the Physiologic Society. Cambridge Meeting 1978.

30. Levin, R.J. and Wagner, G.: Human Vaginal Fluid-Ionic Composition and Modification by Sexual Arousal. From the Proceedings of the Physiologic Society, 10-11 December, 1976. *J. of Physiol*. 266: 62-63, 1977.

31. Levin, R.J. and Wagner, G.: Influence of Atropine on Sexual Arousal and Orgasm in Women. In: *Abstracts of the Third International Congress of Medical Sexology*. Rome, 1978.

32. Maurus, M., Mitra, J. and Ploog, D.: Cerebral Localization of the Clitoris in Ovariectomized Squirrel Monkeys. *Experimental Neuro*. 13: 283-288, 1965.

33. Abel, G.G. et al.: Women's Sexual Response During REM Sleep. Presented at the 131st American Psychiatric Association Meeting. Atlanta, Georgia, May 11, 1978.

D. The following contain recent information on the neurophysiology and neuro-pharmacology of sexual desire.

34. Everitt, B.J.: Cerebral Monoamines and Sexual Behavior. Chapter 30 in *Handbook of Sexology*. Money, J. and Musaph, H. (Eds.), Amsterdam, London, and New York: Excerpta Medica, 1977.

35. Herbert, J.: The Neuroendocrine Basis of Sexual Behavior in Primates. Chapter 31 in *Handbook of Sexology*. Money, J. and Musaph, H. (Eds.), Amsterdam, London, and New York: Excerpta Medica, 1977.

36. Gorski, R.A., The Neuroendocrine Regulation of Sexual Behavior. In *Advances in Psychobiology, Vol. 2*. Newton, G. and Riesen, A.H. (Eds.) New York: Wiley International Publication, J. Wiley & Sons, 1974.

37. Montagna, W. and Sadler, W.A. (Eds.) *Reproductive Behavior*, New York and London: Plenum Press, 1973.

38. Fernstrom, J.D. and Wurtman, R.J.: Brain Monoamine and Reproductive Function. *International Review of Physiology, Vol 13; Reproductive Physiology*. Greep, R.O. (Ed.) Baltimore-London-Tokyo: University Park Press, 1977.

39. Davidson, J.M.: Neurohormonal Bases of Male Sexual Behavior. *International Review of Physiology, Vol 13: Reproductive Physiology*. Greep, R.O. (Ed.) Baltimore-London-Tokyo: University Park Press, 1977.

40. Heath, R.G.: Pleasure and Brain Activity in Man: Deep and Surface Electro-encephalograms During Orgasm. *J. Nerv. and Ment. Disease* 154: 3-18, 1972.

41. MacLean, P.D.: Brain Mechanisms of Primal Sexual Functions and Related Behavior. In: *Sexual Behavior: Pharmacology and Biochemistry*, Sander, M. and Gessa, G.L. (Eds.) New York: Raven Press, 1975.

42. Pfaff, D.: Luteinizing Hormone-Releasing Factor Potentiates Lordosis Behavior in Hypophysectomized Ovariectomized Female Rats. *Science* 182, 1973.

43. Moss, R.L. and McCann, S.; Induction of Mating Behavior in Rats by Lutenizing Hormone-Releasing Factor. *Science* 181, 1973.

44. Belluzzi, J.D. and Stein, L.: Enkephalin May Mediate Euphoria and Drive Reduction Reward. *Nature* 266: 566-558, 1978.

45. Goldstein, A.: Opioid Peptides (Endorphins) in Pituitary and Brain. *Science* 193: 1081-1086, 1976.

II. TREATMENT

Sex therapy approaches to the treatment of orgasm and excitement phase disorders are described in *Human Sexual Inadequacy*, Masters, W. and Johnson, V. (Little, Brown, 1971) and in *The New Sex Therapy* by H.S. Kaplan (Brunner/Mazel, 1974). *The Illustrated Manual of Sex Therapy* (Quadrangle, 1975) by H.S. Kaplan contains a summary of the behavioral aspect of treatment. A self-help approach to the treatment of orgasm dysfunctions is described in *For Yourself* by Barbach, L. (New York: Doubleday, 1975).

The sections on psychosomatic medicine by Kaplan, H.S. in the *Comprehensive Textbook of Psychiatry*, 1st Ed., Friedman, A. and Kaplan, H.I., Eds. (Williams and Wilkins, 1967) contain basic psychophysiologic concepts that are applicable to the sexual dysfunctions.

Information on the pharmacologic, behavioral, and psychoanalytic approaches to the treatment of phobias and phobic anxiety states are described in:

46. Klein, D.F.: Delineation of Two Drug Responsive Anxiety Syndromes. *Psychopharmacologia* 5: 397-408, 1964.

47. Klein, D.F. et al.: Antidepressants, Anxiety, Panic and Phobia. In: *Psychopharmacology: A Generation of Progress*. Lipton, M., DiMascio, A., and Killam, K.F. (Eds.) New York: Raven Press, 1978.

48. Zitrin, C.M., Klein, D.F. and Woerner, H.G.; Behavior Therapy, Suggestive Psychotherapy, and Phobias. *Archives of Gen. Psychiat.* 35: 307-316, 1978.

49. Wolpe, J.: *Psychotherapy by Reciprocal Inhibition*. Stanford, Ca.: Stanford University Press, 1958.

50. Freud, S.: Analysis of a Phobia in a Five-Year Old Boy (1909). In : *The Complete Psychological Works of Sigmund Freud*. Vol. X, London: Hogarth Press, 1955.

Concepts and clinical approaches to the treatment of success and pleasure conflicts may be found in the following:

51. Canavau-Gunpert, D., Garver, K., and Grumpert, P.: *The Success-Fearing Personality*. Lexington Mass., Toronto: Lexington Books, 1978.

52. Friedman, M.: *Overcoming the Fear of Success*. New York: Seaview Press. In press.

53. Tec, L.: *The Fear of Success*. New York: Readers Digest Press, 1976.

54. Freud, S.: Some Character-Types met with in Psychoanalytic Work (1915).

In: *Sigmund Freud, Collected Papers*, Vol. IV. Jones, E. (Ed.) New York: Basic Books, 1959.

55. Horner, M.S.: Towards an Understanding of Achievement Related Conflicts in Women. *J. of Social Issues* 28: 157-176, 1972.

Some of the statistical surveys and studies upon which current concepts of norms of sexual behavior are based include the following:

56. Kinsey, A.C., Pomeroy, W.B. and Martin, C.E.: *Sexual Behavior in Human Male*. Philadelphia: Saunders, 1948.

57. Kinsey, A.C., Pomeroy, W.B., Martin, C.E. and Gebhard, P.H.: *Sexual Behavior in the Human Female*. Philadelphia: Saunders, 1953.

58. Hunt, M.: *Sexual Behavior in the 1970's*. New York: Dell, 1972.

59. Pietropinto, A. and Simenauer, J. *Beyond the Male Myth*. New York: Signet, 1978.

60. Hite, S. *The Hite Report*. New York. Macmillan, 1976.

There is a scarcity of solid information on the outcome of treatment of sexual disorders. The following represent some of the best data that have been accumulated thus far.

61. Masters, W. and Johnson, V.: *Human Sexual Inadequacy* Boston: Little, Brown 1970.

62. O'Conner, J.F. and Stern, L.O.: Results of Treatment in Functional Sexual Disorders. *N.Y. State Jnl. Med.* Vol. 72, 1927-1934, 1972.

63. Spitzer, R.L. and Klein, D.F. (Eds.): *Evaluation of Psychological Therapies*. Baltimore: Johns Hopkins Press, 233-250, 1976.

64. Hogan, D.R.: The Effectiveness of Sex Therapy: A Review of the Literature. In: *Handbook of Sex Therapy*, LoPiccolo, J. and LoPiccolo L. (Eds.) New York and London: Plenum Press, 1978.

III. OTHER REFERENCES

A. The following articles contain recent information on medical aspects of sexual dysfunction.

65. Schiavi, R.C.: Androgens and Male Sexual Function: A Review of Human Studies, *Journal of Sex and Marital Therapy*, Vol. II, No. 3, Fall 1976.

66. Raboch, J. and Starka, L.: Reported Coital Activity of Men and Levels of Plasma Testosterone, *Archives of Sexual Behavior*, Vol. II, No. 4, 1973.

67. Seagraves, T.R.: Pharmacologic Agents Causing Sexual Dysfunction. *Journal of Sex and Marital Therapy*, Vol. 3, No. 3, Fall 1977.

68. The Sexually Dysfunctional Diabetic Report *Sexual Medicine Today*, Feb 1979.

69. The New Arterial Bypass that Reverses Organic Impotence. *Sexual Medicine Today*, Jan. 1979.

70. Ellenberg, M.: Impotence in Diabetics: The Neural Factor. *Am. Intern. Med.* 75: 548-554, 1967.

71. Kolodny, R.D.: Sexual Dysfunction in Diabetic Females. *Diabetes* 20: 557-559, 1971.

72. Kolodny, R.D.: Sexual Dysfunction in Diabetic Men. *Diabetes* 23: 306-309, 1974.

B. The literature on disorders of sexual desire is rather scant. It includes the following articles of interest:

73. Kaplan, H.S.: Hypoactive Sexual Desire. *J. of Sex and Marital Therapy* 1977, 3, 3-9.

74. *DSM-III. Third Diagnostic and Statistical Manual of the American Psychiatric Association.* Washington, D.C.: American Psychiatric Association, 1979.

75. Araoz, D.L.: Hypnosis in Treating Hypoactive Sexual Desire. *Am. J. of Clinical Hypnosis.* 1977.

76. Lopiccolo, L.: Low Libido States. Presented at the meeting of the American Association of Sex Therapists, Philadelphia, 1979.

77. Lief, H.: What's New in Sex Research? Inhibited Sexual Desire. *Medical Aspects of Human Sexuality* Vol. II, 7: 94-95, July, 1977.

C. The following references are of particular relevance for the theory and treatment of sexual disorders.

78. Money, J. and Musaph, H.: *The Handbook of Sexology.* Amsterdam, London, New York: Excerpta Medica, 1977.

79. Kernberg, O.F.: *Borderline Conditions and Pathological Narcissism.* New York: Aronson, 1975.

80. Kernberg, O.F.: Love the Couple and the Group: Psychoanalytic Perspectives. Presented at a Symposium on objects relation theory and love at the Michigan Psychoanalytic Society, Detroit, Nov. 1977.

81. Kernberg, O.F.: Adolescent Sexuality in the Light of Group Process. Presented at the Fifth Reunion of the Pan American Forum for the Study of Adolescence, San Francisco, 1979.

82. Kernberg, O.F.: Boundaries and Structure of Love Relations. *J. of the Am. Psychoanalytic Assoc.* 25, 1: 81-114, 1976.

83. Berne, E.: *Transactional Analysis in Psychotherapy.* New York: Grove Press, 1961.

84. Perls, F.S.: *Gestalt Therapy,* New York: Grove Press, 1961.

85. Sager, C., Kaplan, H.S. et al.: The Marriage Contract: In: *Progress in Group and Family Therapy.* Sager, C.J. and Kaplan, H.S. (Eds.) New York: Brunner/Mazel, 1972.

86. Salzman, L.: *The Obsessive Personality.* New York: Aronson, 1968.

INDEX

616.6   DISEASES OF UROGENITAL
KAP   SYSTEM
KAPLAN, HELEN SINGER
DISORDERS OF SEXUAL DESIRE

	DATE DUE		

Col. Black Library
Augusta Mental Health Inst.
Augusta, ME. 04332